CHINESE FUNERARY BIOGRAPHIES

CHINESE FUNERARY BIOGRAPHIES

An Anthology of Remembered Lives

EDITED BY

Patricia Buckley Ebrey, Ping Yao, and Cong Ellen Zhang

UNIVERSITY OF WASHINGTON PRESS

Seattle

Chinese Funerary Biographies was made possible in part by a grant from the Chiang Ching-kuo Foundation for International Scholarly Exchange.

Composed in ArnoPro, typeface designed by Robert Slimbach

UNIVERSITY OF WASHINGTON PRESS
uwapress.uw.edu

LIBRARY OF CONGRESS CATALOGING-IN-PUBLICATION DATA
Names: Ebrey, Patricia Buckley, 1947– editor. | Yao, Ping (Professor of history), editor. | Zhang, Cong Ellen, editor.
Title: Chinese funerary biographies : an anthology of remembered lives / edited by Patricia Buckley Ebrey, Ping Yao, and Cong Ellen Zhang.
Description: Seattle : University of Washington Press, [2019] | Includes bibliographical references and index.
Identifiers: LCCN 2019014764 (print) | LCCN 2019022301 (ebook) | ISBN 9780295746425 (ebook) | ISBN 9780295746401 (hardcover : alk. paper) | ISBN 9780295746418 (pbk. : alk. paper)
Subjects: LCSH: Inscriptions—China. | Epitaphs—China. | China—Biography. | Funeral rites and ceremonies—China. | Burial—China. | China—Social life and customs—Sources.
Classification: LCC CN1160 .C438 2019 (print) | LCC CN1160 (ebook) | DDC 929.351—dc23
LC record available at https://lccn.loc.gov/2019014764
LC ebook record available at https://lccn.loc.gov/2019022301

The full Chinese text of the biographies translated in this volume is available at https://doi.org/10.6069/9780295746425.s01.

COVER ILLUSTRATION: Rubbings of peony scrolls on epitaph tablets. Tomb of Xianyu Tinghui, Xi'an, Shaanxi, Tang dynasty, 723 CE.

CONTENTS

Acknowledgments ix

Translation Conventions xi

Chronology of Imperial China with Subjects of Epitaphs xiii

Introduction 3

1. **Three Short Eastern Han Funerary Biographies**
   Epitaphs for Ma Jiang (34–106), Wu Zhongshan (ca. 92–172),
       and Kong Dan (fl. 182)
   TRANSLATED BY PING YAO AND
       PATRICIA BUCKLEY EBREY 23

2. **A Chinese General Serving the Northern Wei State**
   Entombed Epitaph for the Late Wei Dynasty Overseer of Military
       Affairs, Sima Yue (462–508)
   TRANSLATED BY TIMOTHY DAVIS 30

3. **A Twice-Widowed Xianbei Princess**
   Epitaph with Preface for the Great Enlightenment Temple Nun
       Surnamed Yuan (Yuan Chuntuo, 475–529)
   TRANSLATED BY JEN-DER LEE 39

4. **Authoring One's Own Epitaph**
   Self-Authored Epitaph, by Wang Ji (590?–644)
   Inscription Dictated While Near Death, by Wang Xuanzong
       (633–686)
   TRANSLATED BY ALEXEI KAMRAN DITTER 47

5. **Wives Commemorating Their Husbands**
   Epitaph for Cao Yin (fl. 7th century), by Madam Zhou (fl. 7th century)
   Epitaph for He Jian (686–742), by Madam Xin (fl. 742)
   TRANSLATED BY PING YAO   59

6. **A Married Daughter and a Grandson**
   Entombed Funerary Inscription for My Daughter the Late Madam
      Dugu (785–815) and Entombed Record for My Grandson
      Who Died Young (Quan Shunsun, 803–815),
      by Quan Deyu (759–818)
   TRANSLATED BY ANNA M. SHIELDS   66

7. **A Nun Who Lived through the Huichang Persecution of
   Buddhism**
   Epitaph for Daoist Nun Zhi (Zhi Zhijian, 812–861), by Zhi Mo
      (fl. 860)
   TRANSLATED BY PING YAO   75

8. **An Envoy Serving the Kitan Liao Son of Heaven**
   Epitaph for Han Chun (d. 1036), Court Ceremonial Commissioner,
      by Li Wan (fl. 1012–1037)
   TRANSLATED BY LANCE PURSEY   83

9. **Epitaphs Made Widely Available**
   Funerary Biographies for Three Men from Luzhou: Liang
      Jian (d. 1042), Wang Cheng (d. 1042), and Chen Hou
      (1074–1123)
   TRANSLATED BY MAN XU   101

10. **A Friend and Political Ally**
    Funerary Inscription for Mr. Culai (Shi Jie, 1005–1045), by Ouyang Xiu
       (1007–1072)
    TRANSLATED BY CONG ELLEN ZHANG   111

11. **Preserving a Father's Memory**
    Funerary Inscription for Chao Juncheng (1029–1075), by Huang
       Tingjian (1045–1105)
    TRANSLATED BY CONG ELLEN ZHANG   122

12. **A Gentleman without Office**
    Epitaph for Scholar Residing at Home Wei Xiongfei (1130–1207),
        by Wei Liaoweng (1178–1237)
    TRANSLATED BY MARK HALPERIN   130

13. **Wives and In-Laws**
    Funerary Inscription for [My Father-in-Law] Mr. Zou of Fengcheng
        (Zou Yilong, 1204–1255) and Funerary Inscription for [My Wife]
        Madam Plum Mansion (Zou Miaozhuang, 1230–1257),
        by Yao Mian (1216–1262)
    TRANSLATED BY BEVERLY BOSSLER   138

14. **A Clerk Promoted to Official under the Mongols**
    Funerary Inscription for Mr. Su (Su Zhidao, 1261–1320), Director of
        the Left and Right Offices of the Branch Secretariat for the Lingbei
        Region, by Yu Ji (1271–1348)
    TRANSLATED BY PATRICIA BUCKLEY EBREY   158

15. **A Mongol Rising to the Defense of the Realm**
    Epitaph for Grand Guardian Sayin Čidaqu (1317–1365), by Zhang Zhu
        (1287–1368)
    TRANSLATED BY TOMOYASU IIYAMA   172

16. **A Merchant Aspiring to Gentlemanly Virtue**
    Funerary Biography of the Gentleman Residing at Home
        Cheng Weiqing (1531–1588), by Wang Shizhen
        (1526–1590)
    TRANSLATED BY YONGTAO DU   182

17. **A Ming General Turned Warlord**
    Funerary Inscription for Military Officer Mao (Mao Wenlong,
        1579–1629), by Mao Qiling (1623–1716)
    TRANSLATED BY XING HANG   190

18. **A Brother Remembers His Sister**
    Epitaph for My Sister Madam Fang (Qian Huan, 1600–1668), by Qian
        Chengzhi (1612–1698)
    TRANSLATED BY MARTIN W. HUANG   212

19. **A Chinese Bannerman Expert in Waterworks**

Epitaph for Director General of River Conservancy Jin Wenxiang
(Jin Fu, 1633–1692), by Wang Shizhen (1634–1711)

TRANSLATED BY R. KENT GUY   222

20. **A Woman Determined to Die**

Epitaph for the Joint Burial of Scholar Wu (Wu Xi, 1666–1687) and
His Martyred Wife, Madam Dai (1666–1687), by Mao Qiling
(1623–1716)

TRANSLATED BY JOLAN YI   241

21. **A Wife's Sacrifices**

Living Funerary Inscription for My Wife, Madam Sun (1769–1833),
by Fang Dongshu (1772–1851)

TRANSLATED BY WEIJING LU   250

22. **A Wife's Moving Tribute**

Epitaph for Mr. Zeng (Zeng Yong, 1813–1862), by Zuo Xijia
(1831–1896)

TRANSLATED BY GRACE S. FONG   259

Teaching Guide   269
Contributors   276
Index   281

ACKNOWLEDGMENTS

This collection of funerary biographies owes its greatest debt to the Henry Luce Foundation/ACLS Program in China Studies, which funded the 2017 Collaborative Reading Workshop "Records of the Dead, Records for the Living: Reading Muzhiming." This workshop, organized by Ping Yao and Cong Ellen Zhang, brought together fourteen scholars who study fourth- through nineteenth-century China. Each participant distributed a fully annotated translation of one or more funerary biographies, and in the workshop we were able to get down to the nitty-gritty level of scholarly interchange. We had enough time to discuss each translation in detail, to consider not only the meaning of specific expressions but also the larger social and cultural contexts. We also explored the development of funerary biographies as a genre and their use as historical sources.

In the final workshop session, we brought up the idea of redoing our translations to make them more accessible to students and other readers with a general interest in Chinese history and culture. The authors agreed to write new introductions to their translations, reduce the use of footnotes, and try to make their translations as comprehensible to nonexperts as possible. We also decided to recruit scholars to do additional translations so that we could present biographies from a more diverse set of individuals. Those who joined us after the workshop include Lance Pursey, Tomoyasu Iiyama, Xing Hang, Yongtao Du, R. Kent Guy, and Grace S. Fong. We wish to thank them all for helping make this a more well-rounded collection of readings.

We would also like to thank the College of Natural and Social Sciences at the California State University, Los Angeles, for providing the funds for the workshop venue, and Professor Jason Chiu for helping with the workshop logistics.

TRANSLATION CONVENTIONS

Since nineteen translators contributed to this volume, and the original texts date from the second to the nineteenth centuries, it is impossible to be entirely consistent in how terms and words are translated. Our goal was to keep the translations readable and to handle situations in similar ways whenever reasonable.

Place names. After each new place name, we give the name of the modern province in which it is located in brackets. We translate *xian* as "county" but decided not to translate *zhou* because the standard translations for it differ greatly, depending on the time period. It is, however, always a unit larger than a county.

Personal names. Whereas in English we often refer to people by their surnames, for Classical Chinese it was more common to use personal names. Here we have added surnames to avoid confusion. It is common in epitaphs to use an honorific term after the surname of the deceased meaning something like "lord" or "sir." Here we uniformly use "Mr." for men. In addition to having a *ming* (name or formal name), most upper-class Chinese men also acquired a *zi*, which is rendered here as "courtesy name." After his death, a man's *ming* became known as *hui* (taboo name). In the case of women, whose personal names are rarely given in epitaphs, we sometimes use "Lady" to indicate that the woman had a title but generally use "Madam."

Dates and reign titles. We give dates in their original form, using the name of the reign period and the stems-and-branches term for the year. This is followed in brackets by the Western year with which it overlaps most. Also called the sexagenary cycle, the stems-and-branches system uses the sixty possible combinations of the ten "stems" and the twelve "branches." Reign titles were chosen by the emperor and until 1368 were often changed, sometimes to mark an auspicious occurrence, sometimes to indicate a shift in policy or other event. Many emperors had five or more reign periods, depending on how long they reigned. After the first Ming emperor did not change the name of his reign during his thirty years on the throne, his successors followed his practice, as did the emperors of the subsequent Qing dynasty, with the result that Ming and Qing emperors are often referred to by their reign names (the Qianlong emperor, for example).

Ages. For simplicity, when a text says the subject died at forty-nine *sui,* we simply translate that he died at forty-nine. Where we have actual birth and death dates, to the month and day, we convert the age to Western reckoning, but that is rare. On the day a baby is born, he or she is described as being one *sui,* meaning in his or her first year of life. Each New Year's Day, he or she becomes one *sui* older. Consequently, someone described as two *sui* could be anywhere from two days old (if born on the last day of the previous year) to a day short of two years old (if born on the first day of the previous year). On the average, an age in *sui* will be a year older than an age in Western reckoning.

Subjects of sentences. In Chinese, it is not necessary to supply a subject when it is obvious from context. We have generally supplied the subject without putting it in brackets, to help the flow of the narrative.

Titles of offices. As a rule, we use the translations of office titles given by Charles Hucker in *A Dictionary of Official Titles in Imperial China* (1985). When such titles are not part of a proper name, they are capitalized only when they might otherwise be misinterpreted as a more general descriptive term. For example, "minister of justice" is clearly an official title in English, but "General of the Left" is not, and so it is capitalized.

Allusions. Literary allusions range from a phrase that alludes to an obscure poem that many people would not recognize to everyday sayings that everyone understands without necessarily knowing their source. These are translated variously: by paraphrasing the meaning, by providing a brief gloss in brackets, or by adding a note to explain the reference.

CHRONOLOGY OF IMPERIAL CHINA
WITH SUBJECTS OF EPITAPHS

Warring States period (475–221 BCE)
Qin dynasty (221–206 BCE)
Western Han (202 BCE–9 CE)
Eastern Han (25–220 CE)
　　Ma Jiang (34–106)
　　Wu Zhongshan (ca. 92–172)
　　Kong Dan (fl. 182)
Three Kingdoms period (220–265)
Western Jin (265–316)
Eastern Jin (317–420)
Southern Dynasties (317–589)
Northern Dynasties (386–581)
　　Northern Wei (386–534)
　　　Sima Yue (462–508)
　　　Yuan Chuntuo (475–529)
Sui dynasty (581–618)
Tang dynasty (618–907)
　　Wang Ji (590?–644)
　　Wang Xuanzong (633–686)
　　Cao Yin (fl. 7th c.)
　　He Jian (686–742)
　　Lady Dugu (785–815)
　　Quan Shunsun (803–815)
　　Nun Zhi Zhijian (812–861)

Five Dynasties (907–960)
Liao dynasty (916–1125)
   Han Chun (d. 1036)
Song dynasty (960–1279)
  Northern Song (960–1126)
    Liang Jian (d. 1042)
    Wang Cheng (d. 1042)
    Shi Jie (1005–1045)
    Chao Juncheng (1029–1075)
    Chen Hou (1074–1123)
  Southern Song (1127–1279)
    Wei Xiongfei (1130–1207)
    Zou Yilong (1204–1255)
    Zou Miaozhuang (1230–1257)
Yuan dynasty (1234–1368)
  Su Zhidao (1261–1320)
  Sayin Čidaqu (1317–1365)
Ming dynasty (1368–1644)
  Cheng Weiqing (1531–1588)
  Mao Wenlong (1579–1629)
Qing dynasty (1644–1912)
  Fang Qian Huan (1600–1668)
  Jin Fu (1633–1692)
  Wu Xi (1666–1687)
  Madam Dai (1666–1687)
  Madam Sun (1769–1833)
  Zeng Yong (1813–1862)

CHINESE FUNERARY BIOGRAPHIES

Introduction

HISTORY COMES ALIVE WHEN WE LEARN NOT JUST OF INSTITU-
tions, ideas, and events, but also of individual people. For this reason,
biographies are among the most valued historical sources.[1]

Biography has long been a major strand of history writing in China.
The great Han period historian Sima Qian (d. 86 BCE) included accounts
of about 150 individual people in his monumental work, *Historical Records*
(Shiji). His records of individuals had all the main components of a biography: they gave subjects' formal and courtesy names, the county or prefecture they came from, and chronological summaries of their political
career if any. Sima Qian sometimes quoted conversations to make his
account more vivid. After finishing the account of the subject's career, he
might say more about other aspects of the person's life, such as his writings, his personality, and his brothers and sons. Although the majority of
individuals he featured were rulers and their ministers, Sima Qian did not
think only political figures deserved to have their lives recorded: he compiled biographies of men and women notable for other reasons, ranging
from their philosophical contributions to their business acumen. After
Sima Qian, the tradition of biography writing that he initiated was continued and expanded by state history-writing projects. The resulting
dynastic histories are rich in accounts of leading individuals involved in
the government plus some remembered for other accomplishments or virtues. State-sponsored biographical writing drew from and in turn influenced private compilations. Especially notable are accounts of exemplary
women, filial children, men of note from a specific place, and, in later

periods, painters, calligraphers, eminent monks or nuns, and much else. With the growing compilation of local histories from the Song period (960–1279) on, more and more people's lives were recorded, generally through the cooperation of members of the local elite and the local government.

This book focuses on privately written biographies (not government-compiled ones) and, within private biographies, ones written as a way to commemorate the dead, a tradition that can also be traced back to the Han period (206 BCE–220 CE). As epitaphs developed over time as a literary genre, they borrowed elements from the tradition of biography writing for the official histories, but they also were shaped by other elements of Chinese culture, especially the family system, the practice of ancestral rites, and the value placed on filial piety.

The biographies translated in this volume are called in Chinese *muzhiming*, literally "entombed account with inscription," but are here variously referred to as epitaphs, funerary biographies, or funerary inscriptions. Tens of thousands of these funerary biographies survive from imperial China (221 BCE–1911). For many centuries, traditional historians have used them to supplement the official histories. When the subject of a funerary biography is also known from a dynastic history biography, the funerary biography often provides more detail on the private side of the subject's life, such as his wife's family name and where he was buried. In addition, the authors of the official histories, wanting to apportion praise and blame, did not shy away from recording character flaws and political misdeeds. Since one of the main functions of an epitaph was to create a positive image for kin to emulate and other members of the elite to admire, they describe the subject in laudatory terms and are silent on his or her failings.

Funerary biographies, because of their inclusion of telling details about personal conduct, family life, local conditions, and social and cultural practices, can be tremendously helpful in giving the reader a sense of the ways of thinking of their period and the realities of daily life, especially among the elite class. Epitaphs are especially valuable for the glimpses they give of the lives of a wide range of people not well documented in such sources as dynastic histories and gazetteers. Women, who rarely enter standard historical sources unless they were celebrated as chaste widows or other paragons of virtue, are well represented in funerary biographies (though still not nearly as well as men). Similarly, one can find many epitaphs for men who never managed to leave much of a mark politically and who are not recorded in any other source. Even boys and girls who died young and were not normally recorded in genealogies or biographies of their parents were subjects of epitaphs and fondly remembered by family members.

Modern historians have also been drawn to funerary inscriptions for the rich, quantifiable data they provide for the study of family, demographic, and social history. Funerary biographies regularly give date of death and age at death, enabling one to calculate birth and death dates. They also identify the families of marriage partners, which allows documenting marriage circles and kinship networks. Most men's and women's funerary biographies also give the names or at least the number of their children and often also whether they were still living or had died young, giving us evidence of fertility and mortality. Quantifiable data mined from funerary biographies have been used to document changes in age at marriage and preferred marriage partners. Ongoing digital humanities projects, such as the Chinese Biographical Database (CBDB), draw heavily on epitaphs to document elite family migration, regional development, and political and intellectual networks. Wide use of these historical sources has added greatly to our understanding of family life, ritual and religious practices, as well as elite self-identification and strategies to maintain their social status, such as restrictive marriage circles.

Historians of women have been at the forefront of drawing from *muzhiming*. Both funerary biographies and biographies in didactic accounts of model women share the goal of praising women for fulfilling familial roles and acting as moral exemplars. But epitaphs routinely include more nuanced depictions of a woman's emotional experiences and the various ways that she negotiated delicate family relationships. Moreover, biographies in official histories and didactic literature usually concentrate on one pivotal moment in a woman's life, whereas epitaphs offer a fuller picture of a woman's roles at various stages of her life. Funerary biographies of women were often written by a close relative, such as a husband or brother, though a son might also ask an eminent writer to take information he would provide and use it to write the epitaph for his mother. Although there are many more extant funerary biographies for men than for women, as sources for documenting women's lives, nothing rivals epitaphs.

This volume provides full translations of thirty examples of private biographical accounts written from the second to the nineteenth centuries. Only about a fourth of the subjects were people of national stature based on their intellectual, administrative, or military credentials. Some of the biographies were selected for the access they give us to the more private side of life, such as the feelings of parents for their children. Others were selected to show something of the diversity of the lives recorded in private biographies, from generals, low-level government functionaries, and religious clergy to non-Han military officers and imperial relatives. All of them help illuminate a period in time and a social and political milieu. To read these biographies as sources for the lives of the deceased, it is important to put them in historical context. For this reason, the translators of each biography first sketch its historical context.

Epitaphs were not just words, but also physical objects. From the fifth century on, a *muzhiming* was generally a square-shaped piece of stone, some 40 to 160 centimeters (16 to 64 inches), engraved on one side with a biography of the occupant of the tomb in which it was buried (figure 1). The inscriptions are conventionally divided into two parts, a prose preface (*xu*) and a rhymed elegy (*ming*). The staple elements of the preface include the name of the deceased, death and burial dates, ancestral and biographical information, outstanding virtues and talents, and, for men, career-related accomplishments. The length of the preface varies greatly, from a few hundred to several thousand words. The rhymed elegy is typically much briefer. The elegy normally repeats information contained in the preface in more poetic language, supplemented with poetic allusions that mourn the loss of the deceased and express the longing of the living.

The inscribed stone was protected with a stone cover on which the name of the deceased and, when applicable, his or her title, were engraved in archaic script. The cover was often adorned with images of auspicious animals and decorated patterns that reflected Chinese cosmological ideas.

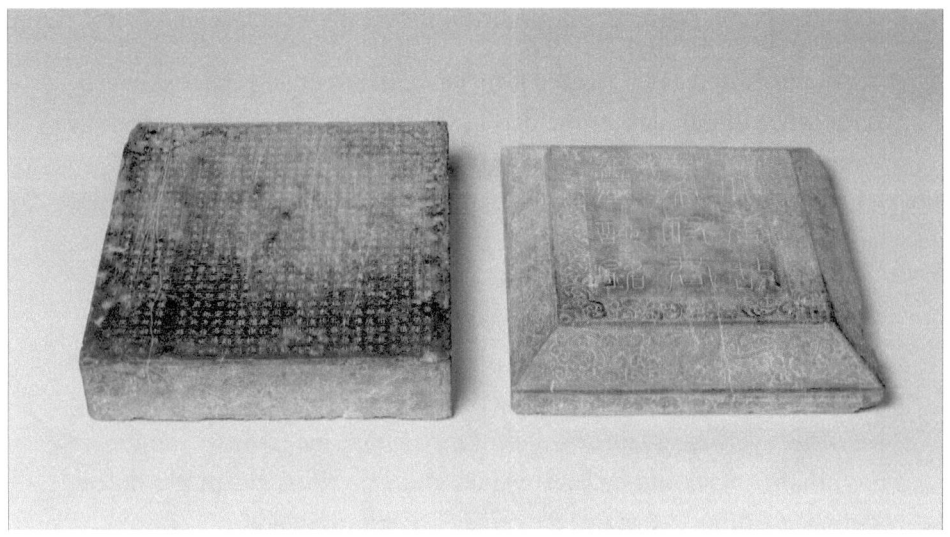

Stone inscribed with the epitaph of Xu Derun. (d. 688), along with its cover. The two pieces of limestone are approximately 59 centimeters on each side, and both the top and bottom stones are about 13 centimeters tall. In the collection of the Metropolitan Museum of Art, New York.

At burial, this set of engraved slabs would be placed near the deceased, either on top of or in front of the coffin, or in the tomb's entryway.

The production of a *muzhiming* required multiple steps and could be extremely time-consuming. Generally, when it was a father who had died, the process began with the preparation of his "record of conduct" (*xing-zhuang*), often by a family member or close friend. One of the mourners would then ask a man known for his literary talent to write the epitaph. Famous writers would receive many such requests and would not accept them all. Occasionally emperors would order a court official to compose a colleague's funerary biography. Sometimes writers were known to have volunteered their service to the deceased's families. In more than a few cases, scholarly men prepared their own *muzhiming* (see Selection 4).

The *muzhiming*, like other tomb goods, was meant to help the tomb's occupant transition from this life to the underworld, to ensure his or her well-being in the afterlife, and to pronounce to the spirits his or her identity and status. As burial objects, funerary inscriptions first and foremost marked the location of the tomb and identified the occupant. They also served to protect the deceased from harmful forces and claimed ownership of the burial plot for the deceased's physical remains and spiritual essences. Moreover, the accounts of the deceased's virtues and accomplishments would comfort the dead as well as inform the underworld authorities of his or her high standing. The inscriptions also served to preserve a record of the deceased's virtue for all time. For the living, *muzhiming* functioned as powerful tools of remembrance and family preservation. The process of epitaph preparation allowed blood relatives to muse over, commemorate, and cherish their ancestor's words and deeds, thus strengthening family solidarity. Funerary biographies reinforced dominant social and cultural values and proved useful in promoting family standing, two major concerns of elite households.

After the manuscript was delivered, often over long distances, the deceased's family had the option of either using the brushwork of the epitaph author or commissioning a calligrapher for better artistic effect. Many did end up hiring a calligrapher, which would require more time and funds. For this reason, *muzhiming*, in rubbings and as artifacts, provide invaluable material for the study of calligraphy and the evolution of the distinct scripts. Generally speaking, although the funerary inscription was written out in the regular script, the name and official title of the deceased on the cover was often done in the seal or clerical script. The finished product was then committed to stone by local artisans. Understandably, the aesthetic inclinations and educational level of the artisans would have a large impact on the visual effect of the end product as they re-created the calligraphers' work. As excavated cases have shown, a calligrapher or a carver would occasionally make a mistake, omitting a word or writing the wrong character.

Taking into account the time needed for the multiple parties to communicate with each other and make adequate arrangements, it could easily take months or more before an inscribed stone was ready for burial. And costs could mount. Historical records are mostly silent on the exact prices charged and amounts paid. When specifics were mentioned in passing, they often involved prominent writers and artists, highly influential families, or unusual burial circumstances. Suffice it to say, the time and expense needed for epitaph preparation could result in long delays in burial. Simpler options did exist. As the made-to-order works (Selection 9) contained in this volume demonstrate, professional workshops existed to provide "funeral packages," including *muzhiming*, that would lessen both the cost and the time required. The availability of this type of service, possibly as early as the late Tang (618–907), indicates that the popularity of *muzhiming* in mortuary rites had spread to prosperous families outside the literati elite.

The interment of the inscribed stone did not mark the end of an epitaph's life. Copies were made and circulated as rubbings and in anthologies, genealogical records, family instructions, and the collected works of individual authors. Not only did these texts circulate among family and friends, but they were also admired for their literary and artistic values within the larger literati community. Over the years, grave robbing, mud slides, construction projects, and archeological excavations have brought to light a large number of stone epitaphs, either in their entirety or as fragments, steadily adding to the body of material historians can draw on.

The most common complaint about funerary inscriptions from the late Tang on was their overly flattering language. Many a Song epitaph writer expressed his frustration and outrage when dealing with overly demanding "clients." As Zeng Gong (1019–1083), one of the most productive Northern Song (960–1127) epitaph writers, put it, sons and grandsons trying to elevate their ancestors at any cost was an age-old problem. "Among sons and grandsons, who would not want to glorify their ancestors?" Even descendants of evil people went to great lengths to brag about and exaggerate their ancestors' accomplishments. Zeng placed much of the blame on epitaph writers, too ready to produce an account that would please the family. "For this reason, epitaphs have become unreliable."[2]

The historical development of funerary inscriptions began in Qin (221–206 BCE) and Han times, when a variety of different texts were placed in tombs. Written on silk or carved on more permanent material, these texts served to identify the deceased, protect the tomb, and inform the spirits and underworld bureaucracy of the status and privileges of the grave's occupants. Engravings of genealogical and biographical records were also found on coffins, tomb goods, offering stands, and the structural elements of the tomb, including the entrances, pillars, lintels, and walls. Most of these tomb "goods" were costly, and their adoption was limited to influential and well-to-do families. Archeological evidence has nonetheless confirmed the general belief that some form of identification of the dead was necessary even for people of the humblest statuses. Hundreds of tile and brick inscriptions found at burial plots for Qin and Han laborers and convicts, for example, contained basic information about the deceased's names, family registrations, and death dates. Although made of lesser materials and inscribed with the briefest of records, these objects served to mark the identities of the dead both for official documentation purposes and for their transition from this life to the other world. Scholars have generally considered these tile and brick inscriptions to be a direct antecedent of *muzhiming*.

To date, the earliest entombed epitaph is the epitaph for Ma Jiang, wife of Jia Wuzhong, dated to 106 CE (see the first piece in Selection 1). Ma Jiang's funerary inscription, in its extant form, is about two hundred characters long and contains some of the most basic elements of *muzhiming*: the deceased's biographical information, exceptional virtues and achievements, death and burial dates, grave location, and other specific burial arrangements. Compared to typical works produced in later times, it notably lacks an elegy. Conversely, some other early *muzhiming* contain only an elegy, without a preface. Only twelve *muzhiming* have survived from the entire Han period, a strong indication that other ways to identify the tomb occupant continued to be used.

More common from the Han period were above-ground, tombside stele inscriptions (*mubei*) (see the second and third pieces in Selection 1). This development was closely related to the growing importance of public funeral ceremonies and ancestral rites held at cemeteries. Steles were erected for ranked officials and people of local importance alike by political subordinates, relatives, friends, and local gentlemen. Intended to mark burial locations as well as memorialize the deceased's exemplary accomplishments, they became especially popular in the second and early third centuries. In addition to celebrating the deceased, a special feature of these steles was to include the names of sponsors and donors, making these artifacts ideal material to understand contemporary social networks and elite identities.

Lavish tombs and funerals attended by large gatherings of people eventually provoked a reaction. The Wei (220–265) and Jin (265–316) courts issued a series of imperial edicts banning extravagant burials. In addition to promoting frugality, the official policies especially aimed to limit the construction of shrines and stone steles that exalted powerful local and regional families. The proscriptions failed to end the popular practice but did lead to families turning more often to putting their inscribed stones underground.

Other factors contributed to the gradual ascendancy of *muzhiming* as a major form of commemorative writing. In the fourth century, invasion and occupation of north China by various non-Chinese groups and the flight of the Chinese court to the south led to long-term political and social instability, with the result that many members of the educated elite died far from their ancestral graveyards. Those interred in temporary burial grounds, in tombs that accommodated multiple bodies, or died violent deaths generated much anxiety in the living as they sought effective ways of remembering the dead. Entombed epitaphs, due to their utility as permanent markers of identity, grew in popularity.

Based on published funerary biographies, it was not until the fifth and sixth centuries, during the Northern Wei (386–534), that *muzhiming* became common in tombs of the elite. Of the 660 published entombed epitaphs from the Han through the Northern Dynasties (386–581) and Southern Dynasties (420–589), more than half (356) date from the Northern Wei. The surge in numbers coincided with the relocation of the Northern Wei capital south to Luoyang in 494. Among the sinicization policies of Emperor Xiaowen (r. 467–499) was an order that Xianbei troops brought south bury their dead in Mangshan near Luoyang instead of returning them to their ancestral homelands farther north. The Xianbei ruling house and Chinese elite also chose these hills for their burial grounds (see Selections 2 and 3).

By the second half of the fifth century, *muzhiming* had acquired their standard form. Not only did they supply detailed genealogical and biographical information, including names, ancestry, marriage alliances, wife and children, agnatic and affinal kin, and office-holding record for men, but they also highlighted the deceased's moral character and accomplishments. They were also coming to be recognized as an independent literary genre. This can be seen from the use of the term *muzhiming* in the inscribed titles (450s), the inclusion of epitaphs in the key anthology *Selections of Refined Literature* (Wenxuan, 520s), and the presence of epitaphs in the collected works of individual authors.

Funerary biographies have survived in large numbers from the Tang and Song dynasties. Compared to the several hundred extant pieces from earlier times, some eight thousand *muzhiming* have survived from the Tang. Nearly a thousand epitaphs were included in *Complete Prose of the Tang Dynasty* (Quan Tang wen), a work compiled in the early nineteenth century from other books then extant, such as collected works and anthologies. Another seven thousand or so have been unearthed, mostly from the Mangshan area and along the corridor between Luoyang and Chang'an, the two Tang capital cities, where the most socially and politically influential clans lived and where their ancestral graveyards were located.

Starting from the second half of the Tang, funerary biographies grew substantially longer; whereas only a few earlier epitaphs were over one thousand words, the longest Tang works ran to two to three thousand characters. Song epitaphs tended to be even lengthier, with a fair number over five thousand characters and some approaching ten thousand. Tang and Song *muzhiming* were also larger than earlier ones, normally exceeding 70 centimeters (28 inches) in width and length, whereas average-sized stone inscriptions from the Jin and Northern Wei dynasties fell between 40 and 50 centimeters (16 to 20 inches). The subjects of Tang and Song *muzhiming* grew much more diverse over time. Although a large percentage continued to feature men and women from the most politically and socially distinguished families, people outside this elite society—including Buddhist and Daoist monks and nuns (Selections 3 and 7), minor officials, local gentlemen without office (Selection 12), merchants (the third piece in Selection 9), palace women, concubines, maids, and wet nurses, even children (Selection 6)—were portrayed in growing numbers through the Tang and Song. The geographical distribution also changed. Whereas the capital areas had the largest concentration of burial plots for members of Tang great clan families, in the Song, funerary biographies were prepared for people from much more diverse regional backgrounds by authors who hailed from equally disparate places. The most striking evidence for this is the inscriptions found in southeastern Shanxi that seem to have been supplied by funeral experts who could produce a funerary biography for almost anyone, probably using a book of samples (see Selection 9).

Two periods, the late eighth to early ninth centuries and the early to mid-eleventh century, were particularly important in the history of funerary biographies, in line with the large political, social, and cultural transformations from the Tang to the Song. Especially relevant are the decline of the great families toward the end of the Tang and the growing influence of the literati elite in the Song. Compared to their medieval aristocratic counterparts, whose status relied in large part on illustrious pedigree and endogamous marriage practice, the new scholar-official class was a much more socially and geographically diverse group, who distinguished themselves through scholarship, examination success, and government service. This change in the composition and orientation of the country's most prominent elite class directly affected *muzhiming* content, especially in terms of the representation of ideal male and female behavior as well as the meanings given to individual and familial achievements.

The growing popularity of funerary biographies in Tang and Song times led to better preservation of them. Although *muzhiming* was accepted as a literary genre by the fifth century, only the poetic elegy portion of an epitaph was included in collected works. The prose preface was often omitted because it was not yet considered essential to the genre. In comparison, Tang epitaphs were kept in their entirety and compiled in a separate, independent category in the collected works of individual authors. Another noticeable change in the same period concerns the style of *muzhiming* writing. Epitaphs from the Period of Disunity (220–589) and early Tang were written in highly stylized parallel prose (see Selections 2, 3, and 4). Starting from the ninth century, the Ancient-Style Prose Movement, led by men like Han Yu (768–824), Liu Zongyuan (773–819), and Quan Deyu (759–818), made possible the lively portrayal of individual lives using anecdotal and intimate details written in much freer prose (see Selection 6).

The triumph of the Ancient-Style Prose literary movement also provided Song writers with new flexibility in how they organized their compositions. Northern Wei and Tang authors normally followed a strict sequential order in their depiction of the deceased. After introducing the deceased's name, ancestral and familial information, and early life, the epitaph would usually proceed to depict the major events in his or her life, immediate family members, and death and funeral arrangements. In contrast, Song authors did not let these conventions limit them. It was not out of the ordinary for a Song epitaph to begin with a statement such as "On such and such day, Mr. A died in the capital [at home, or on his official post]," "Mr. B [the grieving son], wearing mourning clothes and wailing loudly, showed up at my door and implored me to write his late mother's funerary biography," or "In such and such year, I got to know Mr. C when we were both serving in such and such prefecture." Such unconventional, attention-grabbing openings were often followed by meticulous accounts of associations between the author and the deceased or their close kin. The variations in structure and narrative not only marked new directions in epitaph writing, but they also pointed to the creative energy Song authors put into composing a fascinating biographical account (see Selections 10, 11, 12, and 13).

Pre-Tang funerary biographies rarely list their authors. Tang authors regularly identified themselves from the eighth century onward. Among the authors who are identified are a few women (Selection 5), generally writing in much the way that men did when writing about close relatives.

The Tang is also notable for the participation of highly celebrated calligraphers in the production of funerary inscriptions. The brushwork of Ouyang Xun (557–641), Yu Shinan (558–638), Zhang Xu (675–750), Yan Zhenqing (709–784), and many others added greatly to the prestige of the finished product. Equally important, the participation of major calligraphers led to widespread imitation of their calligraphic styles from rubbings of funerary inscriptions and thus contributed to the evolution of the regular script used for them. For these reasons, starting from the Song period, rubbings of epitaphs became collectible for both their literary and their artistic merits. By the eleventh century, rubbings and hand-made copies of stone epitaphs were available for purchase by complete strangers who simply treated *muzhiming* as literary or artistic productions. Consequently, epitaphs did not simply serve to please the dead and perpetuate ancestral memory. They became a public, highly effective platform for families as well as epitaph authors to mark social status and promote social and cultural ideals.

The growing public use of epitaphs reflects a shift in the audience for *muzhiming* from the spirits of the deceased and the underworld toward the living. This change can also be seen in how epitaph writers referred to their relationship with the deceased or the deceased's family. Song writers routinely recounted the circumstance under which a person requesting the epitaph asked the author to write it and how the author was convinced to oblige. The writer might imply that his long-term friendship with the subject or the family and his intimate knowledge about the deceased's outstanding character and achievements obligated him to help preserve the deceased's legacy (Selections 10 and 11).

Another sign that funerary biographies were becoming more an affair of the living than of the dead can be seen in the changes in their content. Following earlier precedents, Tang and Song epitaphs regularly mentioned their subject's ancestry and family background. The space that this component took up, however, shrank over time. Epitaphs from the first half of the Tang routinely detailed the deceased's great clan origins. Ninth- and tenth-century funerary inscriptions were less specific in this respect. By the eleventh century, only a small number of funerary inscriptions would trace the deceased's descent for centuries. This diminishing interest in ancestry reflects the decreasing importance of pedigree to social standing during this period.

Shortening accounts of ancestry helped make room for extended discussion of descendants and their achievements. Early Tang epitaphs rarely provide a full list of the deceased's children, most often only the son or grandson in charge of the burial. It was not until the second half of the dynasty that daughters' names appeared regularly. From the beginning of the ninth century, the depiction of all offspring, even children born to concubines, became increasingly common in parents' *muzhiming*. By the mid-eleventh century, a typical *muzhiming* would include complete information about the marriages of the deceased's sons and daughters; his or her paternal and maternal grandchildren; and sons' and grandsons' schooling, examination success, and official service record. In this context, mothers, especially widows, were increasingly given credit for educating their children and for nurturing sons' scholarly and bureaucratic ambitions. This increasing focus on the deceased's immediate family members contributed to ever lengthier *muzhiming*.

Descendants, sons in particular, were made especially visible in late Tang and Song epitaphs in another respect: the *muzhiming* became nearly as important as a means to celebrate a son's filial exertions as it was to laud the dead. Song funerary inscriptions are replete with poignant anecdotes about sons going to great lengths to obtain a parent's epitaph from a person of literary repute. Sons are described as traveling long distances in states of deep grief and waiting for months, even years, in order to convince a famous writer to author their parent's funerary biography. This celebration of the son's filial devotion to securing the best possible funerary biography for his parent led to an interesting phenomenon. Of the hundreds of Tang and Song epitaph authors, the large majority chose not to compose their own parents' funerary biographies. To use the Northern Song as an example, of the 373 epitaph writers whose work was included in *Complete Prose of the Song Dynasty* (Quan Song wen), only 15, or 4 percent, authored a *muzhiming* for a parent. Instead, these highly accomplished authors turned to their friends and colleagues to extol their parents' virtues and, in the process, to celebrate the filiality of the epitaph-requesting son. The celebrated writers who eventually consented were probably responding to market demand as they wrote longer and longer epitaphs.

After the Tang dynasty, part or all of China was repeatedly ruled by non-Han royal houses. The Kitan Liao (916–1125) and Jurchen Jin (1115–1234) ruled only parts of China (Jin considerably more than Liao), but first the Mongol Yuan (1234–1368) and then the Manchu Qing (1644–1912) came to rule both north and south China. Selections included here from those dynasties deal in several different ways with the contact between

Han and the non-Han rulers (see Selections 8, 14, 15, and 19). Interestingly, the authors of these inscriptions do not highlight ethnic differences between the central subject and those he worked with or married. Was this because ethnic difference was indeed a matter of little significance in everyday life, because it was too obvious to need discussion (somewhat like class), or because its presence was a sensitive subject?

No full tally exists of the funerary biographies extant from later dynasties—Liao through Qing. It is probably safe to assume that more were written in the later dynasties than in the Tang owing to population growth, the expansion of the literati class, and the spreading use of *muzhiming* as a funeral practice for ordinary men and women. Increasing literacy and the prosperity of the publishing industry further contributed to the transmission and preservation of the textual versions of the funerary inscriptions. The recently compiled *Complete Prose of the Song Dynasty*, for example, contains about 4,500 funerary biographies, most preserved in their authors' collected works but some excavated. One Qing compilation includes 5,500 *muzhiming*.[3] The reason not as many *muzhiming* have been published for later dynasties reflects a lower priority given to both excavating and publishing findings from more recent centuries, in large part because of the abundance of other sources for late imperial China. Moreover, within the commemorative writing genre, *muzhiming* did not enjoy the same dominance that it had in the Tang and Song because the bereaved frequently turned to other literary forms, such as personal memoirs and sets of poems, to express their grief.

Most of the Tang-Song developments in the style of funerary biographies continued in the post-Song period. Funerary biographies remained a respected literary genre, and certain authors wrote many of them. Yu Ji, the author of Selection 14, for instance, wrote eighty-nine, and Mao Qiling, the author of both Selection 17 and Selection 20, wrote eighty-five. Funerary inscriptions provide a valuable source on merchants (Selection 16) and military men (Selection 17). For these later periods, we have selected epitaphs for women in a higher proportion than found in the whole surviving corpus because women are less well documented in other sources. Funerary biographies written by women's close relatives seem especially revealing. We include one by a brother (Selection 18) and one by a husband (Selection 21). We also have a funerary biography written by a wife for her husband (Selection 22). Fewer than fifty funerary biographies written by women survive from imperial China, mainly from the Ming and Qing periods, providing rare chances to hear women's voices.

We invite readers to peruse these funerary biographies in any order. Each can stand on its own, but there is much to learn by comparing them across time. One could read those for women together, for instance, or those for military men.

In considering private biographies and the ways they differ from ones in the state histories, readers might find it interesting to consider the thoughts of an eleventh-century man on that issue. Zeng Gong was of the opinion that, although writing history and writing funerary inscriptions shared similar goals, they differed in one area: history recorded all factual information, including both good and bad deeds. Not everyone, however, deserved an epitaph. To Zeng, ancients began to produce *muzhiming* lest "the outstanding deeds of the accomplished, the virtuous, the talented, the ambitious, and the righteous might be forgotten by posterity." Their deeds must be chronicled, inscribed, and subsequently enshrined in temples or deposited in tombs. This way, "the deceased will have no regret. The living will have paid their respect [by acknowledging their deeds]. The good people of the world, happy to see the preservation of these records, are motivated to establish themselves [in similar ways]."[4] Zeng's view on this major difference between history and funerary biographical writing gave epitaph authors and descendants much to think about as they shaped the deceased's legacy. At the same time, Zeng hinted that fear of being deemed undeserving of an epitaph and thus forgotten to history was socially beneficial, as it motivated good behavior.

Notes

The full Chinese text of the biographies translated in this volume is available at https://doi.org/10.6069/9780295746425.s01.

1. There is now a large literature, in both Chinese and English, on the topics discussed in this introduction. For some of the most accessible of these studies, see the Further Reading list at the end of this introduction.

2. Zeng Gong, in Zeng Zaozhuang 曾棗莊 and Liu Lin 劉琳, eds., *Quan Song wen* 全宋文 (Shanghai: Shanghai cishu chubanshe, 2006), 57:246–47.

3. *Qingdai beizhuan quanji* 清代碑傳全集 (Shanghai: Guji chubanshe, 1988).

4. Zeng Gong, *Quan Song wen*, 57:246.

Further Reading

STUDIES OF FUNERARY BIOGRAPHIES AS TEXTS OR INSCRIBED STONES

Barbieri-Low, Anthony. "Carving Out a Living: Stone-Monument Artisans during the Eastern Han Dynasty." In *Recarving China's Past: Art, Archaeology, and Architecture of the "Wu Family Shrines,"* by Cary Y. Liu, Michael Nylan, Anthony Barbieri-Low, et al., 485–511. New Haven, CT: Yale University Press, 2005.

Brown, Miranda. "Han Steles: How to Elicit What They Have to Tell Us." In *Rethinking and Recarving: Ideals, Practices, and Problems of the "Wu Family Shrines" and Han China*, edited by Cary Y. Liu and Naomi Noble Richard, 180–95. Princeton, NJ: Princeton Art Museum, 2008.

Choo, Jessey Jiun-Chyi. *Inscribing Death: Burials, Texts, and Remembrance in Tang China, 500–1000 C.E.* Honolulu: University of Hawai'i Press, forthcoming.

———. "Shall We Profane the Service of the Dead? Burial Divination and Remembrance in Late Medieval *Muzhiming*." *Tang Studies* 33 (2015): 1–37.

Davis, Timothy M. *Entombed Epigraphy and Commemorative Culture in Early Medieval China: A History of Early Muzhiming.* Leiden: Brill, 2015.

Ditter, Alexei. "The Commerce of Commemoration: Commissioned *Muzhiming* in the Mid- to Late Tang." *Tang Studies* 32 (2014): 21–46.

Ebrey, Patricia Buckley. "Later Han Stone Inscriptions." *Harvard Journal of Asiatic Studies* 40.2 (1980): 325–53.

Egan, Ronald C. *The Literary Works of Ou-yang Hsiu.* Cambridge, UK: Cambridge University Press, 1984.

Lu, Huiwen. "Calligraphy of Stone Engravings in Northern Wei Luoyang." In *Character and Context in Chinese Calligraphy*, edited by Cary Y. Liu, Dora C. Y. Ching, and Judith G. Smith, 78–103. Princeton, NJ: Princeton University Art Museum, 1999.

Schottenhammer, Angela. "Characteristics of Song Epitaphs." In *Burial in Song China*, edited by Dieter Kuhn, 235–306. Heidelberg: Edition Forum, 1994.

Yang, Ruowei. "The Liao-Dynasty Stone Inscriptions and Their Importance to the Study of Liao History. *Gest Library Journal* 6.2 (1993): 55–72.

Zhang, Cong Ellen. "Bureaucratic Politics and Commemorative Biography: The Epitaphs of Fan Zhongyan." In *State Power in China, 900–1400*, edited by Patricia Buckley Ebrey and Paul Jakov Smith, 192–216. Seattle: University of Washington Press, 2016.

Zhao, Chao. "Stone Inscriptions of the Wei-Jin Nanbeichao Period." *Early Medieval China* 1 (1994): 84–96.

STUDIES OF FUNERARY CULTURE AND COMMEMORATION OF ANCESTORS

Brashier, K. E. *Ancestral Memory in Early China.* Cambridge, MA: Harvard University Asia Center, 2011.

———. *Public Memory in Early China.* Cambridge, MA: Harvard University Asia Center, 2014.

Brown, Miranda. *The Politics of Mourning in Early China.* Albany: State University of New York Press, 2007.

Choi, Mihwa. *Death Rituals and Politics in Northern Song China.* Oxford: Oxford University Press, 2017.

Fong, Mary H. "Antecedents of Sui-Tang Burial Practices in Shaanxi." *Artibus Asiae* 51 (1991): 147–98.

Guo, Jue. "Concepts of Death and the Afterlife Reflected in Newly Discovered Tomb Objects and Texts from Han China." In *Mortality in Traditional Chinese Thought,* edited by Amy Olberding and Phillip. J. Ivanhoe, 85–115. Albany: State University of New York Press, 2011.

Huang, Martin W. *Intimate Memory: Gender and Mourning in Late Imperial China.* Albany: State University of New York Press, 2018.

Hulsewé, A. F. P. "Texts in Tombs" *Asiatische Studien* 18–19 (1965): 78–89.

Huntington, Rania. *Ink and Tears: Memory, Mourning, and Writing in the Yu Family.* Honolulu: University of Hawai'i Press, 2018.

Lai, Guolong. *Excavating the Afterlife: The Archaeology of Early Chinese Religion.* Seattle: University of Washington Press, 2015.

McMullen, David. "The Death of Chou Li-chen: Imperially Ordered Suicide or Natural Causes?" *Asia Major,* 3rd ser., 2.2 (1989): 23–82.

Poo, Mu-chou. "Ideas Concerning Death and Burial in Pre-Han and Han China." *Asia Major,* 3rd ser., 3.2 (1990): 25–62.

Steinhardt, Nancy Shatzman. "Yuan Period Tombs and Their Inscriptions: Changing Identities for Chinese Afterlife." *Ars Orientalis* 37 (2009): 140–74.

Wu Hung. *The Art of the Yellow Springs.* Honolulu: University of Hawai'i Press, 2010.

———. "From Temple to Tomb: Ancient Chinese Art and Religion in Transition." *Early China* 13 (1988): 78–115.

STUDIES OF WOMEN'S HISTORY DRAWING EXTENSIVELY ON FUNERARY BIOGRAPHIES

Barr, Allan H. "Marriage and Mourning in Early-Qing Tributes to Wives." *Nan Nü: Men, Women and Gender in China* 15.1 (2013): 137–78.

Bossler, Beverly. "A Daughter Is a Daughter All Her Life: Affinal Relations and Women's Networks in Song and Late Imperial China." *Late Imperial China* 21.1 (2000): 77–106.

Carlitz, Katherine. "Mourning, Personality, Display: Ming Literati Commemorate Their Mothers, Sisters, and Daughters." *Nan Nü: Men, Women and Gender in China* 15.1 (2013): 30–68.

Ebrey, Patricia Buckley. *The Inner Quarters, Marriage and the Lives of Chinese Women in the Sung Period.* Berkeley: University of California Press, 1993.

———. "The Women in Liu Kezhuang's Family." In *Women and the Family in Chinese History,* by Patricia Buckley Ebrey, 89–106. New York: Routledge, 2003.

Halperin, Mark. "Domesticity and the Dharma: Portraits of Buddhist Laywomen in Sung China." *T'oung Pao* 92.1 (2006): 50–100.

Lee, Jen-der. "The Death of a Princess-Codifying Classical Family Ethics in Early Medieval China." In *Presence and Presentation: Women in the Chinese Literati Tradition,* edited by Sherry Mou, 1–37. New York: St. Martin's Press, 1999.

———. "The Epitaph of a Third-Century Wet Nurse, Xu Yi." In *Early Medieval China: A Sourcebook,* edited by Wendy Swartz, Robert F. Campany, Yang Lu, and Jessey Choo, 458–67. New York: Columbia University Press, 2014.

———. "The Life of Women in the Six Dynasties." *Journal of Women and Gender Studies* 4 (1993): 47–80.

Yao, Ping. "Good Karmic Connections: Buddhist Mothers and Their Children in Tang China (618–907)." *Nan Nü: Men, Women and Gender in China* 10.1 (2008): 57–85.

———. "Women in Portraits: An Overview of Epitaphs from Early and Medieval China." In *Overt and Covert Treasures: Essays on the Sources for Chinese Women's History,* edited by Clara Wing-chung Ho, 157–83. Hong Kong: Chinese University Press, 2012.

———. "Women's Epitaphs in Tang China (618–907)." In *Beyond Exemplar Tales: Women's Biography in Chinese History,* edited by Joan Judge and Ying Hu, 139–57. Berkeley: University of California Press, 2011.

STUDIES OF SOCIAL AND CULTURAL HISTORY DRAWING EXTENSIVELY ON FUNERARY BIOGRAPHIES

Bossler, Beverly J. *Powerful Relations: Kinship, Status, and the State in Sung China (960–1279).* Cambridge, MA: Council on East Asian Studies, Harvard University, 1998.

Chaffee, John W. *Branches of Heaven: A History of the Imperial Clan of Sung China.* Cambridge, MA: Harvard University Asia Center, 1999.

Ebrey, Patricia Buckley. *The Aristocratic Families of Early Imperial China: A Case Study of the Po-ling Ts'ui Family.* Cambridge, UK: Cambridge University Press, 1978.

Halperin, Mark. *Out of the Cloister: Literati Perspectives on Buddhism in Sung China, 960–1279*. Cambridge, MA: Harvard Asia Center, 2006.

Hymes, Robert P. *Statesmen and Gentlemen: The Elite of Fu-chou, Chiang-hsi, in Northern and Southern Sung*. Cambridge, UK: Cambridge University Press, 1986.

Iiyama, Tomoyasu. "Steles and Status: Evidence for the Emergence of a New Elite in Yuan North China." *Journal of Chinese History* 1.1 (2017): 3–26.

Lu, Weijing. "Personal Writings on Female Relatives in the Qing Collected Works." In *Overt and Covert Treasures: Essays on the Sources for Chinese Women's History*, edited by Clara Wing-ching Ho, 403–26. Hong Kong: Chinese University Press, 2010.

Shields, Anna M. *One Who Knows Me: Friendship and Literary Culture in Mid-Tang China*. Cambridge, MA: Harvard University Asia Center, 2015.

Tackett, Nicolas. *The Destruction of the Medieval Chinese Aristocracy*. Cambridge, MA: Harvard University Press, 2014.

Xu, Man. "China's Local Elites in Transition: Seventh- to Twelfth-Century Epitaphs Excavated in Luzhou." *Asia Major*, 3rd ser., 30.1 (2017): 59–107.

STUDIES OF THE CHINESE BIOGRAPHICAL TRADITION

Durrant, Stephen. *The Cloudy Mirror: Tension and Conflict in the Writings of Sima Qian*. Albany: State University of New York Press, 1995.

Judge, Joan, and Hu Ying, eds. *Beyond Exemplar Tales: Women's Biography in Chinese History*. Berkeley: University of California Press, 2011.

Twichett, Denis. "Chinese Biographical Writing." In *Historians of China and Japan*, edited by W. G. Beasley and E. G. Pulleyblank, 95–114. London: Oxford University Press, 1961.

———. "Problems of Chinese Biography." In *Confucian Personalities*, edited by Arthur F. Wright and Denis Twitchett, 24–39. Stanford: Stanford University Press, 1962.

———. *The Writing of Official History under the T'ang*. Cambridge, UK: Cambridge University Press, 1992.

Three Short Eastern Han Funerary Biographies

Epitaphs for Ma Jiang 馬姜 (34-106), Wu Zhongshan 吳仲山
(ca. 92-172), and Kong Dan 孔耽 (fl. 182)

TRANSLATED BY PING YAO AND PATRICIA BUCKLEY EBREY

These epitaphs, among the earliest to survive, were not for people of
national significance and include one woman. They concentrate on
sketching the deceased's character while also providing basic data on
death and burial.

THE EARLIEST SURVIVING INTERRED INSCRIPTION IS "FUNERARY
Biography for Madam Ma Jiang," dated 106 CE. Discovered in 1929 in
Luoyang, the epitaph not only provides biographical information about
Madam Ma, but also praises her virtue. Although relatively short, it contains all of the most basic elements of *muzhiming*: biographical information about the deceased, her achievements and virtues, her relatives, a
description of the funeral arrangements, the name of the author of the
epitaph, and the family member who commissioned the epitaph.

Modern archeologists were not the first to record the texts of acciden-
tally discovered stone inscriptions. By the Song dynasty, many educated
men made rubbings of stones that they found bearing inscriptions dating back to the Han period. They also began publishing notes on the

rubbings in their collections. One such collector, Hong Kuo (1117–1184), recorded the full text of 185 inscriptions along with his notes on them, including not just inscriptions to mark graves, but also many other kinds, such as inscriptions for temples, road-building projects, or to commemorate an especially admired local official. The second and third pieces included in this selection are from his *Explications of Works in Clerical Script* (Li shi). From Hong Kuo's time on, scholars with antiquarian interests published inscriptions dating from earlier dynasties.

Most of the epitaphs that survive from the Han period were inscribed not on stones that were buried with the coffin, but on standing stones erected above the grave. In that period, the texts on the stones were often relatively brief. The funerary biography for Wu Zhongshan, the second given below, is unusual in that no one in the subject's family seems to have held government office. It also has a high proportion of borrowed or otherwise unusual characters. The last of the three funerary biographies here, for Kong Dan, is for a man who served in local government at a subordinate level, though it explains that for a while he filled in for a regular official who was ill. However, like Mr. Wu's, his biography focuses mostly on his personal character. What makes him stand out is that he wrote his own funerary biography and had a funerary shrine built while he was still living. The inscription even mentions how much he paid for the construction.

Funerary Biography for Madam Ma Jiang

On the twenty-first day of the seventh month, in the seventh year of the Yongping reign period [64 CE], Jia Wuzhong, the fifth son of [Jia Fu], General of the Left and Specially Advanced Duke of Jiaodong of the Han dynasty, died. He was then twenty-nine years of age. His wife, Ma Jiang, was the daughter of [Ma Yuan], the Wave Breaking General, who was also the Duke of Xinxi and Zhongcheng, and the elder sister of the Brilliant Virtue Empress [39–79, consort of Emperor Ming, r. 57–75]. She gave birth to four daughters. At the age of twenty-three, her husband, Mr. Jia, died. Madam Ma resolutely held to the lofty principle of chastity and toiled diligently for years. She raised her daughters well and glorified the ancestors. Two daughters were elevated to be consorts in the Xian [illegible] Jie Palace; another was married to the Duke of Ting, surnamed Zhu; and yet another was married to the Duke of Yanggao, surnamed Liu. Her home was full of those wearing red and purple [robes of high office] and recipients of royal favors and ranks. This was all because of Madam [illegible]. With her motherly virtues, Madam [illegible] protected the entire clan. At the age of seventy-three, [she passed away] on the [illegible] day of the seventh month, the first year of the Yanping reign period [106]. The emperor paid his condolences, and the Two Palaces[1] [illegible] provided imperial items [to be used for the funeral] in accordance with the rites. She was then buried on the tenth day of the ninth month at the old cemetery in Mangmen [illegible]. Her descendants feared not being able to make her virtues known and thus carved this on the stone to record [broken here].

Source: Zhao Chao 趙超, *Han Wei Nan Bei chao muzhi huibian* 漢魏南北朝墓誌彙編 (Tianjin: Tianjin guji chubanshe, 1992), 1.

Stele for the Deceased Commoner Wu Zhongshan

Dated early in the twelfth month of the first year of the Xiping reign period [172].

Mr. Wu Zhongshan when young established a name for good deeds. He would take on any sacrifice himself and in frugality had no equal. He did not covet official advancement but hid away in the world of men. The commandery and county requested his services, but he never even went close enough to see the city walls. He persisted in his life of poverty and hardship, having no aspirations for fame and glory.

Mr. Wu was the second among three brothers. He deferred to the elder and guided the younger, and the three of them went around together. The eldest and the youngest unfortunately died young. As the seasons passed, Mr. Wu's years exceeded eighty. Before his lifetime was exhausted, he met misfortune [and died]. His sons and grandsons, swallowing their tears, called his soul back but to no avail, as he was far from the world. How bitter it is!

Mr. Wu's virtue was exceptional. He extended kindnesses to his local community. When people far and near would ask him for things, he would not tell them that he had nothing himself. In the spring and fall, he would take loans so that he could give to the needy.

Without going contrary to people's intentions, he would guide them using reason. In the markets and courtyards, he would provide food to those who were starving. He also gathered food for orphans under his care. For those who died, he would arrange burials. For the orphans, he would arrange marriages. When those with debts were unable to repay them, he would not merely lament it but would repay them on their behalf. How could people know of all his kind acts of generosity!

Mr. Wu had three children, two of them grown men when he died. They inherited very little because, when he had any surplus, it went in all directions. Not only were they unable to construct [an elaborate tomb with] colorfully painted towers, halls, and viewing pavilions, but it was even difficult for them to deal with their relatives or provide more than a thin coffin and a slight outer coffin, of modest size.

The orphans grieved for their departed father, distraught day and night, feeling as though something was missing. They decided to build a cover so that, if the spirits have consciousness, they will enjoy the flourishing rivers and hills. How beautiful! May his descendants have ten thousand years.

Source: Hong Kuo 洪适, *Li shi* 隷釋, *Shike shiliao xinbian* edition, 9.3a–4a, with readings from Huang Gongzhu, *Liang Han jinshi wenxuan pingzhu* (Hong Kong: Taiping shuju, 1966), 143–45.

Stele for the Spirit Shrine of Kong Dan (fl. 182), Administrator of Liang

Mr. Kong's name was Dan, and he was the oldest of three brothers. His forebears have flourished since the Yin dynasty [i.e., Shang dynasty, 16th c. to 1045 BCE]. Since the Yin house placed its emphasis on inner substance, Mr. Kong took as his courtesy name Boben, "Elder Brother Basic." At first, when the region of Lu suffered the collapse of [Wang Mang's] Xin state, the descendants scattered; since [ancestor] Shuyang, they have been settled here.

When Mr. Kong was young, he studied *The Classics of Ritual* [Liji]. During a period of general hardship when people took to eating human flesh, he made a hut of dirt and thatch and wore himself out gathering wild vegetables to feed his parents. Kind, honest, quiet, and faithful— such traits came to him naturally and did not have to be learned.

Once Mr. Kong's income had improved a little, he remembered with regret his deceased grandmother and so decided to honor her with a shrine. He expressed his filial sadness and regret as in the "Gentle Wind" and "Smartweed" [poems in *The Book of Songs* (Shijing)]. He erected a building and planted cypress trees around it. His filial sentiment was so sincere that it moved the spirits: a large snake appeared on the stone, disappearing later. Mr. Kong also set free caged birds and released trapped animals.

Mr. Wu's younger brother had a lofty spirit, but what he accumulated was virtue, not property. Mr. Kong invited him to live with him for decades. Even if his brother made unreasonable requests, he would respond to him generously. Therefore, Heaven was moved and gave evidence of it by the [auspicious sign of the] interlocking of the branches of trees.

Because Mr. Kong was generous with other people and was very talented, his fame spread widely. The county asked him to serve as a clerk of the registrar, and the commandery requested his advice. When the head of the commandery, Mr. Shen of Wucheng, became ill, he delegated his responsibilities to Mr. Kong, who administered all of the civil affairs under the seal of the magistrate of Gushu County.

As the years passed and he grew old, Mr. Kong returned home. With the yellow hair of old age, bent shoulders, and handsome grandchildren, he enjoyed a happy old age. Observing the deterioration of metal and stone, he came to realize that everything has its beginning and its end. Thus [he built this shrine] in order to make plans to obtain blessings for thousands of years and the favor of Heaven.

Watching the craftsmen build the shrine gave him great satisfaction. The inner room of the shrine has free access to the outside on four sides, and there is a long walkway. It cost altogether 300,000 [coins] and was completed in the sixth month, summer, of the fifth year of the Guanghe reign period [182], the *renxu* year.

Mr. Kong's son respectfully and admiringly praised him in verse as follows:

Mr. Kong's virtue came by nature. He was benevolent and pure.
Because of his compassion, a divine snake appeared.
Heaven sent down portents in the interlocking of branches.
Mr. Kong took pity on the birds and animals and set them free.
He enjoyed a prosperous life, and his fame spread.
He understood the nature of life and was able to anticipate the future.
In order to perpetuate [his name] for millions of years, his achievements have been recorded.
To show his worthiness, a stone shrine has been inscribed.

[Note in smaller characters:]
I, Mr. Kong's son, De, have recorded my father's deeds based on what he himself wrote. When he was seventy-two, he erected this shrine himself. I have sadly finished the inside. At this time, I have already served in the commandery several times as a clerk and local inspector. Obeying his instructions, I have recorded [my father's] activities, doing the calligraphy myself. The stone craftsmen Zhu Shi and Zhu Zu of this county together undertook the construction.

Source: Hong Kuo, *Li shi*, 5.5a–7a.

Note

1. During the Han dynasties, the Two Palaces were commonly referred to as East Palace and West Palace, as were their occupants, the empress dowager and the emperor respectively. The term could also refer to the emperor and the crown prince.

Further Reading

Brown, Miranda. *The Politics of Mourning in Early China*. Albany: State University of New York Press, 2007.

Ebrey, Patricia. "Later Han Stone Inscriptions." *Harvard Journal of Asiatic Studies* 40.2 (1980): 325–53.

Kinney, Anne Behnke, trans. *Exemplary Women of Early China*. New York: Columbia University Press, 2014.

Yao, Ping. "Women in Portraits: An Overview of Epitaphs from Early and Medieval China." In *Overt and Covert Treasures: Essays on the Sources for Chinese Women's History*, edited by Clara Wing-Chung Ho, 153–83. Hong Kong: Chinese University Press, 2012.

A Chinese General Serving the Northern Wei State

Entombed Epitaph for the Late Wei Dynasty Overseer of Military Affairs, Sima Yue 司馬悅 (462–508)

TRANSLATED BY TIMOTHY DAVIS

This epitaph reveals the complicated political history of an era when northern and southern courts coexisted, and people who lost power at one might be welcomed at the other.

IN 1979, THE TOMB OF SIMA YUE (462–508) WAS DISCOVERED 1.5 miles southwest of the Meng County seat in Henan.[1] Although it had been looted, the tomb still contained a dozen earthenware vessels and a well-preserved epitaph. The recovered inscription, translated below, provides an opportunity to explore the important role of the Sima family of Wen County (the royal family of the Jin dynasty) in the complicated political history of the Period of Disunity—an era characterized by the blending of Xianbei (Turco-Mongolic) and Chinese culture, which shaped the economic, social, military, and political patterns of the subsequent Sui and Tang dynasties in profound ways.

When the Eastern Han dynasty collapsed in the early third century, the Chinese realm split into three kingdoms. The Kingdom of Wei (220–265) in the north had the largest population and controlled the traditional capital region of Chang'an and Luoyang. However, owing to the machinations of the Sima family of Wen County, the royal family of the Wei state steadily lost power. The prominence of the Jin regime derived from Sima Yi's (179–251) successful military campaigns against Wei's neighboring state to the southwest. Following Sima Yi's death, his sons continued to control the court through their firm hold on military power. Eventually, in 265, Sima Yi's grandson, Sima Yan (236–290), accepted the abdication of the last Wei ruler and began his reign as the founding emperor of the Western Jin dynasty, which unified the Chinese realm in 280.

That unification, however, proved to be less enduring than anticipated, as civil war erupted among Sima Yan's many sons. This protracted conflict was followed by several campaigns initiated by non-Chinese peoples (Xiongnu, Jie, Di, Qiang, and Xianbei) against a weakening Jin authority. By 317, the regime was no longer able to ward off these challenges to its sovereignty and reluctantly abandoned its capital in Luoyang and fled south—a transition that marked the beginning of the Eastern Jin period. With this psychologically stunning and economically devastating development, China experienced a period of protracted political division lasting over 270 years, as a succession of northern and southern states contended for legitimacy. It was during the most enduring of the Northern Dynasties, the Northern Wei, ruled by the Tuoba clan of the Xianbei people, that the subject of the epitaph under consideration and his immediate forebears were active.

Sima Yue's grandfather, Sima Chuzhi (390–464), was an eighth-generation descendant of Sima Yi's younger brother Sima Kui. All we know of the intervening genealogical connections is that Sima Chuzhi was seventeen when his father was killed by a member of his administrative staff. Chuzhi accompanied his father's body to Danyang (Jiangsu) near the Eastern Jin capital, Jiankang (Nanjing, Jiangsu), for burial. While at the capital, the ambitious general Liu Yu (Liu Song Emperor Wu, r. 420–422), who had been consolidating his authority for years, embarked on an aggressive plan to seize control of the Jin state. Several members of the Sima family were victims of this coup. Chuzhi's uncle and elder brother were both killed, and Chuzhi himself only managed to escape by hiding in a Buddhist monastery. He crossed the Yangzi River and sought protection with an uncle, then the governor of a province in Hubei. When his uncle's provincial troops were defeated by forces loyal to Liu Yu, Chuzhi had no choice but to flee to the north.

When the Northern Wei emperor sent representatives to see if Chuzhi posed a threat, Chuzhi argued that that he could serve the regime more effectively if he had official recognition. The emperor subsequently bestowed upon him the title of General Campaigning in the South and made him governor of Jingzhou (southern Henan). Chuzhi helped the Northern Wei defeat a major campaign waged by the second Liu Song ruler to retake Luoyang and territory south of the Yellow River. In his later years, Sima Chuzhi married the Princess of He'nei and was appointed to the position of palace attendant. His son, Sima Jinlong (d. 484), became even more integrated into the Xianbei elite. He married the daughter of the Prince of Longxi and on passing away was buried just outside the capital at Pingcheng (Datong, Shanxi). His tomb has been excavated in modern times, revealing hundreds of splendid burial objects. In the 490s, the Northern Wei emperor Xiaowen (r. 471–499) undertook an ambitious plan to structure the Northern Wei state according to Chinese models. During the five-year period from 494 to 499 CE, he issued a series of edicts designed to close the cultural gap between Xianbei and Chinese. He banned the wearing of non-Chinese clothing, required the use of the Chinese language at court, insisted on employing Chinese weights and measures, ordered courtiers to replace their Xianbei names with Chinese names (the imperial family's surname was changed to Yuan), and urged members of the elite class to mourn their dead according to Confucian practices. And, most important, he decided to relocate the Northern Wei capital from Pingcheng in the north to Luoyang. The move, carried out in 494, was intended to strengthen Northern Wei control over conscription, taxation, and the agrarian economy in the productive southern regions of the empire. One year after the relocation of the capital, Emperor Xiaowen issued an edict, ordering elites residing at Luoyang to be buried at the new capital rather than having their remains returned to their northern homelands. In other words, the Tuoba elite were reclassified as natives of Luoyang.

Sima Yue, the subject of the epitaph translated below, was the third son of Sima Jinlong. In the first paragraph of his epitaph, the author lays out the impressive titles and offices held by his father and grandfather. By highlighting Sima Yue's fine pedigree, the author both acknowledges the achievements of the Sima ancestors and fortifies the family's claims to an enduring elite status. The second paragraph begins by celebrating the many excellent attributes and moral qualities that Sima Yue possessed, even in his youth. It then alludes to his steady promotion to positions in the bureaucracy and his exemplary service in those offices. The narrative effectively persuades the reader that Sima Yue's staunch loyalty to the Northern Wei state was merely the continuation of the tradition of faithful service initiated by his grandfather and father.

The third paragraph of Sima Yue's epitaph informs the reader that not only did he accompany the court to Luoyang in 494, but the emperor's younger brother, the Prince of Xianyang, recognized him as a "peerless and elegant" gentleman. Apparently, part of this admiration for Sima Yue derived from his ability to "treat all men of the local lands fairly," meaning he was effective at negotiating with the Chinese who were already living in the area, helping to smooth the transition to a more direct Northern Wei rule of the region. As a result of his successes, he was given greater trust and responsibility as a military leader.

Sima Yue was also involved in protecting the Northern Wei lands south of the Huai River from the encroaching Liang armies. The fourth paragraph of his epitaph celebrates his contribution to the defeat of Liang forces. As a reward, Sima Yue was appointed governor of Yuzhou (eastern Henan and northern Anhui). Unfortunately, he was unable to enjoy this special honor for long, as he was murdered by some of his own subordinates in 508. The rebels managed to overcome Sima Yue's bodyguard, then executed him and sent his head to the Liang emperor Wu. The epitaph describes this tragedy in less explicit terms: "hostilities were triggered and stealthily launched; that such calamity would arise was not anticipated."

The nearly two-and-a-half-year gap between Sima Yue's death in 508 and his burial in 511 is probably attributable to the fact that the family did not wish to bury his dismembered body without first retrieving his severed head. Not long after the quelling of the rebellion, a Northern Wei general retook the territory from the Liang and negotiated to exchange two prisoners for Sima Yue's head. Following this exchange, Sima Yue's burial went forward.

A close reading of the epitaph produced for Sima Yue helps us better understand many aspects of the early medieval experience in China, including the motives behind shifting political loyalties, the fragility of elite prestige, the complexities of ethnic identity, and the results of encounters between peoples with deep ties to the steppe and those imbued with the classic values of traditional Chinese civilization.

Epitaph for the Late Wei Dynasty Overseer of Military Affairs for Yuzhou Bearing [Plenipotentiary] Credentials, General Chastising the Caitiffs, Founding Viscount of Yuyang County, and Governor of Yuzhou, Sima Yue

The gentleman's taboo name is Yue; his courtesy name, Qingzong. He was a native of Xiaojing Village, in the metropolitan township of Wen County [37 miles northeast of Luoyang, Henan], He'nei Commandery, Sizhou. He was the grandson of the late palace attendant, Grand General Chastising the South authorized to open an office with accouterments equal to the Three Dignitaries, the Steadfast Prince [Sima Chuzhi (d. 465)], and he was the third son of the late palace attendant authorized to open an office with accouterments equal to the Three Dignitaries, secretary of the Ministry of Personnel, minister of works, His Honor the Vigorous Prince [Sima Jinlong (d. 484)]. Before this, the family was a commoner lineage, and yet the prince [Sima Chuzhi] was enfeoffed Prince of Langye. Hence, the Steadfast and Vigorous princes together extended this high rank for two generations.

The gentleman was endowed with a spirit that harmonized the purest vital essences—one infused with the valiant bearing of alp and river. His divine understanding was exceedingly profuse; shining in the dim it penetratingly broke forth. With a stern and stouthearted manner and outstanding intellect, he exceeded others in upholding moral principles. An eminently flourishing bloom, even at a young age he stood apart from the crowd. Facing hardship, he maintained lofty composure and established staunchly pure moral conduct; [his reputation was as] the so-called sounding bronze and reverberating jade.[2] When fourteen, having become a descendant disciplined by the Way, he entered to serve as an attendant in the forbidden precincts. During the Taihe reign period [477–500], when the ministers and prefects were just inaugurated, mainstay officials were selected, and he was admirably viewed as a leader. Owing to the gentleman's capacity for understanding and enlightened judgment, whether at the earth's extremities or throughout the civilized lands within the seas, he was selected for promotion and appointed chief registrar and shortly thereafter transferred to the posts of Marshal for the Grand General and commander of the two precincts. He assisted high-ranking officials and worked on managing and coordinating the reallocation of lands.

When the imperial carriage moved on to Luoyang [494] and the royal domains were first established, [the court] made careful selection from among the nine tributaries [of ranked men]. The imperial younger brother, the Prince of Xianyang [Yuan Xi (d. 501)], because of his fondness for the extraordinary abilities of worthies, brilliantly oversaw and tended to the broad selection of peerless and elegant men. Unless one was able to treat all men of the local lands fairly, in no case was he allowed to occupy a leadership position. Because the gentleman's fine reputation was broadcast from his youth, his good name flourished and fruited, and he was appointed General Tranquilizing the Boreal Region and Mounted Escort of Sizhou [Henan]. He provided supporting assistance with his admirable ways, his influence shone brightly, and he set down an orderly track.

The gentleman was familiar with and revered the landmark texts and canons, and his parental instruction led to continuous harmony. His son was wed to an exemplary princess, and his daughter, well-favored, became an honored consort.[3] Marital connections were plaited together and layered up, and his kin connections supported the purple imperial house. Going out [from the court], he took charge of the two domains; his transforming kindness flowed forth, and he was praised. In sequence, he served as prefect of Yingzhou and Yuzhou, and the black-haired masses of the Yangzi region received his grace. [As for how to] subdue and conquer the enemy, he calculated and strategized, and his aligning plans were all-encompassing and far-reaching; his tactics resulted in the capture of Yiyang [Xinyang, Henan] and generally stabilized Sui [Suizhou, Hubei] and Anlu [Xiaogan, Hubei] [commanderies], and he rolled up the region of the three passes like a mat and opened the frontier for a thousand leagues. His meritorious achievement quickly became apparent, and he was further appointed to administer the lands of Yuzhou [located in eastern Henan and northern Anhui]. But hostilities were triggered and stealthily launched; that such calamity would arise was not anticipated. At the age of forty-seven, he passed away at Yuzhou on the seventh day of the tenth month in the first year [508] of the Yongping reign period.

The emperor sorrowfully lamented [the gentleman's death]; those at court and in the countryside sighed with grief. If death and life are mandated by Heaven, their length or brevity having fixed terms, then even a worthy one may yet encounter such calamity. Owing to his novelty and uniqueness, the distress of the multitude can be comprehended. The palace attendant Gou Rongxian was dispatched to offer condolences and to make a sacrifice, and a thousand bolts of silk were bestowed to take care of funerary affairs. Moving on to *jiashen*, the eighteenth day of the second month, in which the new moon was on a *dingmao* day, in the fourth year [511], divination determined that his coffin should be lowered in the grave in the West District of Wen County on the south side of the ridge mound. The court dispatched an internuncio with an imperial patent granting him the titles General Pacifying the East and Governor of Qingzhou [Shandong]. His posthumous name is Zhuang ["Dignified"]. He was buried according to the proper rituals. We inscribe this crypt stone so that his exemplary life may be illuminated and his fragrant reputation made brilliant. The elegy reads:

Fulgent and flourishing is this vast lineage,
Its stunning radiance [spread across all within] the four seas.

A jasper root produced jade leaves,
For generations its members served as Wei ministers.
The gentleman received the nectar of those blooms,
At birth possessing the features of a fine soul.
As a mirror in darkness penetratingly shines,
His wit and intelligence were perfected early.
At home, he was filial and concordant,
And he toiled with devotion on behalf of the royal court.
Comparable to the luster of jade,
Or chimes and bronze bells.
Like a solitary pine,
Beset with clouds yet remaining green.
As moonlight gleaming,
Disperses fog to peerlessly shine.
Dignified and discerning like the dragon or *lin*-unicorn,
The Two Palaces accorded him glory.[4]
From the eastern hall to the western terrace,
He went forth to take his place possessing a fragrant reputation.
For him they split the bamboo [patent conferring authority]
    over two domains,
His transformative power flowed and the people intoned [his
    praises].
As pastor to Yingzhou and Yuzhou,
His awe shook the border cities.
He pacified those remote and placated those nearby,
His grace saturated the peasants of the river regions.
His merits were established and his name became outstanding,
He should have enjoyed extensive years.
How could he suffer such a fate,
Forced to hide his form?
Having prognosticated for the burial and determined a proper
    time,
We divined for his dwelling place among the range of hills.
Soaring funeral banners freely flutter,
He will dwell in the shrouded enclosure.

The door leaves have been closed,

Frost appears among the tomb mounds.

May it be that by cutting this stone for the gloom,

And by making perpetual sacrifices, we can extol his worthiness.

Installed on *xinsi*, the fifteenth day of the second month, with a new moon on *dingmao*, during the fourth year [a *xinmao* year] of the Yongping reign period of the Great Wei [511].

Source: Zhao Chao 趙超, *Han Wei Nan Bei chao muzhi huibian* 漢魏南北朝墓誌彙編 (Tianjin: Tianjin guji chubanshe, 1992), 57–59.

Notes

1. The Meng County seat has been renamed Mengzhou City; it is located 37 miles northeast of Luoyang on the north side of the Yellow River. The epitaph's dimensions are 108 cm × 78 cm; it is 12 cm thick.
2. Mencius used this musical imagery to explain how Confucius was the Alpha and Omega of the moral gentleman.
3. Sima Yue's eldest son, Sima Fei, married the Princess of Huayang, daughter of Northern Wei emperor Xuanwu (r. 499–515); his daughter Sima Xianzi (491–521) was selected to serve the same emperor as an imperial concubine.
4. The Two Palaces refers to the emperor and the crown prince.

Further Reading

Davis, Timothy. *Entombed Epigraphy and Commemorative Culture in Early Medieval China: A History of Early* Muzhiming. Leiden: Brill, 2015.

Graff, David A. *Medieval Chinese Warfare, 300–900.* London: Routledge, 2002.

Holcombe, Charles. "The Xianbei in Chinese History." *Early Medieval China* 19 (2013): 1–38.

Lewis, Mark Edward. *China between Empires: The Northern and Southern Dynasties.* Cambridge, MA: Harvard University Press, 2009.

Swartz, Wendy, Robert Ford Campany, Yang Lu, and Jessey J. C. Choo. "Part 1: The North and the South." In *Early Medieval China: A Sourcebook,* edited by Swartz, Campany, Lu, and Choo, 11–87. New York: Columbia University Press, 2014.

A Twice-Widowed Xianbei Princess

Epitaph with Preface for the Great Enlightenment Temple Nun
Surnamed Yuan (Yuan Chuntuo 元純陀, 475–529)

TRANSLATED BY JEN-DER LEE

The biography of Yuan Chuntuo, who joined a convent and chose not
to be buried with her husband, demonstrates alternative intellectual
and institutional possibilities for women and serves as a useful entry
to historical analysis of ethnicity, class, and gender.

THE NORTHERN WEI WAS FOUNDED BY THE TUOBA CLAN OF THE
nomadic Xianbei people. The Xianbei came originally from the region
northwest of the Yellow River and emerged as a power contending for
supremacy in the latter half of the fourth century. In 439, the Xianbei
succeeded in incorporating all of north China into their state, known as
the Northern Wei. Over time, the Xianbei adopted policies designed to
more effectively rule a population of Chinese peasants. In 493, the reign-
ing Emperor Xiaowen (467–499) initiated a program to adopt Chinese
practices. He moved his capital to Luoyang, a city south of the Yellow
River that had earlier been the capital of the Eastern Han and Western
Jin dynasties. He then ordered Xianbei aristocrats to adopt Chinese dress,
speak Chinese at court, intermarry with Han elite families, and even
forsake their Xianbei names and take Chinese ones. The Tuoba imperial
clan set an example by changing its name to Yuan.

Besides supporting Confucian teachings, the Northern Wei court also patronized the Daoist and Buddhist religions. Buddhism, which had arrived in China in the Han, flourished in the centuries that followed. So many Buddhist temples were built in the city of Luoyang that, after the fall of the Northern Wei, a book was written to reminisce about their splendor. Buddhism had a special appeal to women. The two female rulers of the Northern Wei, Empress Dowager Wenming (441–490) and Empress Dowager Ling (491–528), were both patrons of Buddhism. Becoming a Buddhist nun offered women an alternative to marriage and family life. In the case of women whose husbands had died, joining a convent was a respectable choice, often supported or even encouraged by their families.

Yuan Chuntuo (475–529), the subject of this piece, lived in this precise period of political transformation and cultural diversity. Her epitaph was excavated in the early twentieth century, but the image of its rubbing was not published until decades later, and research on its content only appeared in the 1990s. In the late twentieth century, as scholars looked for sources on Chinese women's history, this sixth-century nun began to attract attention with her distinctive origin and eventful life.

Yuan Chuntuo was born to the royal family of the Northern Wei. Her grandfather was an heir apparent who never ascended the throne but was given an imperial title posthumously. Her father, portrayed in the epitaph mainly as a loving parent, was a prince whose activities at court contributed to the succession of Emperor Xiaowen.

Madam Yuan was first married in her teens to the non-Han Mu family, longtime military allies of the ruling Tuoba clan. Widowed before long, she was betrothed again as a successor wife to a general of Han ethnicity. Women's remarriage was not rare in this period. Rather, it was often used strategically for aristocratic families to form multilateral alliances. Though her first marriage was short-lived, it did produce a daughter whose son she would depend on later in her life. That her grandson's last name was also Yuan testifies to continued intermarriage with the ruling house.

Madam Yuan Chuntuo witnessed and perhaps involuntarily participated in the sociocultural transition of her times. Her elder brother Yuan

Cheng (467–519), referred to as Prince Wenxuan in the epitaph, was the mastermind behind Emperor Xiaowen's planned transformation movement. Yuan Cheng also seems to have taken the initiative in marrying Chuntuo to the Han general Xing Luan (464–514), known not only for his erudition and comeliness but also for his military prowess.

Xing Luan had a son from his previous marriage, and Yuan Chuntuo was praised for having brought up the child properly. She was from this point in her life portrayed in the epitaph as aspiring to Confucian ethics and fulfilling all womanly virtues advocated in the Classics. However, the fact that she entered the Buddhist religious order after Xing Luan's death demonstrated alternative intellectual and institutional possibilities for women of her time. The Northern Wei court, unlike the subsequent Tang government, did not require all Buddhist monks and nuns to register with and live in designated temples. We know Yuan Chuntuo stayed with her grandson; unfortunately, however, we cannot be sure whether she lived with her daughter throughout her life.

It is also difficult to identify the author of this epitaph since no name was inscribed at the beginning or the end. The lengthy and positive description of Yuan's second marriage suggests that the piece may have been commissioned by the Xing family and composed from its perspective. But Yuan Chuntuo's actions spoke louder than words when it came to the issue of women's identity. At odds with classical prescriptions, she did not spend her old age with the Xings but with her daughter's son. Again contrary to aristocratic practice of the time, she stated, on her death bed, her desire not to be buried with her deceased husband.

Madam Yuan Chuntuo lived to the age of fifty-five, just about the average life expectancy for aristocratic women in her period. She was entombed one month after she passed away, in the winter of 529. Despite all the despair and lamentation, the author closes her epitaph with a wish on behalf of families and friends that "the fragrance of the thoroughwort beds and orchid fields never vanish," a literary flourish often found in funerary writings. Indeed, fifteen hundred years later, Yuan Chuntuo's name does survive, and her family origin, royal background, and experiences as a woman twice widowed reveal some of the nuances of ethnicity, class, and gender.

Epitaph with Preface for the Great Enlightenment Temple Nun Surnamed Yuan, Successive Wife of the Deceased Duke Pingshu, Surnamed Xing, Posthumous Title Wending, Chariot and Horse General in Chief of the [Northern] Wei

Madam's name was Chuntuo and her Buddhist ordained name, Zhishou. She was the granddaughter of Emperor Jingmu [428–451], whose temple name was Gong, and the fifth daughter of Prince Rencheng [447–481], whose posthumous name was Kang.

Like coiled roots and mountain peaks, her character stood out from the jade forest. Her appearance was upright and pretty, and her manner naturally graceful. She was bright as a child and elegant as a little girl. Prince Rencheng loved her more deeply than his other daughters. He often held her in his arms and let her sit on his lap. When she was seven, Prince Rencheng passed away. Her filial piety was inborn, not needing to be taught. She cried day and night as if she were shedding blood and dining on sorrow.

When she was fifteen, she was married to the Mu family. She devoted herself to women's work and cultivated all the womanly virtues. When her husband died, her other half thus collapsed; she was severed from the three followings and decided to remain a widow. She thought of the virtues of Jiang [queen of King Xuan of the Zhou] and began to sing the songs of the yellow swan [of celibacy]. But her elder brother, the Grand Mentor whose posthumous name was Prince Wenxuan, firmly would not allow her to follow her moral principles and sentiments.

Her second husband, Duke Wending [Xing Luan], came from a noble family with sublime virtues. Xing Luan's talent met the needs of both a military general and a prime minister. He served during the reign of Emperor Xiaowen and got along very well with the ruler. His reputation put him among the top officials since antiquity, and his merits soared over his contemporaries. Madam Yuan was beautifully wedded to become the duke's spouse. Their relationship was as well-matched as zither and harp, as harmonious as egg-shaped ocarina and bamboo flute. Their interaction did not rely on words, and they treated each other with respect.

Madam Yuan served her mother-in-law with all propriety and single-handedly attended to her unfailingly. She treated her husband's concubines with nothing but generosity, and she got along cordially with them all. Since his son Xun, Cavalier Attendant-in-Ordinary, lost his mother when he was a baby, Madam Yuan brought him up with profuse kindness. She reared him with both abundant love and ample discipline, and provided him with both great righteousness and profound benevolence, treating him better than her child by birth. Her teaching was like that of Mencius's mother, who cut off the woven cloth on the loom [to emphasize the importance of consistent learning], and she helped the son establish a worthy reputation.

Moreover, Madam Yuan was insightful and perceptive, and she surpassed her peers with her quick wit. She read all the poetry, documents, rituals, and laws that she came across, and she mastered plaiting, tasseling, knitting, and weaving as soon as she laid hands on them. She talked infrequently and spoke discreetly. Her character was like white jade with no flaws. She respected and kept promises more than she treasured gold.

She served in the palace with towels and handkerchiefs, and would not wear sumptuous clothing. She cleaned the noble house with a basket and broom, and would only dress in washed old clothes. She truly could be the leader of womanhood for her time and a model of motherhood for a thousand years. Was it only because she learned of people's deeds by listening to their words and knew people's feelings by observing their expressions?

When her husband passed away, she wanted to consolidate his virtues. She would not shed tears during the night but would cry with sorrow in the morning. Thus, she lamented: "I have lived a difficult life and endured the hardship of being widowed twice. I am ashamed to have married more than once and feel embarrassed not to have a steadfast heart. Serving another man without holding to my virtue, I was not able to help his lineage flourish. Happiness comes from adversities, and effects rise from causes."

Consequently, she discarded her mundane burdens and dedicated herself to Buddhist learning; [like a sailing boat] she gave up her favorite ford and rested in correct waters. She broadly collected Buddhist sutras and extensively studied the ordinances. She treasured the six methods to reach the shore of nirvana and looked on gold by the thousands as if it was grass and straw. She had just accomplished the ten good deeds to obtain rewards when she perished. [Yuan] Weiqing, Prince Xihe, was born to the Mus and therefore was Madam's grandson through her daughter's line. He was the talent of the royal family, and his reputation was extremely good. He was appointed as the governor of the capital to the great benefit of the imperial city. On a visit to him, Madam fell fatally ill. She passed away in his official villa in the Yingyang Commandery [Henan] that winter on the thirteenth day, the day of *xinyou*, of the tenth month, of which the first day was *jiyou*. Her death was lamented by her offspring and by Buddhist monks and nuns and laymen. She regained consciousness right before she died and explicitly requested that she be buried alone in a separate place from her husband so that she could fulfill her wishes for Buddhist cultivation. Her children, out of respect for her, dared not go against her will.

As such, on the seventh day, the day of *jiashen*, of the eleventh month, of which the first day was *wuyin*, she was buried, after proper divination, 15 *li* [ca. 4 miles] northwest of Luoyang city, southwest of Mangshan, east of the mountain nicknamed Ma'an. Once the gold and jade are ruined, dust and dirt get in. We respectfully carved the account of her life onto a stone tablet to be interred in the spring hut [tomb], expecting that fragrant and luxuriant grass will follow. The elegy reads:

> The gold phase of the Jin dynasty lost its vitality, and the water
>   phase [of the Northern Wei] came to prosper.
> How wonderful the two ancestral emperors who flew like drag-
>   ons and glided like phoenixes!
> They were succeeded by emperors of cultural and military accom-
>   plishments and their glory piled up, their brightness doubled.

Their wisdom followed their virtues, and they ruled the territory
of the Zhou and the populace of the Han.
Madam Yuan was endowed naturally with gentleness and born
with tender goodness.
Her behavior equaled the tranquility of the dried-up tree and the
preciousness of the river bream.
It was like water lily blooming on a small island in clear water
and sun shining over layers of roof beams.
She was like the truffles in the valley and vines that attract
orioles.
Her wedding was prepared fully according to propriety, with
jade girdle rings resounding.
Her brilliance was equivalent to [Mencius's mother's] breaking
of the looms, and her wisdom was
like [Shuxiang's mother] burying the sheep's head [to save Shux-
iang from being implicated in crimes].
She kindheartedly gathered the nine clans and harmoniously
interacted with different branches of the family.
Alas, smooth time had its limit, and the shifts in fortune were
unpredictable.
She was the primary wife of a noble and then became a
widow.
After her heaven collapsed, how could she not be saddened?
She left the earthly realm and entered the Buddhist field.
The hidden seclusion was quiet and silent, and the heavenly way
was vast and obscure.
Life is temporary and fate transient.
The days are short while the nights are long.
Once one goes to the sunset place, one cannot return to the sun-
rise field.
Dew formed on the green arbor, and winds howled through the
white poplar.
Even so, the fragrance of the thoroughwort beds and orchid
fields would never vanish.

This was set up on the seventh day, *jiashen*, of the eleventh month, of which the first day was *wuyin*, of the second year of the Yong'an reign period [529].

Source: Yan Juanying 顏娟英, ed., *Beiwei Fojiao shike tapian baipin* 北魏佛教石刻拓片百品 (Taipei: Institute of History and Philology, Academia Sinica, 2008), 69–70.

Further Reading

Lee, Jen-der. "The Death of a Princess-Codifying Classical Family Ethics in Early Medieval China." In *Presence and Presentation: Women in the Chinese Literati Tradition*, edited by Sherry Mou, 1–37. New York: St. Martin's Press, 1999.

———. "The Epitaph of a Third-Century Wet Nurse, Xu Yi." In *Early Medieval China: A Sourcebook*, edited by Wendy Swartz et al., 458–67. New York: Columbia University Press, 2013.

———. "The Life of Women in the Six Dynasties." *Journal of Women and Gender Studies* 4 (1993): 47–80.

———. "Women, Families and Gendered Society." In *Cambridge History of China*, vol. 2: *The Six Dynasties*, edited by Albert E. Dien and Keith N. Knapp. Cambridge, UK: Cambridge University Press, 2019.

4

Authoring One's Own Epitaph

Self-Authored Epitaph, by Wang Ji 王績 (590?–644)

Inscription Dictated While Near Death,
by Wang Xuanzong 王玄宗 (633–686)

TRANSLATED BY ALEXEI KAMRAN DITTER

These self-authored epitaphs problematize the assumption that autobiographies provide a more "authentic" portrait of their subjects' identities. Both also demonstrate the early phase of the Ancient-Style Prose Movement and the influence of Daoism during the Sui and Tang dynasties.

TWO OF THE EARLIEST EXTANT EXAMPLES OF SELF-AUTHORED TANG epitaphs are those written by Wang Ji (590?–644) and Wang Xuanzong (633–686). The lives of these two individuals together span the first century of China's political reunification, first under the short-lived Sui dynasty and then under the more enduring Tang dynasty. This century witnessed a number of remarkable political, social, and cultural achievements, ranging from the establishment of the two new capital cities of Chang'an and Luoyang and the dramatic expansion of China's political and cultural influence within Asia to the development of the civil service examination system, the growth of Daoism and Buddhism within Chinese society, and the nascence of the "Return to Antiquity" or "Ancient-Style Prose" movements that would dominate prose composition in later centuries.

The content and style of these two epitaphs reflect in particular the last two developments. They illustrate how ideals and practices of Daoism permeated the intellectual and religious life of elites during this period. The epitaph of Wang Ji, moreover, exemplifies the simpler diction and syntax that would later be promoted by advocates of the Ancient-Style Prose Movement. His epitaph in this regard provides a strong contrast to the more structured and allusively dense epitaph of Wang Xuanzong, which uses the more ornate style favored in formal writing in the early Tang period.

Autobiographies are relatively scarce in any form within the Chinese literary tradition. As such, these self-authored epitaphs—two of only sixteen extant self-authored epitaphs from the Tang dynasty—are important sources not only for their historical content but also for the insight they provide into practices of posthumous representation and self-fashioning of identity in medieval China. These works are invaluable as well for interrogating the assumption that autobiographies provide more "authentic" portrayals of their subjects' identities than other historical sources. Despite their authors speaking as though they wielded exclusive autonomous control over their own posthumous representation, these works, in particular Wang Xuanzong's epitaph, were ultimately susceptible to the same sorts of editorial manipulations—such as framing subjects' lives in a way designed to enhance reputation or support claims important to surviving family members—observable in more conventional examples of the medieval Chinese epitaph.

Wang Ji was born around 590 into an illustrious elite family with a long tradition of Confucian learning and imperial service. Wang Ji himself, however, was an exception to these traditions. His education encompassed more than just the conventional Confucian curriculum, with his studies ranging in scope from fortune-telling to fencing. What's more, despite his intelligence, erudition, and advantageous family connections, he enjoyed only a sporadic and unremarkable career as an official. He was recommended for office on the basis of being "Filial and Brotherly, Incorrupt and Pure" in either 610 or 614 but served only brief stints in low-ranked positions, first as a proofreader in the Palace Library and then as vice-magistrate of Liuhe County. He retired a short while later, pleading illness (although one early biography alleges the actual problem had been that his heavy drinking interfered with his ability to perform his duties). At the beginning of the Tang dynasty, he was summoned to the capital, where he was given the title Expectant Official. He remained there for six years without ever receiving an assignment before retiring for a second time. During the Zhenguan reign period (627–649), he requested and received an appointment as an assistant in the Imperial Music Office, a position he desired because its director was a famed brewer. Within a year, however, some months after the death of the director, Wang retired, for the third and final time, to family land he had inherited in the countryside between Chang'an and Luoyang.

Wang Ji's self-authored epitaph constructs his identity as a principled gentleman living within yet apart from the world around him. This separation from the world is reflected in the language of the epitaph, which makes extensive use of negative phrases. Throughout the epitaph, for example, Wang repeatedly describes himself in terms of what he does not do (respond to questions, acknowledge distinctions, calculate benefits, distinguish himself), does not have (friends or colleagues, accomplishments, destinations, or reasons), or is not (well known or familiar to those in power). In so doing, Wang Ji erases many of the social ties epitaphs were intended to emphasize and render permanent: ancestry and lineage, prominent social connections, and positive contributions made to the empire through official service.

Daoist influences permeate Wang's epitaph. Wang's diction echoes that of many Daoist writings, which similarly used negative constructions. His epitaph, moreover, often alludes directly or indirectly to Daoist works, in particular *Zhuangzi*. Wang Ji's self-chosen courtesy name, "No Particular Accomplishment" (Wugong), alludes to the "Wandering Far and Unfettered" chapter of *Zhuangzi*, which states, "The Spirit Man has no particular accomplishment."[1] His impolite body posture, disdain for polite discourse, and the intentionless nature of his comings and goings similarly echo tropes found in various chapters of *Zhuangzi* and other Daoist writings. Finally, the rhymed elegy portion of his epitaph quotes two lines from the "Great Source as Teacher" chapter of *Zhuangzi* verbatim: "He looked upon life as a dangling wart or swollen pimple, / And looked upon death as its dropping off, its bursting and draining." These lines allude to an anecdote in which Confucius explains to his disciple Zigong the difference between "men who roam outside the lines" and those who "roam inside the lines." The former, Confucius explains, "look upon life as a dangling wart or swollen pimple, and on death as its dropping off, its bursting and draining. Being such, what would they understand about which is life and which is death, what comes before and what comes after?"[2] Wang thus identifies himself as one of those who "roam outside the lines," someone who cannot be expected to adhere to the conventional social behaviors of more ordinary men.

Wine is mentioned frequently within Wang Ji's extant corpus of writings, and his epitaph is no exception. For Wang Ji, drunkenness was a metaphor for an enlightened understanding of the Way. He viewed being drunk (i.e., being in a state in which "one is aware of one's incapacity to distinguish reality from illusion or to make right judgments") as analogous to being enlightened (a state in which one recognizes that "all perceptions of reality are illusory and that he is no more able to perceive the reality of the Way than the drunken man is able to perceive the reality of the mundane world in his impaired state").[3] The "virtue of wine" thus links Wang's "roaming around" and unconventional social behavior with his broader Daoist perspective on life.

Wang Xuanzong lived a generation later than Wang Ji. Although his life is comparatively less well documented than Wang Ji's, his epitaph is far more detailed. This in no small part is due to Wang Xuanzong's autobiographical account being embedded within a larger narrative frame authored by Xuanzong's brother, Wang Shaozong (fl. seventh c.). This frame serves multiple functions. To begin with, it supplies information conventionally included within epitaphs that was absent from Xuanzong's own account. This includes the date and place of Xuanzong's death, the names of eminent associates, and details about his career and accomplishments. The frame also functions rhetorically. It provides details about the context within which the self-narrated account was recorded, offering evidence of its authenticity and the reliability of the recorded draft. It also provides additional justification and support for burying Wang Xuanzong in the manner that he desired. Whereas the self-narrated epitaph merely states Xuanzong's wish to be interred within his stone chamber on Mount Song, the narrative frame communicates Xuanzong's equanimity in the face of his imminent demise, his personal admonition that the funeral be simple, the support of other notables for his choice of burial location, and his family's insistence that he take the sobriquet Master of Great Harmony against his wishes. Finally, it highlights both the prominent Daoists with whom Wang Xuanzong associated and the written works that he produced.

Unlike Wang Ji, whose relationship with Daoism is primarily philosophical, Wang Xuanzong is described in his epitaph as a practitioner of the Shangqing tradition of Daoism. This tradition was the foremost of the three major Daoist traditions (Shangqing, Tianshi, Lingbao) throughout the late medieval period (sixth to tenth centuries). The origins of this tradition can be traced to the revelations collected within the *Authentic Declarations* (Zhen'gao, also translated as *Declarations of the Perfected*). These revelations were purported to have been communicated by Daoist divinities and saints to the calligrapher and mystic Yang Xi (330–ca. 386) over a period of several nights. The doctrines and practices of the Shangqing tradition synthesize various intellectual and religious strands, including traditions of immortality seeking, ecstatic mysticism, and practices and concepts from Tianshi Daoism. Shangqing Daoism and Daoism in general flourished during the first century of the Tang dynasty at least in part due to the strong support of the imperial Tang family, who shared the same surname, Li, as the Daoist sage Laozi and claimed to be descended from him. The Tang founding emperor, Gaozu (r. 618–635), and his grandson, Gaozong (r. 649–683), were especially strong supporters of Daoism, ordering the construction of Daoist temples in every province and the reproduction of all existing Daoist texts as well as adding the *Daodejing* to the list of texts tested in the civil service examination. Gaozu was especially supportive of Shangqing Daoism, as were Gaozong and Empress Wu Zetian (r. 690–705). The latter two both made personal visits to the Daoist grand master Pan Shizheng (585–682) (the "Ascended to Perfection Master Pan" mentioned in Wang Xuanzong's epitaph) multiple times, which illustrates the depth of their personal investment in Shangqing Daoism.

Self-Authored Epitaph and Preface

Wang Ji had a father and mother but did not have colleagues or friends. The courtesy name he made up for himself was "No Particular Accomplishment." People sometimes asked him about his name, but he merely lolled with splayed legs and did not respond.[4] He probably chose it because he felt he contained the Way within himself and had "no particular accomplishment" in his times. He understood principles completely on his own without reading a book. He did not acknowledge honor and shame and did not calculate benefit or harm in determining what to do.

He started his career by earning a salary as an official and passed through a number of positions while only advancing a single rank. His talents were lofty but his position lowly, and he merely managed to avoid criticism. He was unknown to the emperor and unfamiliar to high officials, and at forty and fifty years old he still had not distinguished himself.[5]

He therefore retired and returned home, roaming around his hometown on account of the virtue of wine. He sold his services as a fortune-teller here and there, and time and again he would read books. When in motion he seemed to have no destination in mind, and, when he settled down, he seemed to have no reason for stopping. There were none among his fellow villagers who could ever fathom his intentions. He had previously farmed Eastern Embankment, so he took the sobriquet Master of Eastern Embankment. On the day he died, he made up a rhymed elegy for himself, which said:

There is a hermit of the Tang,
Wang Ji of Taiyuan.

seemingly stubborn, seemingly foolish,

appearing unreasonable, appearing excitable.

There are only three paths to his courtyard,

And merely four bare walls to his hall.[6]

Acknowledging neither moderation nor restraint,

how could he have either kith or kin?

"He looked upon life as a dangling wart or swollen pimple,

And looked upon death as its dropping off, its bursting and
     draining."

Without thoughts and without worries,

About where to go or what to follow.

An inscribed stone on top of his grave mound;

A grave formed in horse-shoe shape.

Alas for the filial son,

in vain facing the tall pines.

Source: Jin Ronghua 金榮華, *Wang Ji shi wenji jiazhu* 王績詩文集校注
(Taipei: Xin wenfeng, 1998), 310.

Epitaph and Preface of the Hermit of the Central Marchmount, Master of Great Harmony, Gentleman Summoned to Office Wang of Langye of the Great Tang, Dictated While Near Death

*Respectfully recorded and calligraphed by youngest brother [Wang]
Shaozong, Grand Master for Proper Consultation, Acting Vice-Director of
the Palace Library and Reader-in-Waiting of the Eastern Palace, and Concurrent Secretarial Censor*

On the fourth day of the first month of summer of the second year of
the Chuigong reign period [686], [Wang Xuanzong] drifted in and out
of consciousness during the wee hours of the morning. The friends of
my sixth older brother realized that his illness was taking a turn for
the worse. A short time later, while he was staying temporarily at the
government lodge in the Huihe Ward [in Luoyang], he transmitted

the imperceptible to the "not-yet-beginning" and transcended through seeming death within the area of the Yi and Luo Rivers [i.e., Luoyang].[7] Since ancient times there has been death. Alas!

A few days earlier, he had addressed his seventh brother, Shaozong, saying,

> I reside in the mysterious hamlet, preserving my harmony among a community of the benevolent, leaving my tracks alongside the myriad beings while my heart-mind roams in the Great Nonexistence.[8] One mounts the Yang and thus is born, encounters the Yin and thus is extinguished; this is the constant of all things and is something that you most certainly understand. After my transformation, you should abide by the Daoist practice of nonaction while the younger generation performs established Confucian funerary practices. I have heard that "quintessential spirit belongs to Heaven and physical form belongs to earth." I am content anywhere; there is no need to select an auspicious day. A single cart and everyday clothes are sufficient; I do not expect any special effort.

Shaozong respectfully heeded what was said, not daring to neglect [his instruction] or fall short in any way.

At this time, Master Huan Daoyan of the state of Pei was also at my elder brother's side. He thereupon sobbed and responded, "Here are the principles of authenticity and openness. They are what are admired by Daoists. How would those who are affectionate and faithful dare go against them!"

After that, the disciple of Ascended to Perfection Master Pan[9]—a member of our clan named Datong—crossed the Central Marchmount, coming from far away to inquire about Xuanzong's illness. Learning that my elder brother's ordained lifespan was nearing its end, he also extended his counsel, saying to Xuanzong, "If it is not considered taboo, I sincerely hope you might return your spirit to your 'stone chamber' [i.e., cavern] in the central peak [of the Marchmount]. Previously when Ascended to Perfection Master Pan was near death, he ordered that he also be entombed there. You and my teacher often interacted, moreover, and were close friends for a long time. While the time of your death has yet to arrive, you should come back to the grotto mansion." He earnestly pleaded again and again. Only then did Wang Xuanzong accede, saying,

This body is merely my leftover traces. If I leave it behind in the manner you suggest, then there is no need to excavate a separate tomb chamber, which I fear would harm the terrain. Simply consign my body to the mountain hollow, and that's enough. I once wrote an exegesis of *The Authentic Declarations*. I created a secret record of diagrams of the mysterious, separately annotating its contents. These texts do not circulate within the human world. Should you wish not to forget about my aspirations and perhaps preserve them at the burial site, you may simply obtain a slab of dark stone whose surface is naturally level and engrave it with text. All those future descendants will thus know how I exerted my efforts.

Struggling with illness and physically feeble, he brought his feelings to bear and strove his utmost to write down the text of his inscription in its entirety. It contained his essence and lodged his spirit. Its remaining sounds [i.e., his elegy] were recorded as he began to mount the light [i.e., die]. As his vision seemed to become unclear, he had no alternative but to dictate his epitaph orally. Based on the record of his conduct, his affinal kin and close friends coerced upon him the sobriquet Master of Great Harmony so as to recall his Daoist teachings and illuminate their many subtleties. His epitaph states:

Alas! In former days there arose the Tang dynasty, and it happened that I was born during it. Surnamed Wang, named Xuanzong, courtesy name Chengzhen, I am originally a native of Linyi of Langye (Shandong). The tenth-generation grandson of the Duke of Wenxian, counselor in chief of the Jin [Wang Dao (276–339)]. After the fall of the Chen dynasty [557–589], the Wang clan crossed the Yangzi, first residing in Fengyi but midcourse changing residence to Jiangdu [Yangzhou, Jiangsu]. The details of their origins and conferments are fully recorded in the national histories and family records. A conferred lifespan of fifty-five years, all the way until the fourth day of the fourth month of the second year of the Chuigong reign period [686]. Then, in accordance with the number of the great expansion,[10] I will die suddenly. After I die, you may return me to the stone chamber on the central peak where I formerly resided. This is also in accord with the ideas of "entombing without building a tumulus" and "nowhere is the spirit not present."

What's more, the area of the Yi and Luo Rivers in past days was none other than the territory of the Duke of Zhou, a land where my ancestors were retainers and the homeland from whence I myself obtained my surname. Surely returning to be buried on the Central Marchmount is not forgetting where one came from. Clasping my hands as I take my eternal leave, what more is there to say? Showing that all things have an end, I therefore write my elegy, which says:

> Pure, so pure is the Great Clarity,
> Enduring, so enduring is the Great Tranquility.[11]
> Primordial Chaos, no self,
> In its midst, an essence.[12]
> Abruptly becoming a person,
> In proper time obtaining form.
> Principle penetrated, and in stillness there was response,
> Yin accumulated and Yang matched equally.
> Comprehending the constant and thus acquiring inborn
>   nature,
> Ceasing discrimination and thus eschewing attachments.
> Nowhere is the Dao not present,
> Nothing can the spirit not endure.
> Mysteriously transmitting the secret instructions,
> Silently faring to the peaks of the transcendents.

The "ten thousand things" all eventually expire,

How could I linger on?

Returning to the authentic abode,

This chamber, dark, so dark.

Raise no grave mound, plant no trees,

Let there be no record of conduct, let there be no fame.

Consign my physical body to the stone chamber of Mount
Song,

I declare I will follow in the footsteps of the mouth organist
of the Luo River.[13]

And in mystery arrive at the Ten Great Grotto-Heavens,[14]

Hastened by the spirits of the eight directions.

Winds and clouds gather and scatter,

Mountain and rivers empty and fill,

But "the spirit of the valley does not die,"[15]

And my original self is ever-living.

Source: Zhou Shaoliang 周紹良 and Zhao Chao 趙超, eds., *Tangdai muzhi huibian* 唐代墓誌彙編 (Shanghai: Shanghai guji chubanshe, 1992), 1:744.

Notes

1. Translation modified from Brook Ziporyn, trans., *Zhuangzi: The Essential Writings* (Indianapolis: Hackett, 2009), 6.
2. Ziporyn, trans., *Zhuangzi*, 47.
3. Ding Xiang Warner, *A Wild Deer and Soaring Phoenixes: The Opposition Poetics of Wang Ji* (Honolulu: University of Hawai'i Press, 2003), 89.
4. "Lolling with splayed legs" (*jiju*) is often used within Daoist anecdotes to convey a sense of disdain for formality and proper etiquette. The refusal to answer questions similarly suggests the casual disdain for social mores of those possessing a superior understanding of the Dao.
5. This alludes to *Analects* 9.23: "Only when a man reaches the age of forty or fifty without distinguishing himself in any way can one say, I suppose, that he does not deserve to be held in awe." D. C. Lau, trans., *Confucius: The Analects*, 2nd ed. (Hong Kong: Chinese University Press, 1992), 83.
6. "Three paths" is often used as an allusion to the dwelling of a recluse. "Four bare walls" is often used to indicate poverty or a simple lifestyle.

7. "Imperceptible" (*ming*) can be understood as that which is you but cannot be seen. "Not-yet-beginning" (*weishi*) refers to the state in which one existed before one began one's existence. "Seeming death" (*weihua*) refers to the ascension of a Daoist practitioner, in which the corpse would be left behind, thus making it seem as though death had occurred.

8. The "Great Nonexistence," analogous to the "Primordial Chaos" mentioned in the elegy, refers to the original Void, beyond and before the manifestation of the Dao and the emergence of the world that nonetheless contains within the seed for all existence.

9. "Master Pan" refers to Pan Shizheng (585–682), the eleventh grand master in the lineage of Shangqing Daoism.

10. This line alludes to the "Commentary on *The Appended Phrases*," which states: "The total sum of Heaven's and earth's numbers is fifty-five. These [numbers] indicate how change and transformation are brought about and how gods and spirits are activated." See "Commentary on *The Appended Phrases* [Xici zhuan], *Part One*," in *The Classic of Changes: A New Translation of the I Ching as Interpreted by Wang Bi*, trans. Richard John Lynn (New York: Columbia University Press, 1994), 60.

11. "Great Clarity" refers to Heaven; "Great Tranquility," to earth.

12. "Primordial Chaos" is often likened to an egg, an undifferentiated state prior to existence that contains within it the nascent potentiality of all existence.

13. A reference to the Daoist immortal Wang Ziqiao, who was a skilled player of the mouth organ.

14. "Ten Great Grotto-Heavens" refers to dwelling places of transcendents.

15. This phrase appears in the *Daodejing* 6. See D. C. Lau, trans., *Tao Te Ching* (London: Penguin Books, 1963), 62.

Further Reading

Barrett, Timothy H. *Taoism under the Tang: Religion and Empire during the Golden Age of Chinese History*. London: Wellsweep, 1996.

Robinet, Isabelle. "Shangqing (Highest Clarity)." In *The Encyclopedia of Taoism*, edited by Fabrizio Pregadio, 2:858–66. London: Routledge, 2008.

Warner, Ding Xiang. *A Wild Deer and Soaring Phoenixes: The Opposition Poetics of Wang Ji*. Honolulu: University of Hawai'i Press, 2003.

Wells, Matthew V. "(Mis)conceiving the Self in Early China: Memory and Truth in Early Chinese Autobiographical Writing." In *Beating Devils and Burning Their Books*, edited by Anthony E. Clark, 133–54. Ann Arbor, MI: Association for Asian Studies, 2010.

———. *To Die and Not Decay: Autobiography and the Pursuit of Immortality in Early China*. Ann Arbor, MI: Association for Asian Studies, 2009.

5

Wives Commemorating Their Husbands

Epitaph for Cao Yin 曹因 (fl. 7th century),
by Madam Zhou 周 (fl. 7th century)

Epitaph for He Jian 何簡 (686–742),
by Madam Xin 辛 (fl. 742)

TRANSLATED BY PING YAO

These epitaphs, among the earliest written by women, allow us to hear women's voices and consider the ways Tang women perceived spousal relations, gender roles, social status, and even the meaning of life and death.

THROUGHOUT CHINESE HISTORY, GIRLS IN MANY ELITE FAMI-lies were taught to read and write; some would become celebrated writers and poets. During the Tang dynasty in particular, elite women seemed to be quite literate: writings of Tang elite men often mention how their mothers taught them Confucian classics when they were young, sowing the seeds of their future success in the civil service examinations. In addition, epitaphs for Tang elite women routinely report that as children they were avid readers of Confucian didactic texts for women.

What use did Tang elite women make of their literacy? Did Tang women employ their literary skills in areas other than cultivating female virtues and educating their sons? What was the scope of their understanding of literary and philosophical traditions? Fortunately, four female-authored Tang epitaphs have survived, providing evidence that Tang women tried their hand at this increasingly popular genre. In addition, these epitaphs provide us with first-hand evidence of how these Tang women perceived family relations, gender roles, social status, and even the meaning of life and death.

In this selection, I look into two of the four epitaphs authored by Tang women, both for their husbands. "Epitaph for Cao Yin," possibly the earliest known female-authored epitaph in Chinese history, first appeared in the collected works of the Song scholar Hong Mai 洪邁 (1123–1202). Hong noted that the epitaph was unearthed in 1197 in Shangrao (in Jiangxi) by a local official but did not specify whether or not he transcribed the text himself. Very likely Hong did some light editing, as the epitaph does not include Cao Yin's age at death and his funeral arrangements, both standard in Tang epitaphs. From the fact that both Cao Yin's grandfather and his father served at Emperor Gaozu's (618–626) court, we can infer that he likely died during Emperor Taizong's reign (626–649). The second epitaph, "Epitaph for He Jian," was authored by Madam Xin and dates to 742. Though relatively short, its literary style and narrative structure are typical for a Tang epitaph.

The epitaphs for Cao Yin and He Jian present an interesting contrast in terms of Tang family histories. Cao Yin was born to an official family but failed three times to pass the civil service examinations and would die a commoner. He Jian, in contrast, was the first one in his family to succeed in the civil service exams and the first to receive an official appointment. Though these are only individual cases, they nevertheless point to social mobility during the Tang.

More interestingly, the epitaphs convey two completely different voices and attitudes. Cao Yin's life was marked by failure in his career aspiration, and he died young, having been married for only eight years. However, his wife, Madam Zhou, was undisturbed by what would normally be perceived as misfortunes. She declares, "Human beings follow various forms existing between Heaven and Earth, constrained by the patterns of Yin and Yang. Life and death, gathering and dispersing, are no more than ways of the world: What is there to be sad or happy about?" Zhou's statement was inspired by the Daoist philosopher Zhuangzi (4th c. BCE), who drummed on a basin and sang when his wife passed away. In Zhuangzi's view, life and death were just like the progression of spring and fall, summer and winter, merely ways of the natural world.

In contrast to Madam Zhou, the author of He Jian's epitaph, Madam Xin, took her husband's death very hard. She not only vowed never to remarry, but also contemplated committing suicide. Moreover, throughout the epitaph, Madam Xin portrays her husband as a Confucian *junzi* (gentleman, noble man) who exhibited appropriate virtues at every stage of his life. Xin writes beautifully and employs various analogies and phrases that go back to the Confucian classics. From the *Analects*, for example, she cites "subduing oneself and returning to propriety" to describe He Jian's upright character, and she uses Confucius's students Gaochai and Yan Hui to depict He Jian's filial piety and simplicity. From *The Book of Rites*, she borrows the story of Meng Jingzi, possibly a relation of Mencius, to illustrate her husband's profound understanding of ritual. Xin also uses the analogy of the Cypress Boat, the title of a poem about a woman refusing to remarry in *The Book of Songs*, to convey her vow of chastity. Most impressively, the eulogy that Xin dedicates to He Jian makes eloquent use of literary analogies that are rooted in the *Analects*.

The difference in writing style and worldview reflected in these two epitaphs are likely a result of social and geographical differences. Zhou was probably from a local commoner family in today's Jiangxi, where her husband's epitaph was unearthed. Xin, in contrast, lived with her husband in the capital, Chang'an. Zhou married into a family that was falling out of the ruling class. To her, Daoist ideals of pursuing a reclusive life and returning to nature could bring peace of mind. Xin was married to a newly minted Presented Scholar (*jinshi*) and a new recruit of the ruling class; her eagerness to demonstrate the family's commitment to Confucian values is understandable. What the two authors shared was familiarity with Chinese philosophical traditions and their ability to see their lives through these lenses.

The epitaphs for Cao Yin and He Jian also show that marital harmony was much celebrated during the Tang. In fact, spousal love is a recurrent theme among Tang epitaphs, and it was not uncommon for a grieving husband to vow to stay a widower when it came to writing his wife's epitaph. Tang epitaphs also show that many elite men and women chose joint burial, a practice that was considered contrary to Confucian ritual tradition in early China. Among extant Tang epitaphs for married men and women, 45 percent of the individuals were recorded as being jointly buried with their spouses. Considering that many epitaphs of the remaining 55 percent were for deceased whose spouses were still alive or whose spouses were jointly buried with first husbands or first wives, the rate of joint burial was remarkably high. Although most joint burials consist of two separate epitaphs for the deceased, some families opted to have a joint epitaph for the burial. More than two hundred such joint epitaphs have survived, a testament to how much Tang society cherished marital harmony.

Epitaph for Cao Yin

The gentleman's surname is Cao, his given name Yin, and his courtesy name Bifu. His family has lived in Poyang [in Jiangxi] for generations. Both his grandfather and his father were officials at Gaozu's court. Although Mr. Cao took the civil service examinations thrice and failed to pass, he abided by rite and ethics at home. When he died on the road in Chang'an, high-level ministers and officials at the imperial court and reputable elders among the locals all sighed profoundly. I, however, was the only one who was not so distraught. I said to his mother: "Our family owns farmland, enough to support his parents; our house holds his writings, enough to teach his children. Human beings follow various forms existing between Heaven and Earth, constrained by the patterns of Yin and Yang. Life and death, gathering and dispersing, are no more than ways of the world: What is there to be sad or happy about?"

My surname is Zhou, and I am Mr. Cao's wife. I was married to him for eight years and, undeservingly, reaped his kindness and grace. Therefore, I dedicate this eulogy to him:

One's birth is determined by Heaven; so is one's death. If one comprehends this principle, what sorrow is there to speak of?!

Source: Zhou Shaoliang 周紹良 and Zhao Chao 趙超, eds., *Tangdai muzhi huibian* 唐代墓誌匯編 (Shanghai: Shanghai guji chubanshe, 1992), 124.

Entombed Epitaph for the Late Granary Administrator in the Left Awesome Guards of the Great Tang Mr. He of the Lujiang Commandery, with Preface, written by Wife Madam Xin of Longxi

The gentleman's taboo name is Jian and his courtesy name Hongcao. He was a native of Lujiang [in Anhui]. His great grandfather Yuan, grandfather Hao, and father Gui did not serve in office. All of them had a penchant for serenity and tranquility; they avoided the mundane world and lived in obscurity. By the time Jian grew up, he was broadly learned and masterfully skilled. He was gentle, respectful, focused, and solemn. He passed the Presented Scholar (*jinshi*) examination and consequently received his first official appointment as assistant magistrate of Gaoyou, Yangzhou [in Jiangsu]. In this capacity, he acted incorruptibly and benevolently; his uprightness and diligence inspired everyone. He was next appointed as a granary administrator in the Left Awesome Guards but later resigned to mourn his mother. During the mourning period, [Mr. He] was constantly torn apart by grief; his display of emotion was extraordinary. His heart was consumed by sorrow; never once did he stop lamenting. He often wept torrents of tears as Gaochai did. His mourning conduct was as that of Jingzi.[1] Consequently, he became gravely ill and was beyond cure. Acupuncture failed to cure him; medicinal herbs could not save him. He passed away on the nineteenth day of the six month of the inaugural year of the Tianbao reign period [742] at his residence in Guohua Ward, Henan County. He was fifty-seven.

Mr. He, placing no value on gold or jade, instead cherished loyalty and trustworthiness. He did not crave possessions but considered erudition to constitute wealth.[2] We have long heard that people of shabby lanes cannot endure adversity, yet, living in such circumstances, Mr. He was unvarying in his joy.[3]

On the thirtieth day of the seventh month of the same year [742], [Mr. He] was temporarily buried in the city's north section, following ritual. I myself yearned to follow him in death, but it would not be right for our young children to lose another parent. The sorrow of my weeping, can he feel it? I have taken the vow of Cypress Boat and my heart will not change.[4] Hence, I have carved this eulogy onto the stone. It says:

> Recalling my deceased husband,
> He followed propriety[5] and acted benevolently.
> He cultivated morality and practiced what he learned;
> He established himself through refined qualities.
> To his friends, he was trustworthy;
> To his parents, he was a model of filialty.
> Why is the way of Heaven so cruel?
> Destroying this fine person?
> The cemetery is mournfully gloomy,
> Trees along the tombs are dim and blurry.
> For thousands and thousands of years,
> Will he dwell in this place.

Source: Zhou Shaoliang 周紹良 and Zhao Chao 趙超, eds., *Tangdai muzhi huibian* 唐代墓誌匯編 (Shanghai: Shanghai guji chubanshe, 1992), 1540.

Notes

1. Jingzi, or Meng Jingzi (fl. 435 BCE), was said to be the great-great-grandfather of Mencius (372–289 BCE). He was known for having a perfect understanding of mourning rituals (*Analects* 8.4).
2. The phrase "erudite" (*duowen*) comes from *Analects* 16.4, "Jishi." Confucius was said to have advised his disciples to form friendships with men of erudite learning.

3. This sentence refers to Confucius's praise of his favorite student, Yan Hui, for being unvarying in his joy while living on a shabby lane (*Analects* 6.11).
4. "Cypress Boat" is a poem in the *Book of Songs* traditionally considered to be the oath of Gongjiang, a widow who resisted her parents' pressure to remarry (*Book of Songs* 26). A translation can be found in Arthur Waley, *The Book of Songs: The Ancient Chinese Classic of Poetry* (New York: Grove Press, 1996), 38.
5. "Follow propriety" comes from *Analects* 12.1, "Yanyuan." Confucius considered "following propriety" a top quality of a gentleman (*junzi*).

Further Reading

Larsen, Jeanne. *Willow, Wine, Mirror, Moon: Women's Poems from Tang China*. New York: BOA Editions, 2005.

Yao, Ping. "Women's Epitaphs in Tang China (618–907)." In *Beyond Exemplar Tales: Women's Biography in Chinese History*, edited by Joan Judge and Ying Hu, 139–57. Berkeley: University of California Press, 2011.

A Married Daughter and a Grandson

Entombed Funerary Inscription for My Daughter the Late
Madam Dugu 獨孤氏 (785-815) and Entombed Record for
My Grandson Who Died Young (Quan Shunsun 權順孫, 803-815),
by Quan Deyu 權德輿 (759-818)

TRANSLATED BY ANNA M. SHIELDS

These specific, personal, and moving biographies reveal ideals of virtuous conduct for women and young boys in the Tang and paint a world
in which birth and lineage shaped social relations and political stature.

THE SURVIVAL OF LITERARY COLLECTIONS BY EIGHTH- AND
ninth-century men of letters gives us access to many dimensions of their
lives that are not well documented for earlier periods. The large literary
corpus of the official and writer Quan Deyu (759–818) is filled with letters to patrons and other colleagues, social poems of exchange with dozens of fellow scholars, as well as funerary texts for many people, revealing
the extensive network of family and friends he sustained over several
decades. By his day, funerary inscriptions were becoming more prominent and prestigious forms of literary composition, composed for a wider
range of people, and were included more often in writers' collected works.
These funerary texts ranged from entombed inscriptions to "spirit path

steles" (*shendaobei*), which stood by the tomb, to prayers (*jiwen*) that were offered to the deceased before burial. Quan Deyu composed these texts for a diverse group of individuals, from the highest-ranking officials of Tang government down to his own infant grandchildren.

The audience for Tang funerary inscriptions was broad and grew broader over the course of the dynasty. Though the spirit of the deceased must be considered the first and most important "audience" for the text, we know that these inscriptions were copied onto paper and shared widely within social networks via manuscript, and they later could be preserved in a writer's collected works. Thus, despite being carved on a stone that was subsequently buried, medieval epitaphs could have a long life in the community. For example, Tang letters reveal that friends would often send one another copies of funerary inscriptions for deceased mutual friends as a way of sharing knowledge and affection about the friend. Often, different writers were asked to compose the many required inscriptions and prayers for the deceased, which gave several different people the opportunity to tell the story of his or her life. In the practice of temporary burial and reburial, which could happen for many reasons, a family would often commission new inscriptions for reburial, which added new dimensions to the story. At each stage, writers would try to speak to the many people implicated in the life and death of the individual, from close family members to marriage relations and colleagues. And writers of epitaphs also had an eye on posterity, on future readers of their accounts. In the case of the epitaphs for his daughter and grandson translated here, Quan Deyu brought both his grief and his considerable literary skills to the task of commemorating the impact of their short lives.

As a Tang official, Quan was unusually successful in climbing social and political ladders: born to a respected family of officials with a long pedigree, he rose rapidly to prominence in the bureaucracy of the Tang capital of Chang'an, serving as a senior official in five different ministries, overseeing the civil service examinations, and achieving the highest office of grand councilor while in his fifties. He married well, forging an alliance with the daughter of his esteemed patron Cui Gao, from the aristocratic Cui clan of Boling. As the two epitaphs translated here demonstrate, he fully expected that his own children and grandchildren would be properly reared according to appropriate gender norms and make prestigious con-nections to sustain the family's prominence in capital society. All of these assumptions are useful for understanding the social and political content of the inscriptions for his daughter and grandson.

Quan Deyu numbers among a small group of writers from the "mid-Tang" era (roughly 780–827) whose collections include several funerary inscriptions for women and children—proof that such inscriptions held increasing personal, social, and even literary value in Tang culture. Quan Deyu's married daughter and grandson (a child of Quan's oldest son) both died untimely deaths only a month apart in the winter of 815. Far from being formulaic or conventional, the inscriptions he wrote for them are specific, personal, and moving depictions of family members Quan clearly knew well. They also depict some ideals of virtuous conduct for women and young boys in the Tang. In the case of his daughter, Madam Dugu (whose personal name is not included in the inscription), Quan presents her as the refined, humble, and perfect fulfillment of the virtue embod-ied in the Quan lineage, serving her husband, her parents, and her children with Confucian diligence and reverence. In the case of the grandson—whose given name, Shunsun, meant "Obedient Grandson"—Quan depicts him as a studious, filial, and promising boy with remarkable matu-rity and composure, exemplified during his illness and in the face of death. Equally interesting in these inscriptions is the way in which Quan portrays his own grief in response to the two deaths: he appears wracked with sorrow and shock at the death of his daughter and seems unwilling to accept the fact of her untimely passing. But in writing for his grand-son, Quan seems to take solace from the boy's own belief that he would be reborn in the heaven of the Buddhist Pure Land, and he faces his grand-son's death with greater equanimity.

Beyond praising the two subjects for their virtue and diligence, the inscriptions do not offer many particulars about the two lives—in the case of his daughter, it would have been inappropriate for Quan to disclose too much about her personal life, which would have been spent in the domes-tic, private sphere—but they reveal a world in which birth and lineage shaped social relations and political stature, a perspective common in Tang epitaphs. In both inscriptions, Quan is careful to praise his own illustrious father, Quan Gao (724–766), who had been a hero in the Tang fight to suppress the An Lushan Rebellion (755–763) and had sought to reinforce the brilliant reputation of the Quan clan. In the inscription for his daughter, Quan also describes the prestigious marriage alliance achieved for her with Dugu Yu, the son of the highly respected late-eighth-century literatus Dugu Ji (725–777), who had been Quan Deyu's own patron. In fact, one of the more poignant features of the inscription for Madam Dugu is Quan's lament for the collapse of this bond between the two families—the death of his son-in-law followed by the death of his daughter severed this illustrious and probably long hoped-for tie. We also see in the daughter's inscription how Quan's rank and reputation affected the reception of the women members of the family at court when he was appointed grand councilor, the highest-ranking office he ever held. The inscription vividly captures the mutually influential forces of birth, strategic marriage, and political success among Tang elites.

In contrast to his daughter's inscription, where Quan embeds Madam Dugu's life in the social and political fabric of early-ninth-century Chang'an, the inscription for his grandson, who died before he could begin his career or marry, focuses on the boy's potential and also on his conduct as he sickened and approached death. Quan's depiction of Shunsun's decline reveals medieval Chinese Buddhist beliefs in practice: the boy adopted a Buddhist name after he fell ill and at the moment of crisis was able to part from his family without distress, taking strength from praying and facing west, the direction of the Pure Land. In contrast to the inscription for his daughter, where Quan wrestles with the fact of her death, the Buddhist doctrine of reincarnation, which allows for the immortality of the soul through successive rebirths, provides Quan a consoling framework for his grandson's death in the conviction that the boy's soul would be reborn in a future life. This strong contrast between the two inscriptions' emotional responses to the deaths does not necessarily indicate that Quan's attachment to one was greater than to the other. Instead, it reminds us that medieval Chinese writers had many social, religious, and personal perspectives in which to situate the lives of the deceased, and they were keenly aware of the diverse potential readers of their commemorative biographies. The funerary inscription for Madam

Dugu would surely have been shared with members of the Dugu clan as well as the many other elites in their larger network in Chang'an; the inscription for Shunsun, who died before he could be embedded in those larger social networks, would have been most meaningful to the members of Quan's immediate family.

Entombed Funerary Inscription for [My] Daughter the Late Madam Dugu

On the twenty-first day of the tenth month, in the winter of the tenth year of the Yuanhe reign period [815], the wife of the late vice-director of the Imperial Library, Dugu Yu, who was posthumously entitled Prefect of Jiangzhou, and the daughter of the Quan clan of Tianshui, bedridden with illness, passed away in the Guangfu quarter of the capital. Alas, alas! This was my daughter; therefore, I wail and remember her.

Our household has had generations of esteemed virtue, down unto the great integrity and deeds of our former sire, Grand Guardian, Pure and Filial Lord [Quan Gao], who was a model to the people. Therefore, this accumulated merit was concentrated in you, yet you died untimely, blocked from realizing it. This is why I do not understand the bestowals of Heaven.

In conduct, from the time your hair was pinned [at fifteen years old], you were never far from father and mother or elder and younger brothers. Your [marital] home was in the same quarter, and you often visited your parents. When [your future husband] came to ask for your hand in marriage, he had neither achieved official rank nor passed the examination; later he became an attendant at the Historiography Bureau, then a drafter of imperial edicts, all offices he held two or three terms.[1] In a little over ten years, he became lustrous and brilliant, and it was everyone's opinion that a ministerial appointment awaited him.

Within your chambers, you assisted your lord and offered the ancestral sacrifices, happily and calmly, with filiality and goodness. At that time, when I was fulfilling a great duty [as grand councilor] and your husband occupied a post near the throne, you were able to act

with restraint and labor in humility, attaining harmony in the six relations [father, mother, older and younger brothers, husband, and
children]. In the year that I was bestowed a title by the Changxin Palace [813], you and your mother were given audience positions in the
Inner Court; the sounds of jade pendants [from ennoblement] echoed
each other, and all of our acquaintance and kin were proud of you. In
your sentiments and concern for ritual, you were refined and regulated, and those who speak of the Inner Regulations [for womanly
conduct in the household] would say you hit the mark.

Alas! When your husband had just turned forty, he was struck
down [814]; and you passed away without completing the first year of
mourning for him, aged only thirty-one. Why should Heaven requite
us this way? When you were first widowed, fearing that you would
cause me sorrow, you would restrain yourself from showing sorrow
on your face but instead acted gently and humbly. Yet, because deep
despair attacked you within, in the end you were unable to bear it.
Truly grievous!

Earlier, your father-in-law, the Exemplary Lord Dugu Ji, had a
prominent name in his age, but your husband Dugu Yu was orphaned
not long after he was born, and he was unable to serve his father. If
there is awareness in the vast dark, will you from the shared grave be
able to nourish him below? Though you had wisdom and *qi* above
[when alive], will you when you return to the depths? I do not know.

You bore two sons and a daughter; the oldest boy died untimely
before he was a year old. Your second son, Hui, was born ten years ago,
with a refined nature that surpassed others, yet within a year he again
encountered "thistles and smartweed" [the pain of his mother's death
following his father's], and his wailing and shouting was endless. Hui's
uncle the Right Rectifier of Omissions Dugu Lang, swallowing the
painful grief of brothers-till-death, cherished him as if he were not
orphaned. After the divination with tortoise and yarrow stalks [for the
time and place of burial], you will be entombed on the sixth day of the
second month next year in the plain of Shou'an County in Luoyang. It
is fitting now to carve the tombstone to perpetuate your recognition
hereafter.

I have indeed grown old, so how can I compose this? I feared that others would not know my daughter's beauty and substance, and therefore I suppressed my painful grief and composed this rhymed elegy:

> The radiance of your rising sun not yet full day when it sank in
>   gloom;
> Your branches had just flowered forth when they were withered
>   and stricken.
> Virtuous was my daughter in beauty, now to be entombed with
>   her lord in the depths.
> It is enough, it is enough! I know not if her spirit exists [to know
>   my feelings]!

Source: Guo Guangwei 郭廣偉, ed., *Quan Deyu shiwen ji* 權德興詩文集, 2 vols. (Shanghai: Shanghai guji chubanshe, 2008), vol. 1, 26.389–90.

Entombed Record for My Grandson Who Died Young, Ceremonial Groom in the Livery Service of the Heir Apparent

The son of the Quan clan who died young was named Shunsun (Obedient Grandson), and his youthful name was Wenchang. Once he was overcome by illness, he used the way of the [Buddhist] *śramaṇa* and changed his style name to Lord Nezha. He was the great-grandson of the posthumously entitled Grand Protector, Pure and Filial Lord Quan Gao, the grandson of the minister of justice and Duke of Fufeng, Quan Deyu, and the son of the District Defender in Weinan, Quan Qu. He had recently been appointed Ceremonial Groom in the Livery Service of the Heir Apparent.

He lived thirteen years and, on the twenty-second day of the eleventh month of the tenth year of the Yuanhe reign period [815], died untimely in Guangfu quarter. On the twenty-seventh day, we wrapped his body and buried him in Shenhe Field in Wannian County [of the capital, Chang'an]. Since we have closed the coffin, I, his grandfather, weep and make a record for his tomb, as follows.

As a boy, you were quick-witted and intelligent, filial and obedient, reverent and humble; you followed your grandparents' and your parents' instructions without disobedience. Though other sons and grandsons raised to adulthood may be filial and obedient, they are not as good as you, and therefore I gave you your name. You had read *The Classic of Filial Piety*, *The Analects*, and *The Classic of Documents*, and you were especially fond of calligraphy, never leaving your inkstone and mat. In all of your actions and words, you followed reason and spoke with correctness, far beyond ordinary boys. You were just studying the Younger Dai *Book of Rites*, but, before you had finished it, you fell ill.

From spring into winter, through all four seasons, your illness was increasingly severe. At the moment of greatest crisis, you bade farewell to your respected elders and parted with your younger brothers and sisters, calmly and without distress. Then you said to your maidservant, "It is as if all the Buddhist ceremonies in the void are right in front of my eyes—hurry to light the incense, and move my pillow to face west [the direction of the Pure Land]." You pressed your palms to bow and passed away. Initially I had doubted the Buddhist doctrine of the immortality of the soul, but, encountering this experience, I now believe it. Ah, alas! Because you had taken up official service and furthermore had the resolve of a grown man, I wished not to say that you "died young"[2]—but those who know the rites say this is not permissible, and I do not dare transgress them. The family gravesite lies in Luoyang, and we divined an auspicious date to entomb you in the following year; therefore, we temporarily bury you and here cry out:

> Though the soul and breath have no place to go [without a living body],
> Your divine spirit has gone on its way—
> Then what use is there in my tears and weeping?

Source: Guo, *Quan Deyu shiwen ji*, vol. 1, 26.391–92.

Notes

1. Dugu Yu and Quan's daughter were married at some point in 798, when she was thirteen or fourteen; Dugu passed the most prestigious civil service examination, the *jinshi* (Presented Scholar) exam, that year at age twenty-three, recommended by Quan himself.
2. In the title to this epitaph as well as here, Quan uses the term *shang*, which, according to the classics on ritual was the appropriate way to refer to the death of a child between the ages of twelve and fifteen. Quan's grandson Shunsun was thirteen *sui* at his death, and thus the term applied to him.

Further Reading

DeBlasi, Anthony. "Striving for Completeness: Quan Deyu and the Evolution of the Tang Intellectual Mainstream." *Harvard Journal of Asiatic Studies* 61 (2001): 5–36.

Shields, Anna M. "Words for the Dead and the Living: Innovations in the Mid-Tang 'Prayer Text' (*jiwen*)." *Tang Studies* 25 (2007): 111–45.

Tackett, Nicolas. *The Destruction of the Chinese Aristocracy.* Cambridge, MA: Harvard University Asia Center, 2014.

Yao, Ping. "Tang Epitaphs for Confucian, Daoist, and Buddhist Women (*muzhiming*)." In *Images of Women in Chinese Thought and Culture*, edited by Robin R. Wang, 299–315. Indianapolis: Hackett, 2003.

A Nun Who Lived Through the Huichang Persecution of Buddhism

Epitaph for Daoist Nun Zhi (Zhi Zhijian 支志堅, 812–861),
by Zhi Mo 支謨 (fl. 860)

TRANSLATED BY PING YAO

Written by a man for his sister, this epitaph provides a unique opportunity to understand sibling relations among the Tang elite and women's ties with their natal families. It also offers an example of the ways political actions could have adverse effects on women's lives.

BUDDHISM CAME TO CHINA FROM INDIA VIA THE SILK ROAD IN the first century. It found a receptive audience during the Period of Disunity, when Confucianism lost much of its appeal. In uncertain times, Chinese turned to Daoism and Buddhism as a salve for their anxiety and suffering. Even after reunification under the Sui and Tang dynasties, Buddhism flourished, and the literati class came to embrace Buddhism as a religion that provides philosophically subtle ideas about death and the transience of life. Sui and Tang rulers became major patrons of the religion, none more so than Empress Wu, who dominated the government for more than thirty years, first with her husband, Emperor Gaozong

(r. 649–683), and later on her own. To legitimize her rule, she elevated Buddhism to the state religion. As a result, the membership of Buddhist temples and monasteries increased dramatically. Tang women's epitaphs reveal Buddhist influence on Tang perceptions of gender and on women's life experiences. Although nuns made up less than 1 percent of the female population, nearly 5 percent of women's epitaphs were dedicated to Buddhist nuns. Such disproportion works to our advantage in providing valuable information about Buddhist nuns' lives in Tang China.

During the Tang, ordination as a nun or a monk required the imperial court's approval and an official ordination certificate. By the mid-Tang, such certificates had become hot commodities and would more often than not go first to powerful families or to those who paid hefty bribes. Many women who had not yet obtained certificates but did not want to wait to enter the religious life became "nuns living at home" (*zhujiani*). "Epitaph for Daoist Nun Zhi" describes the life of such a nun whose Buddhist faith was greatly challenged in the midst of her turbulent life.

Dated 862, this epitaph was unearthed by grave robbers in Luoyang during the 1920s along with eight other epitaphs for members of Zhi Zhijian's family. In 2004, the epitaph for Zhi Mo, brother of Nun Zhi and author of her epitaph, was excavated, bringing the number of epitaphs for the Zhi family to a total of ten.

Zhi Zhijian was born in 812 to a prestigious family: her grandfather and father were ranked officials at the Tang court, and her nine brothers who survived to adulthood all held office. While still a toddler, Zhi was afflicted by an illness, which led to her conversion to Buddhism at the age of nine. During the Tang dynasty, it was not uncommon for parents of a sick child to have him or her ordained in the hopes that such an expression of devotion would cure the child. When Zhi was eighteen, her mother died, and she seems to have stepped into the role of nurturing her many younger siblings. Perhaps as a consequence, Nun Zhi lived with her family for the rest of her life, first with her parents and later with her brothers. Most likely she was a "nun living at home," a status that would allow a Buddhist nun to look after her family or a female devotee who was waiting for an imperial permit to enter a convent.

Nun Zhi's religious vocation became problematic in 845, when Tang emperor Wuzong (r. 840–846) launched the most devastating religious persecution in Chinese history. The so-called Huichang Buddhist Persecution led to the destruction of 44,600 Buddhist monasteries and temples and the defrocking of as many as 260,500 Buddhist monks and nuns. By then, Zhi was thirty-three years old. With no clear prospect of becoming a wife and mother, she chose an easy way out: she assumed a new religious identity in Daoism; she would be addressed as *lianshi*, Daoist master.

Zhi's later life, between her conversion to Daoism in 845 and her death in 861, mirrored the social turmoil of late Tang China. The first major incident occurred in 853, when her closest brother, Zhi Xiang, fell from political favor and lost his life. For eight years, Nun Zhi was entrusted with taking care of Xiang's widow and daughter. Eight years later, in 861, Nun Zhi went to live with her younger brother, Ne, who held an appointment in Tengzhou (Guangxi) and later in Fuyang (Zhejiang). This journey proved to be fatal: Nun Zhi was caught up in the social unrest, could not get enough to eat, and eventually came down with an infectious malady. She died that year at the age of fifty. This was roughly the average age for the women of her times but much lower than the average age at death for men of the same period or women in earlier periods of the Tang. The political chaos and economic turbulence of the second half of the Tang seems to have had more adverse effects on elite women than on men.

"Epitaph for Daoist Nun Zhi" is one of more than forty published Tang epitaphs written by a man for his sister, about half of them for women who were married. These texts tend to be intimate in recounting the lives of the deceased and tender in emotional tone. They provide us with a unique opportunity to understand sibling relations among the Tang elite as well as women's ties with their natal families.

Zhi's epitaph also presents a concrete example of the impact of the Huichang Persecution on women's lives. It seems Buddhist nuns experienced greater difficulties than monks after the forced laicization. Presumably, defrocked monks could still marry and establish a family. Nuns past marriageable age (according to the data from Tang epitaphs, the average marriage age for Tang women was seventeen) had fewer options. By converting to Daoism, Zhi probably avoided bringing shame on her family.

An intriguing aspect of "Epitaph for Daoist Nun Zhi" is her descent from a non-Han ethnic group—the Lesser Yuezhi people. The surname Zhi appeared in the Chinese written record as early as the fourth century, and it exclusively belonged to the Yuezhi, nomadic pastoralists living in the western part of modern-day Gansu. During the second century BCE, the Yuezhi split into two groups: the Greater Yuezhi migrated west, while the Lesser Yuezhi remained, living largely in the Guanzhong, Dunhuang, Turfan, and Loulan areas (in modern northwest China). During the Tang, the Lesser Yuezhi people were largely assimilated to Han culture; by the end of the Song dynasty, their ethnic identity had completely disappeared.

Nun Zhi's epitaph along with the other nine for Zhis show that, by the ninth century, the Zhi family had cemented their position as members of Tang society's upper echelon. Not only did all the brothers hold office, but their mothers also were from prominent clans. Their maternal granduncle was Cui Neng (d. 824), a prominent official who served both Emperor Xianzong (r. 805–820) and Emperor Muzong (r. 821–824). Zhi Mo and his brothers took wives from the most sought-after families in the Tang. In addition, quite a few family members had apparently migrated to and settled down in the south. The life experiences of Master Zhi and her family seem in no obvious way different from their contemporaries whose ancestry was entirely Han.

Entombed Epitaph with a Preface for Daoist Nun Zhi, the Eldest Daughter of Mr. Zhi of Langye, the Retired Chief Minister of the Court of State Ceremonial, Posthumous Minister of Works of the Tang

Composed by her younger brother Mo, Gentleman for Court Discussion, Probationary Aid to Administrator of the Court of National Granaries, and Concurrent Officer of the Special Reserves Vault of the Ministry of Revenue

My Daoist nun sister was the thirty-second daughter [of our clan in my generation]. Her Daoist name was Zhijian [Unyielding Aspiration], and her childhood name was Xinniangzi [New Daughter]. Her great-grandfather, named Ping, was vice-magistrate of Xunyang District, Jiangzhou, of the [Tang] imperial dynasty. Her grandfather, named Cheng, was vice-supervisor of the Household of the Heir Apparent and posthumous director of the Palace Administration of the imperial dynasty. Her late father, named [word missing], was a retired chief minister of the Court of State Ceremonial and posthumous minister of works. Her late mother, Ms. Tan of Runan, was posthumously conferred the title of Grand Lady of Runan District. Her stepmother, Ms. Cui of Qinghe, was conferred the title of Grand Mistress of the Lu State.

My sister's oldest brother, Yu, died at a young age. Her older brother Fang was magistrate of Duanshi District in Zezhou when he died. Her dear younger brother Xiang was manager of the Requisitioned Labor of Ezhou when he died. [Among her other younger brothers], Xun and Qian died young, whereas Ne, Hui, Mo, Xiang, Rang, Xin, and Yan are all consistently listed among court officials.

My sister will endure forever as a revered soul. Virtue was inborn in her. Although she lost her parents [at a young age], she was never a needy person. She lived by filiality and kindness and possessed an even-tempered personality. While still a toddler, she fell ill from grief. At nine, she took up Buddhism. Day and night, she conducted herself immaculately, yet she did not live in a Buddhist convent. Whenever a family member had an illness or calamity or was far from the others, she would for an entire month observe [the monastic rule of] fasting in the morning and chanting sutras. The sincerity of her piety and love reached the divine spirits.

At the age of eighteen, my sister suffered the calamity of losing her mother, the Grand Lady of Runan. Her unerring mourning demeanor surpassed everyone else's. Thin as a wooden stick and barely surviving, the sight of her moved both the simpleminded and the bright. Although [her siblings] had drifted off to various places, her tender love for them never diminished. She admonished and encouraged the younger brothers for fear that they would not be able to establish themselves. Fond of the ancients, she especially admired Woman Xie's erudition and Mencius's mother's astute selection of a neighborhood.[1] She never slackened in her able assistance, and she exhausted herself mentally and physically.

Well along in life she encountered the Buddhist persecution and consequently changed her faith to Daoism. When calamity fell on the Ezhou household, Xiang entrusted his family to her. From the seventh year of the Dazhong reign period [853], she never left her orphaned niece and widowed sister-in-law even for a brief moment.

In the second year of this emperor's reign [861], my older brother Ne was appointed to the governorship of Tengzhou. It was said that its climate did not differ much from that of Huai and Zhe [in the center of the country]; its fine vegetables and sweet rice would provide suitable food for her to eat. Ne thus extended his brotherly effort to supporting his worthy sister, hoping to make her heart content. He thus attentively accompanied her, via East Luo, to the southern region. Just over ten days after taking office, Ne encountered harassment by the Man people. As soon as my sister began to adjust to the Tengzhou environment, [her brother Ne] was suddenly transferred to Fuyang. While he was under the strain of collecting and shipping off grain supplies day and night, the local food was far from fine. My sister contracted pestilential qi[2] and suddenly passed away. [During her last hours,] she sat upright and expressed her wishes calmly without any uneasiness. At the age of fifty, on the twelfth day of the ninth month, the second year of the Xiantong reign period [861], she died in the official residence in Fuyang.

Alas, the law of the universe is obscure: those who accumulate merit are not given the longest lives; those who are the kindest do not prosper most! Owing to their humble official duties, her brothers Mo and Xiang were not able to meet her [coffin]. [How regrettable that] they could not repay her love when she ascended to the Upper Pure Realm.[3] Guided by the funeral banner, her coffin was taken from Fu to Yi, where it returned to the clan cemetery. On the eighth day of the tenth month, the third year of the Xiantong reign period [862], she was buried in the northwest part of the cemetery near Duzhai Village, Pingle Township, Henan Prefecture, all in accordance with the rites.

At that time, I, Mo, was on official duty at the Reserves Vault. I requested a leave to return to the east. The tomb site was selected after a divination, and the coffin was then interred. The rites were all conducted with our full devotion. I inscribe on this stone with a knife that cuts into my gut, and I wet the brush with my blood. Standing by the tomb, I wail to the sky, my sorrowful voice sending my farewell. This epitaph fails to fully express our feelings; this tradition [of writing an epitaph] merely averts [the disappearance of her life stories due to] changes in worldly affairs.

The rhymed elegy reads:

The sky is bright and clear, but it is far away and ambiguous.
Life is short and mundane. Who understands its twists and
    turns?
It is said that Heaven aids the virtuous; who would expect it
    punished the benevolent?
She was as constant as gold and as pure as jade, but now the
    crane has departed to rest among pine trees.
The unpredictable is fate; the unquestionable is Heaven.
She was alarmingly ill as an infant, her sickness lingering
    lifelong.
She followed Buddhist teaching, but Daoism nurtured her
    virtues.
She recited Buddhist sutras; her heart roamed in the Daoist
    realm.
Even though one's nature is permanent, one's form succumbs to
    changes.
She lived just to middle age; surely that cannot be called
    longevity.
She disappeared to a cinnamon peak, and her coffin now rests
    among the Mang cemeteries.
The clouds of the Song Mountain pass through her tomb from
    the east; the waves of the Luo River run in front of it.

The tomb is now closed, and her soul has returned to a divine
place.
[My pain as] scooping out flesh and cutting off hands, sorrowfully I compose this epitaph.

Source: Zhou Shaoliang 周紹良 and Zhao Chao 趙超, eds., *Tangdai
muzhi huibian* 唐代墓志匯編 (Shanghai: Shanghai guji chubanshe,
1992), 2393.

Notes

1. Woman Xie refers to Xie Daoyun (4th c.) of the Jin dynasty, who was known for
   her literary talent. Mencius's mother moved their home to a neighborhood suitable to her son learning proper behavior.
2. "Pestilential *qi*" refers to an infectious and often fatal disease.
3. The Upper Pure Realm is one of the three Pure Realms, the most divine places in
   Daoism.

Further Reading

Jia, Jinhua, Xiaofei Kang, and Ping Yao, eds. *Gendering Chinese Religion: Subject,
Identity, and Body.* Albany: State University of New York Press, 2014.
Yao, Ping. "Good Karmic Connections: Buddhist Mothers and Their Children in
Tang China (618–907)." *Nan Nü: Men, Women and Gender in China* 10.1 (2008):
57–85.

An Envoy Serving the Kitan Liao Son of Heaven

Epitaph for Han Chun 韓橁 (d. 1036), Court Ceremonial
Commissioner, by Li Wan 李萬 (fl. 1012–1037)

TRANSLATED BY LANCE PURSEY

This epitaph allows us to consider questions of identity, culture, and
ethnicity from the perspective of someone whose family served the
non-Han Kitan Liao dynasty. It is also rich in information about inter-
state relations of the period.

THE YEAR 1005 WITNESSED A MAJOR GEOPOLITICAL BREAK-
through in East Asia. The two rival empires, Song and Liao, concluded
peace negotiations with the Treaty of Chanyuan, bringing to an end
almost a century of instability and conflict following the collapse of the
Tang in 907. This treaty established a border between the two states and
stipulated not only that Song send annual "gifts" of silk and silver, but
also that, in the correspondence between the two empires, each
emperor address the other as elder or younger brother according to who
was senior in age. The mutual recognition of the existence of two emperors
at the same time, of Liao in the "northern court" and of Song in the "southern court," was an unprecedented development. Whereas in the Tang
period states near and far recognized and paid tribute to only one

emperor, the signing of the Treaty of Chanyuan meant that states such as Xia (1038–1227) and Goryeo (in Korea, 918–1392) had to recognize and pay tribute to two states, both Song and Liao. Han Chun (d. 1036), the subject of this selection, served as an envoy for the Liao court both before and after the completion of this treaty. Through his life, we can observe not only the internal politics of Liao, but also its relations with other states. Furthermore, this epitaph allows us to consider questions of identity—cultural and ethnic—from a perspective different from that in the standard histories.

Indeed, if it weren't for archeological sources that have been unearthed since the late nineteenth century, much of what we know about Liao would be shaped by Song perspectives, which are not always helpful, when we take into account Song-Liao relations. This is because, although the Chanyuan treaty brought relative peace, certain political factions in Song were not happy with this treaty; they considered the Kitans to be foreign barbarians and thus parts of the territory under Liao control—the sixteen prefectures of Yan (Beijing) and Yun (Datong, Shanxi)—to be illegitimately occupied territory. Not only did they want the sixteen prefectures to be made part of the Song state, but they also believed that the people in these regions wanted to belong to the Song. Even though the treaty enshrined the legitimate existence of both Liao and Song, these scholar-statesmen struggled to come to terms with this political reality. Their ideas gained further currency in later generations, influencing not only the way Liao was written about by historians in later periods, but also the very survival of historical materials that inform us about the internal workings of the Liao.

From the perspective of Song thinkers, Liao was an anomaly. The imperial house of Liao was descended from Turko-Mongol tribal groups of people that characteristically practiced pastoralism. These groups were active in the region northeast of the Tang empire and were in frequent contact with both the northeastern provinces of Tang and the Uyghur Khanate (744–840). Following the collapse of the Tang at the end of the ninth century, a Kitan leader named Abaoji (r. 916–926) seized on the power vacuum in northeast Asia. On emerging as leader of the Kitans, Abaoji abolished the tribal system of leadership and did away with many of his rivals, declaring himself emperor of Liao in 916 and establishing imperial succession of his house, the Yelü, in the style of Chinese dynastic empires. This new polity expanded quickly, conquering the Bohai state (Liaoning) and subduing the Jurchen groups (in Jilin and Heilongjiang) to the east; in the south, the sixteen prefectures of Yan and Yun (northern Hebei and Shanxi) were ceded to them in an alliance with the Later Jin (936–945). As the Kaifeng-based Song state expanded from 960 onward, it increasingly grew closer to confrontation with this burgeoning empire that reached westward into Mongolia, eastward to the edge of the Korean Peninsula, and southward past the Great Wall into the north China plain.

The population of Liao consisted of a diverse array of groups with both conquered populations and voluntary migrants from the Korean Peninsula, Inner Asia, and north China. This diversity in its population and the practice of traditional steppe customs by the ruling house resulted in power structures and forms of governance that differed from its predecessor Tang and its contemporary Song. The Liao emperor customarily did not govern from a palace or a fixed place but from tents and on horseback; his court moved between seasonal camps and only periodically visited the five capitals and other urban spaces. Reports written by Song envoys recount journeys across the wilderness to these camps to have an audience with the Liao emperor. Such a diverse population was managed by dividing the government into a Northern and a Southern Administration; the Northern Administration oversaw the various tribal groups across the vast north, while the Southern Administration governed the largely agricultural populations with a bureaucratic system that resembled that of the Tang and Song. Alongside these two administrations, there was also a system known as the ordo, which is still not fully understood but appears to make certain regions and parts of the population the direct estate of individual emperors.

In the eyes of Song observers, this pluralism of populations and power structures was a clear signifier that Liao was "not like us" and may have motivated their need to emphasize a strong distinction between what they saw as the mobile Kitan rulers and the sedentary population made up of conquered peoples from north China that the Kitan ruled over.

Contemporary accounts of Liao in transmitted historical sources were written by observers from Song; other material was compiled two centuries later in the Yuan based on surviving records from the Liao court. This means that the ethnic and cultural identities we read about in accounts of Liao did not necessarily reflect how those individuals would have portrayed themselves. Useful here are archeological discoveries being made in northeast China and Inner Mongolia that provide examples of how these individuals presented themselves. So too excavated epitaphs such as the selection presented here, are a valuable window onto the individuals and identities in Northeast Asia in the tenth to twelfth centuries. The subject of this selection here, Han Chun, and the author, Li Wan (fl. 1012–1037), like many others in Liao would be more or less lost to us if it were not for the discovery of this inscription.

How did Han Chun identify ethnically? Was he Han or Kitan? The writer of his epitaph makes no direct mention of Han Chun's ethnicity as Han or Kitan, which could signify an ambivalence toward these categories or that the topic was sensitive. Li Wan does, however, begin the text with an account of the family name "Han," claiming ties between Han Chun's family and a lineage of remote antiquity that came to be based in Jizhou (Hebei). The account then skips forward over a thousand years to the early tenth century with the conquest of Jizhou by Abaoji and the ascent of Han Zhigu, Han Chun's great-grandfather, who served Abaoji in the early years of what would become the Liao state. This ancestry would suggest that Han Chun would identify as Han, or ethnically "Chinese." However, Han Chun is the fourth generation of a family at the center of imperial politics in Liao, with relatives adopted into the house of Yelü and fluent in the Kitan language. Furthermore, we see explicitly that the maternal side of his family at each generation were from the house of Xiao, which frequently married members of house of Yelü. Evidently, Han Chun was not a Han man in the service of foreign conquerors but very much integrated into the ruling house of Liao, genealogically, politically, and culturally. This duality or fusion of identities made members of the Han lineage well suited to high office and diplomatic service; their intimate ties with the ruling house ensured that they were trusted by and loyal to Liao, and their cultural affinities with north China would have been an advantage on missions not only to Song, but also to other countries in the region, as Chinese was the lingua franca.

Han Chun's relatives were not atypical in being accepted into the house of Yelü; diasporic descendants of other lineages from north China enjoyed similar privileges in Liao, filling the official bureaucratic posts and sometimes serving as envoys on diplomatic missions to foreign states. It is hard to know how these individuals felt about serving an emperor and a regime that was not "Chinese" or whether they considered their situation in such terms, indeed whether they even considered themselves as "Chinese." Epitaphs offer limited perspectives on this, and transmitted sources from Song writers may have had a vested ideological interest in perpetuating ideas of "Chineseness"; such ideas were likely intensified by some Song intellectuals uneasy with the relationship between Liao and Song.

Han Chun's epitaph allows us to see this geopolitical situation in action. Han Chun served two emperors in several roles, mainly as a strategist and as an envoy or messenger bearing the imperial seal to foreign lands. On two occasions, he went to Song, the first time immediately after the conclusion of the Treaty of Chanyuan. Besides visiting Song, Han Chun also traveled considerable distances to other lands, visiting Goryeo twice and Xia on one occasion. At the height of his career, he fell into disgrace as a result of an unspecified incident and was sent on a mission to Shazhou (in Mongolia), where he almost died. These trips stood out as big events in his life, but much of his life would have been spent in the heartlands and political center of Liao, though by no means in only one place. He was put in charge of regions all over Liao, at different points of his life, from the southern border to the restive Eastern Capital Circuit; at the time of his death, he was stationed in the Southern Capital, Yanjing (Beijing). At certain points, he followed the imperial entourage and was posted to several ordo. Throughout his career and posthumously, he accrued an array of roles and ceremonial titles, as can be seen in the long title of his epitaph below.

Han Chun's epitaph was composed by Li Wan and commissioned by Chun's surviving sons. Unlike the epitaphs for members of the Han clan excavated in the huge tomb complex in Bayin (Bayan) Ula'n Sum, Baarin Left Banner, Inner Mongolia, which are accompanied by a wealth of material culture and archeological data with which to work, the precise provenance and current whereabouts of Han Chun's epitaph is a mystery. In other words, the text presented here is all we have to understand how people of his day wished to represent Han Chun.

Little is known about Li Wan, and the relationship between him and Han Chun is not clear. He appears twice in the official *History of the Liao* (completed in 1344), where he is listed as a Palace Library proofreader in 1012. He was sentenced to hard labor in the silver mines for submitting a slanderous memorial by his peers accusing examination officials of favoritism. He authored two surviving epitaphs, Geng Yanyi's (1020), in which he presents himself with no titles but only a reference to his descent from the Li clan of Longxi (Gansu), and this one, where he bears a series of ceremonial titles.

The rhetoric and structure of epitaphs from Liao have no pronounced divergences from conventions of the genre seen in examples from Tang and earlier. The tracing of ancestry to remote antiquity is seen not just in cases like that of Han Chun and his family, where we would assume a north Chinese lineage, but also in the epitaphs of members of the houses of Yelü, who claim a lineage that ties their families to the Liu clan of the Han dynasty imperial house, and the Xiao clan of Lanling (Shandong), who claimed to be descended from Xiao He (d. 193 BCE), the right-hand man of the Han dynastic founder Liu Bang (256–195 BCE). Identity has less to do with the authenticity of a claim regarding lineage and more to do with the context within which the claim is being made.

There are over two hundred epitaphs in Chinese from Liao, a third of which are for members of the houses of Yelü and Xiao. In addition, there are epitaphs written in either of the two scripts invented for the Kitan language (commonly known to scholars as the large script and the small script). The Kitan language has been dead for over half a millennium, and extant examples of writing are currently only partially deciphered. The majority of Kitan epitaphs are also for members of the houses of Yelü and Xiao, which demonstrates that members of these two houses had disproportionate access to the material and cultural capital to invest in funerary inscriptions. Some Liao tombs have impressive structures and contain splendid murals and material culture in addition to epitaphs. There are clear divergences in tomb culture between the north and the south of Liao, leading to the labeling of two distinct tomb cultures, Kitan and Liao Chinese. And, indeed, not all tombs contained epitaphs. Overall, the mortuary culture of Liao demonstrates a mixture of cultural options available to elites and a certain diversity of attitudes toward epitaphs. In Han Chun's epitaph below, we see an effort to tie his lineage to classical Chinese tradition but at the same time to center him and emphasize his family's role in the dynastic house and politics of Liao. In terms of identity, we see in the absence of specific ethnic labels that it is hard won high office and imperial favor that Han Chun's relatives wished to celebrate.

Epitaph with Preface for Mr. Han, the Late Court Ceremonial Commissioner for the Southern Establishment, Military Commissioner of the Guiyi Regiment, Internal Surveillance and Supervisory-Level Commissioner of Shazhou, Grand Master of the Palace with Golden Seal and Purple Ribbon, Acting Defender in Chief, Direct Representative of the Emperor in Charge of Military Affairs in Shazhou, Prefect of Shazhou, Censor in Chief, Supreme Pillar of the State, Dynasty-Founding Marquis of Changli Commandery, with a Land Grant of 1,500 Households and a Fiefdom of 150 Households

Composed by Li Wan, Gentleman for Court Audiences, Acting Director of the Right Office of the Department of State Affairs, Senior Compiler of the Historiography Institute, Commandant of Militant Cavalry, and recipient of the Imperial Purple and Gold Fish Pendant

Mr. Han's name was Chun, his courtesy name Zhengsheng. He was a distant descendant of Huan Shu of Quwo [802–731 BCE], whose clan gained ascendency in the lands of Ji [one of the legendary nine prefectures, covering the northeast of China] and was enfeoffed by the state of Han [northwest Henan and southeast Shanxi]. The eldest brother of the clan took the surname of the Han state [403–230 BCE], which was one of the three states to emerge from the former Jin territory—one of the six major players in the Warring States period. The embers of the clan's glory were almost snuffed out under the reign of the First Emperor of the Qin [r. 221–210 BCE], but, with the arrival of the Heavenly Han dynasty, their base was given a new lease of life. When this new regime doled out its territory, the clan was bestowed with land in Yingchuan [Henan]; it is believed that a branch of the family settled in the Dai region [Shanxi]. Some descendants moved to Changli [Chaoyang, Liaoning], which became their native place. How magnificent is the account of this clan's heritage!

Emperor Shengyuan [honorific title for Abaoji] came to command land reaching from the deserts [western Inner Mongolia] to the pine forests [southwest Inner Mongolia and Liaoning] and advanced into the region of Jiqiu [west of present-day Beijing]. Through marriage, the first emperor acquired a servitor from the lands of mulberry plains [here the writer is referring to Chaoyang, Liaoning], who helped him build a platform to sacrifice to the earth at Liucheng [another name for Chaoyang, Liaoning]. Showing deep learning and wisdom, he won the region over to his side. That servitor, whose taboo name was Zhigu, was Mr. Han's great-grandfather. He held the titles of Distinguished Imperial Subject for loyalty, strategy, and exercise of force, military commissioner for the Zhangwu Regiment [Chaoyang, Liaoning], supervisory commissioner for the Southeast Route, Commander Unequaled in Honor, and once acting Left Vice-Director of the Department of State Affairs and Secretariat Director. Just as Bi Wan [seventh century BCE, an official of the Jin state] sired the ancestors of the founders of the Wei state [in the Warring States period] and Zang Xibo [d. 718 BCE] of Lu state [one of the northern states in the Spring and Autumn period] was forefather to the powerful Zangsun clan, Han Zhigu initiated a flourishing lineage and enjoyed a high reputation through the generations.

Han Kuangmei was Mr. Han's grandfather. In his lifetime, he was a Distinguished Imperial Subject for courage and loyalty, collective strategy, fortitude, and service as a stand-by palace guard; army commander of Yanjing [Beijing]; military commissioner of Tianxiong Regiment [Handan, Hebei]; and Commander Unequaled in Honor.

He was posthumously made acting grand preceptor and director for governmental matters, Superior Area Command of the commander in chief in Weizhou [Hebei], Supreme Pillar of State, and Prince of Ye. He possessed a vast talent for administering the state and firmly upheld the bonds between his family and the emperor. He rose to the towering heights of military command and was the first of the clan to attain noble status. He first married the Grand Mistress of Qin and had two sons and one daughter. The eldest was Mr. Han's father. The second son, Yu, General of the Left Gate Guard, died many years ago. The daughter died following her marriage to the son of Mr. Liu, Attendant of Songzhou. Mr. Han's grandfather also married a concubine who had fallen out of the favor of Imperial Prince Yelü Lihu. She was the niece of Empress Shulü Ping and was given the title Consort of the Prince of Ye. They had one son and one daughter. The son died young. The daughter married Zhang Chongyi, who was the grandson of the director of the Chancellery and the father of Mr. Han's wife. He served as Great General of the Left Gate Guard and administrator of Tanzhou [near Beijing]. Mr. Han's grandfather later married the Mistress of Wei, the niece of the Consort of Ye. All of Han Kuangmei's wives were from the house of Xiao [which provided the empresses for the Kitan royal family].

Mr. Han's great uncle was Kuangsi, campaign commander of the Southwest Route [west Inner Mongolia], military commissioner of the Jinchang Regiment, once seconded to the metropolitan governor, grand preceptor, and Prince of Qin. He had great scholarly prowess and was the most prominent of his brothers, paving the way for many more of his clan to become nobles and high-ranking officials. He sired Derang, who was posthumously named Wenzhong [cultured and loyal], grand councilor, acting Grand Mentor, Prince of Jin, who was given the taboo name of Longyun by the emperor. Han Derang was also awarded the royal family name Yelü, making him a member of the imperial house. Such an unprecedented and glorious honor meant he could approach the emperor without removing his sword or his shoes, a privilege that showed his superiority to the many who came before the emperor. Derang was Mr. Han's uncle [son of his grandfather's older brother].

Mr. Han's older cousin [son of Derang] was Suizhen, who was given the name Zhixin by the emperor. He was commander in chief of 400,000 infantry and cavalry, acting director of the Chancellery, Great Prince of the South, and posthumously made director for governmental matters and Prince of Chen. He was a pillar of the state and enjoyed unparalleled prominence, just as Fang Shu and Shao Hu did for King Xuan of Zhou [r. 828–782 BCE], or Gao Tao and Kui did in their service of [the sage] Shun. He also received the surname of the imperial house. Among the other relatives and members of Mr. Han's clan, there were seven who were commissioners or councilors, and nine who accomplished great deeds. There were several hundred in the family who bore imperial pennants, carried the imperial seal, fought in hand-to-hand combat as palace guards, or were allowed to approach the throne through a special, concealed passage. For the sake of brevity, they cannot all be recounted here.

Mr. Han's father was Yu, commissioner of the Palace Visitors Bureau, acting Grand Mentor, and posthumously appointed Defender in Chief. He once marched on Ji [Hebei], and, at Suicheng [Baoding, Hebei], he personally led the charge against the spears and arrows. When the vanguard fell apart and the Right Commander retreated, he fought without fear for his safety and died in battle. His first wife, from the Xiao clan, was enfeoffed as Mistress of Lanling. She bore nine sons in all; Mr. Han was the youngest of those who survived.

Mr. Han was endowed with considerable talent with weapons and in combat. He was strong and robust, accomplished and magnanimous. He bore his inherited nobility without pretension and cultivated a natural authority that made him deeply sincere. He was an exceptional rider and archer, with a profound grasp of the classics of military strategy. He applied himself to his studies and was qualified for office.

At first, he was appointed Court Service Official on the West of the Palace Domestic Service, but he was then moved to the Memorial Forwarding Office, where he was tasked with administering the northern borders [Mongolia] and accepting the submission of the foreigners [Xia] to the west of the Yellow River [in Shanxi]. When the imperial palace issued an order of submission [of the Xia], a messenger was sent out to deliver it at full speed. That messenger was Mr. Han, bearing the order [from the Liao emperor] enfeoffing Li Jiqian [963–1004] as Prince of Xia. Having ridden all through the night to reach his destination, he left behind his exhausted horse and rode a message station horse back. On returning, he reported the completion of the mission, which pleased the emperor. He was subsequently promoted to commissioner of the Imperial Storehouse.

In the twenty-third year of the Tonghe reign period [1005], payments from Song to Liao were agreed to by peace treaty [the Treaty of Chanyuan], and so troops could now return home. It was like in the time of Lilu [ancient mythological king], when the spirit of fulfilling one's duty spread far and wide; like the time of Getian [ancient mythological king], when all living creatures promoted righteousness. The Zhao [ruling house of] Song sent silver and silks to express their goodwill, and livestock were sacrificed to cultivate harmonious relations. The [Liao] court sought talents who could think and talk on their feet. Mr. Han was appointed to assist in delivering birthday greetings [to the Song court]. Arriving at Biandu [the Song capital, Kaifeng, Henan], he was granted three million cash as a gift. On his return, he was appointed commissioner of the Office of Presentations and then made vice-commissioner of the Visitors Bureau.

Not long after [in 1010], Chen Bian killed the ruler of Goryeo, and so the Huiju route [that connected Liao and Korean Peninsula] was obstructed. Ten thousand cavalry were moved to march against them; six armies assembled to launch a campaign. Mr. Han possessed the qualities both of Xi Gu [682–632 BCE], whom none could surpass at selecting commanders by their knowledge of *The Book of Songs* and *The Classic of Documents*, and Dou Xian [d. 92 CE], who was the greatest at choosing generals based on competence in charioteering and riding. And so he was made Left Primary Officer of the administrative office of the Courageous Guards. When the army returned, he was further appointed General of the Left Gate Guard and put in charge of military affairs for Guihuazhou, close to the land of the historical Loufan people [in Shanxi], neighboring the Baixi [Ningcheng, Inner Mongolia]. The customs of this place were coarse, and the people were dogged by raiders. But, from the moment Mr. Han alighted from his carriage, all submitted to his benevolent instruction. At the end of his tenure, he was made the military director in chief of the Zhangmin Ordo [of Emperor Jingzong]. He firmly controlled the territory and brought reassurance to its populace. Accompanying the entourage of the court, he would review the crimes and sentences of the many provinces.

Leaving the imperial entourage, Mr. Han was made grand commander of the palace army of the regent of Yanjing [southern capital of the Liao, present-day Beijing], and then military director in chief of Yizhou [Hebei]. He managed the rank and file of his army; he resisted the strong and comforted the weak. In command of a substantial war chest, his camps were calm and disciplined. He was transferred to military director in chief of the Hongyi Ordo [the ordo of Emperor Taizu] and appointed grand commander of the army of the emperor's guards and surveillance commissioner of Lizhou [Liaoning], tasked with leading the emperor's personal units.

But, as the ancient sages astutely warned, one should be wary when matters are going extremely smoothly. As the former generations foretold, no situation remains unchanged for long. Suddenly calamity struck his home, and he was quickly implicated and detained on the emperor's orders. Though *The Classic of Documents* commands "innocent until proven guilty," he was not treated in that way. Then again, *The Analects* record that Confucius trusted that his disciple Gongye Chang was innocent despite knowing his alleged crimes. So, although Mr. Han was sentenced to caning, he was not stripped of any rank or office, showing that the emperor took his former achievements into consideration.

The following year [1020], he was sent on a mission to Shazhou to deliver the appointment of Supreme General Cao Gongshun as Prince of Dunhuang. He journeyed ten thousand *li* on less traveled roads, past hundreds of waystations across the desert. Lacking long rivers, the land was a wilderness without lush vegetation. Going beyond the boundaries of Kedun [Bulgan, Mongolia], he went deep into Tartary [the central Mongolian highlands]. When he ran out of food and equipment, the emperor sent three hundred goats and a relief force of a hundred men.

As envoys to the Western Protectorates [a Han dynasty name for Central Asia], he and his entourage made their way across the vast uncultivated expanses with the sun and stars as their guide, exposed to the elements as they passed remote posthouses, desolate save for the odd cry of sand grouse. The frontier was unmarked, vast and trackless but for smoking beacons. Out of the blue, an old illness flared up again, and with no carriage he had to be carried on horseback. When he arrived at Yanquan [location unknown], he immediately carried out the emperor's mission. With an ulcer in his stomach, his health deteriorated rapidly. He collapsed and did not regain consciousness until dusk, waking to find his ailment had abruptly healed. Some say that Mr. Han's loyal service moved the gods to help him.

The journey back east was fraught with peril. He advanced only at night so as not to run into any bandits; pushing on under cover of darkness, he was remarkably undaunted by the dangers. He overcame the arduous desert trails, traversed the boundless expanses, and arrived before the emperor bearing tribute from these distant places. Emperor Shengzong granted him a long audience and generously rewarded him with gifts of two hundred ounces of silver, eighty lengths of felt, and one hundred bolts of silk. Shortly afterwards he was made chief military inspector of seven prefectures—Qian, Xian, Yi, Jin, Jian, Ba, and Baichuan [all in Liaoning]. He was also reappointed military director in chief of Zhangmin Ordo and reclaimed his old position Great General of the Left Gate Guard.

In the fifth year of the Taiping reign period [1025], a variety of tributes came and many goods were traded. The generals had grounded the navy, and troops stayed west of [i.e., did not cross] the Liao River. Proper order between the imperial government and the eastern vassal states was established. Mr. Han was sent on a mission to Goryeo [Korean Peninsula] to present birthday greetings to their king. In the winter of that year [1025], he was appointed surveillance commissioner of Fangzhou in charge of the military affairs of Yizhou [both in Hebei] and military commissioner of the state farms along the border, and served as military administrator of the infantry and cavalry. This region had Shanggu [historical region in Hebei] at its back and the former territory of the Zhongshan state [414–296 BCE] in its sight. As Chulizi did not need to rely on attacking Pu, and Yang Hu's enemy accepted a gift of medicine without fear of poison, both sides of the border got along without interfering in each other's business.

Before long, Mr. Han became military commissioner of Changning Regiment [Beipiao, Liaoning] and the internal supervisory surveillance commissioner of Baichuanzhou. In the autumn of the eighth year of the Taiping reign period [1028], the rebel Dayanlin usurped Xiangping [Liaoyang] and encroached on the Sushen region [Jilin and southern Heilongjiang]. The court was enraged and ready to put down the rebellion, crushing it with a formidable force, just as Yuan Shao [d. 202] defeated Gongsun Zan [d. 199] and Sima Yi [179–251] conquered Gongsun Yuan [d. 238].

Mr. Han was put in charge of four regiments—Konghe, Yiyong, Husheng, and Huyi—and assigned to the Administration of Siege Warfare. After defeating these bandits, he was made military commissioner for the Yongqing Regiment [Jinxian, Hebei] and supervisory-level surveillance commissioner for Beizhou, Bozhou, and Jizhou. He led the Yiyong Regiment and stationed them east of the Liao River. The emperor awarded him two hundred ounces of silver dishes and a fine garment and transferred him to Shenzhou [Shenyang, Liaoning]. Then the barbarians once more revolted, and Heye [near Liaoyang, Liaoning] was ravaged. There were raids on the towns and watchtowers. The bandits arrived like a swarm of mosquitoes, their poison biting everyone. They were like vipers, lying in wait in the long grass. Mr. Han laid out his strategy and vigorously carried out his grand scheme. He cut off the main route to Xuantu [Liaoning and west Jilin, China, and Hamgyong in North Korea] and crossed the turbulent region of Zimeng [around Liaoyang, Liaoning]. He built ramparts in seventeen locations that armies camped in and defended. Through his efforts, the bandits did not raid any farther west.

Before finishing his tenure, Mr. Han was sent south as envoy to Song and was once again awarded three million cash. Unfurling the imperial pennants, he set out, his carriage flying full speed across the border. As before, he was ritually greeted at the gates of the city and likely treated to many feasts. He would toast the pact between his ruler and theirs, and enjoy the hospitality extended to a guest. On his return, he was appointed Court Ceremonial Commissioner for the Northern Establishment, military commissioner for the Guiyi Regiment, and internal supervisory surveillance commissioner for Shazhou. Two years into this tenure, he was promoted to Court Ceremonial Commissioner for the Southern Establishment and acting Defender in Chief.

In the fifth year of the Chongxi reign period [1036], he was in Yanjing [Beijing] making preparations in anticipation of the emperor's sojourn in the city. He had the imperial palaces renovated for the comfort of His Majesty; he lavishly decorated the temples and ancestral shrines so the emperor might seek wisdom there. He mobilized many official bureaus and conscripted much labor [for these projects]. Working tirelessly, all day and night, in both the heat of summer and the cold of winter, he got ill from the strain of the pressure; he consulted doctors, but his illness was too far gone. Though someone like Shu Suntong [d. ca. 183 BCE] can decipher the meaning of strange characters, even Guo Wen [alchemist who lived sometime in the Jin period] found it hard to determine the herbs that would prolong his life when he fell ill.

On the twenty-fifth day of the ninth month, Mr. Han passed away in the main room of his official residence as Court Commissioner. The emperor took pains to cherish his memory and was bitterly sad that such a good person had been put through so much in his life. In addition to the usual gifts to the deceased's estate, he made the exceptional gesture of donating five hundred thousand cash toward funeral expenses. He also gave Mr. Han posthumous offices so as to make known his virtues and achievements. Such was the emperor's utmost gratitude for his service.

On the seventeenth day of the second month of the following year [1037], the family buried Mr. Han on the eastern-facing slope of Mount Baiya in Liucheng. He was buried together with his first wife, in the same plot as his father and grandfather, as is ritually appropriate. Mr. Han was sent far away to Mingsha [western Gansu], an inhospitable place, and stayed in that strange land at the ends of the earth.

Yet, in taking on such danger, he gained peace and, in bearing misfortunes he blamed no one. He died a natural death. On the day of his death, he held the title of Internal Surveillance and Supervisory-Level Commissioner for Shazhou. Is this not strange?

Mr. Han married three times. His first wife bore him two daughters, of which the eldest died young and the second was married to Xiao Qide, general of the Zuori Regiment. His second wife, Madam Xiao, bore him three daughters. The first was wed to Commandant Xiao Zhu, and the second was wed to Zhang Mei of the Left Palace Duty Group, who was grandson of Zhang Yun, military commissioner of the Datong Regiment [Datong, Shanxi], Lord Specially Advanced and Acting Grand Preceptor. The third was married to Kang Derun, Usher for the Interpreter-Clerk Office, but he died young. All daughters served their parents-in-law well and got along with their sisters-in-law. They were all as beautiful as flowers and as pure as jade.

Mr. Han's current wife, Miss Zhang, is the daughter of Zhang Chong, Great General of the Left Gate Guard and administrator of the military affairs of Tanzhou [Beijing]. Their marriage was arranged by Empress Dowager Chengtian. Madam Zhang piously upheld the inner principles of the home and spoke tenderly. Her elegance was matched by her fertility, her obliging way matched by her womanly virtue. Madam Zhang bore three sons. The eldest was Qijia'nu, who was an invalid and stayed indoors; he adhered to Buddhism and died five years before his father. The second son was Yisun, who has been appointed Left Audience Usher. The third son was Yixun, who has been capped but is yet to start an official career. Both listened to the advice of their father and took after him as exceptional horsemen. They grew thin from grief at their father's sudden death, and their affection for him grew deeper. They mourned their father all autumn and divined a far-off auspicious day for the burial. They feared that the riverbanks and valleys might shift [potentially hiding the grave site or exposing the tomb], so they invited me to record his deeds. [Seeing his final resting place,] I am reminded of Fu Yi's [555–639] warming and unsparing words "lush mountains and white clouds" and [the phrases from] Jiang Yan's [444–505] strong and elegant verse "crawling grass" and "graveside trees." I have sketched his genealogy to crudely engrave upon this tomb.

The elegy reads:

> His forefather was Tangshu [r. 1042–? BCE] and later Tuidang
> [active 203–157 BCE]; their descendants moved to Jicheng
> and encountered the sagely emperor.
> Four princes blessed the clan with fortune, making seven glori-
> ous ministers.
> The pennants of ambassadors cast mingling shadows, as they
> would embark bearing the imperial seal.
> Our master arrived, and rejuvenated a splendor long dissipated.
> Why did he have to succumb so suddenly to this illness? It is still
> hard to get answers from the heavens.
> Mourning banners flutter outside guest houses, an engraved
> stone is interred in the tomb.
> A long tunnel built with cemetery earth, carved out from the
> dragon's ear of a high hill.
> The dew shedding tears on fresh grass, the wind howling
> through the poplars.
> The spring of the distant Long Mountains [in Dingxi, Gansu]
> sobs silently
> This home for the spirit and this profuse sacrificial offering will
> endure without end.

The calligraphy is by Shang Yin, Prefecture Nominated Presented Scholar, written in the second month of the sixth year of the Chongxi reign period [1037].

Source: Liu Fengzhu 劉鳳翥, Tang Cailan 唐彩蘭, and Qing Gele 青格勒, eds., *Liao Shangjing diqu chutu de Liaodai beike huiji* 遼上京地區出土的 遼代碑刻彙輯 (Beijing: Shehuikexue wenxian chubanshe, 2009), 62–65.

Further Reading

Hansen, Valerie, François Louis, and Daniel Kane, eds. *Perspectives on the Liao [Theme Volume]. Journal of Song-Yuan Studies* 43 (2013).

Standen, Naomi. *Unbounded Loyalty: Frontier Crossings in Liao China.* Honolulu: University of Hawai'i Press, 2007.

Tackett, Nicolas. *The Origins of the Chinese Nation: Song China and the Forging of an East Asian World Order.* Cambridge, UK: Cambridge University Press, 2017.

Twitchett, Denis, and Klaus-Peter Tietze. "The Liao." In *The Cambridge History of China,* vol. 6: *Alien Regimes and Border States, 907–1368,* edited by Denis Crispin Twitchett and John King Fairbank, 43–153. Cambridge, UK: Cambridge University Press, 2013.

Wittfogel, Karl A., and Fêng Chia-Shêng. *History of Chinese Society: Liao (907–1125).* Philadelphia: American Philosophical Society, 1949.

Epitaphs Made Widely Available

Funerary Biographies for Three Men from Luzhou:
Liang Jian 梁戩 (d. 1042), Wang Cheng 王誠 (d. 1042),
and Chen Hou 陳矦 (1074–1123)

TRANSLATED BY MAN XU

These three epitaphs reveal the use of templates for funerary biographies in Luzhou in the early Song and the eventual adoption of the more typical style as Luzhou became better integrated into the Song economy and Song culture.

THE STYLE AND CONTENT OF EPITAPHS NOT SURPRISINGLY changed over time. Epitaphs in the Tang drew attention to their subjects' prestigious pedigrees. In the Tang-Song transition, this changed in line with the shift from an aristocratic elite to a literati elite successful in the civil service examinations. Song scholar-officials wrote epitaphs for people whom they knew or had heard of, and they always indicated authorship in the texts. Epitaphs preserved in Song collected works differ from Tang examples in emphasizing their subjects' education, character, and career achievements. The individualized Song style set the tone for epitaph writing in late imperial China.

In recent years, about one hundred newly discovered epitaphs from Luzhou, Shanxi, a peripheral region in north China, are changing our understanding of this Tang-Song shift in epitaph writing. Despite its early prosperity and close contact with the Tang capitals, Luzhou suffered from political and social disorder from the late eighth century on. By the Song, when the economic center of the country shifted southward, Luzhou had declined into an economically and culturally backward region. Neither the subjects nor the authors of the Song Luzhou epitaphs are mentioned in other extant Song sources. For more than a century after the beginning of the Song, Luzhou epitaphs remained anonymously authored and lacking in detail. They record subjects' prestigious distant ancestors, employ archaic language, and adopt flamboyant metaphors and rhetoric. All these stylized features point to a surprising Tang-Song cultural continuity that historians had not detected earlier. The typical "Song-style" epitaphs did not appear in Luzhou until the second half of the eleventh century, when the local elite had better educational opportunities and became participants in the national elite culture.

In the first century of the Song dynasty, many Luzhou epitaphs use identical words and phrases, indicating the use of common templates. The epitaphs of Liang Jian and Wang Cheng below are two examples. They are both dated to 1042 and begin with the same preface on the transience of life. They then introduce the subject's family, including spouses and descendants, often using the same expressions to refer to people's moral qualities. Finally, after recording the dates and places of burial, both epitaphs end with the same rhymed elegy. Like other early Song Luzhou epitaphs, these two are brief and vague, giving more attention to descendants than to the deceased. The full listing of the names of all descendants made the account of descendants considerably longer than that of the deceased. From the perspective of descendants, these made-to-order epitaphs were desirable commodities that expressed their filial piety and demonstrated their social standing.

Identical wording and similar calligraphy make it likely that the first two epitaphs translated here came from the same local funeral workshop. Producing a stone inscribed with a funerary biography may have been a service option offered by professional funeral managers. In contrast to the men who left collected works, who saw the epitaphs they wrote as their own literary creations, local professionals who sold similar epitaphs to multiple customers in Luzhou very likely based their work on some sort of handbook and did not claim authorship. Elaborate phrases and classical rhetoric were ready-to-use and easily replicated. They were combined with concrete information that the deceased's family provided. The funeral service provider may have offered the family alternative ways to describe the people in the epitaph, saying something like: "For the widow, shall I write: 'She cultivated the three followings in her youth, and her four virtues are complete. All her kin are pleased with her motherly behavior, and her relatives value her wifely conduct'? Or would you prefer something else?" Many customers undoubtedly accepted the default phrasing. Song Luzhou epitaphs often include mistranscriptions that local customers were unlikely to detect, as funeral managers' limited educations made writing mistakes unavoidable.

From the mid-eleventh century on, Luzhou elites started to compose more detailed epitaphs in accordance with the "typical Song style." Following a series of empirewide educational reforms that established government schools across the country, an increasing number of Luzhou men studied for the civil service examinations and were exposed to the national elite's literary culture. In the last fifty years of the Northern Song period, most Luzhou epitaph writers, like their counterparts elsewhere, claimed authorship and produced individualized essays with emphasis on the personal experiences of the deceased (though their essays never reached the level of leading literary figures like Ouyang Xiu and Huang Tingjian, whose epitaphs are translated in Selections 10 and 11). The new scholar-official class was connected by kinship, marriage, and neighborhood links to Luzhou's nonscholar elites, whose standing was based on land or wealth. Scholar-officials were invited by the descendants or relatives of deceased landlords and merchants to write epitaphs for them, in which they elaborated on the subjects' business enterprises and celebrated their success.

The third epitaph translated here is an example of this sort of individualized epitaph for a man from a well-off family. Chen Hou's (1074–1123) epitaph was composed by his affinal relative Meng Ruwei, a candidate for the civil service examinations. According to Meng's narrative, Chen grew up in a wealthy family with extensive landholdings. None of his ancestors had held official positions. He was trained from youth to manage the family business and proved highly competent at it. He used his wealth well, providing aid to the poor and befriending local scholars. He even married his second daughter to a degree holder and planned to invite scholars to tutor his sons. The epitaph author describes Chen's character in Confucian language, praising his scholarly aspirations and moral probity. At the same time, he is comfortable mentioning a merchant's pursuit of profit, not a Confucian value. Such a positive attitude toward business ventures is found in a number of other Song Luzhou epitaphs but is rarely seen in epitaphs outside Luzhou.

Funerary Epitaph for Mr. Liang of the Great Song, with Preface

Alas, there is life and death, something true in both the past and the present. There were people who could carry a boat, hold a bronze vessel, step on hanging cloth, or cover a big cart wheel with leather and use it as a shield. They were powerful enough to defeat the sun and strong enough to move a mountain. But they could not escape their destined time to die.

Mr. Liang's taboo name was Jian. His ancestors were from Anding Commandery of Jingzhou [in Gansu]. They relocated for official posts, divided into multiple branches, and ended up as residents of Shangdang County in Luzhou. Mr. Liang had great virtues, was benevolent, and talked eloquently. He behaved like a scholar and manifested the proper way to be a person. Local people respected him, and neighbors acclaimed his dignity. He should have lived as long as pine trees and have matched the age of the tortoise and the crane. But he became extremely sick and suddenly died at the age of sixty-six.

His first wife, Madam Guo, died young. The second wife, Madam Zhang, also died long ago. His is survived by his third wife, Madam Li, who cultivated the three followings in her youth, and her four virtues are complete.[1] All kin are pleased with her motherly behavior, and her relatives value her wifely conduct. Mr. Liang had three sons: the eldest is Jing (married to Madam Li), followed by Ji (married to Madam Jia), and then Xin (married to Madam Wang after his first wife, Madam Chen, died).

The eldest son, Jing, is incorruptible and ambitious, has extraordinary virtues, esteems righteousness, disregards wealth, and puts others before himself. The daughter-in-law, Madam Li, fully understands the etiquette of the inner chambers and follows and illuminates the wifely way. She manages ancestral sacrifices devotedly and serves food [to her parents-in-law] diligently.[2]

[Mr. Liang] had nine grandsons: The eldest is Feng (married to Madam Ma after his first wife, Madam Hao, died some time back), followed by Yuan (married to Madam Wang), Wu Four, Brother Five, Chen Six, Kedou, Five [illegible], Brother Eight, and Brother Ten. He had five granddaughters: the eldest is the wife of Mr. Chang, followed by Sister Three, Girl Four, Girl Five, and Girl Six.[3] He had one great-grandson, Child Fu.

The son Jing is grateful for the kindness of his mother's diligent care and sighs with the loneliness of children who lose their parents. Therefore, he chose an auspicious site where an ox rested.[4] In the second (*renwu*) year of the Qingli reign period [1042], on the tenth (*jiashen*) day of the second (*yihai*) month, he made a joint burial for his parents . . . in Zhang Village, which is [illegible] *li* southwest of [illegible]. It is in accordance with ritual to bury in a grave properly. At the time [of the burial], clouds blocked the sun, and old grass was covered with frost. They sighed with grief, filled with sorrow.

The rhymed elegy reads:

Alas, Mr. Liang! He was well known in Luzhou.
Human life is transient, as difficult to preserve as [the light] of a
     candle in the wind.
All the relatives were mournful as he was buried under a desolate
     mound.
The gate of the tomb was permanently closed and will remain
     closed for thousands of years.

Considering that changes happen from generation to generation, and hills made of earth and stone get flattened, [Mr. Liang's descendants] had a stone inscribed to record the facts of his life.

Source: Peking University Library rubbing, D302:6598.

Funerary Epitaph for Mr. Wang of the Great Song, with Preface

Alas, there is life and death, something true in both the past and the present. There were people who could carry a boat, hold a bronze vessel, step on hanging cloth, or cover a big cart wheel with leather and use it as a shield. They were powerful enough to defeat the sun and strong enough to move a mountain. But they could not escape their destined time to die.

Mr. Wang's grandfather's taboo name was Zan. The Wang family were the descendants of the Shang king Yuanzi. They relocated for official posts, divided into multiple branches, and ended up as residents of Shangdang County in Luzhou. Mr. Wang had great virtues, was benevolent, and talked eloquently. He behaved like a scholar and manifested the proper way to be a person. Local people respected him, and neighbors acclaimed his dignity. He should have lived [illegible].

[Mr. Wang's] grandmothers were Madam Song and Madam Jia. They died like fragrant lotus flowers falling. Peach blossoms fell to cover their beautiful faces and jadelike appearance. They should have reached the realm of the sun terrace. Mr. Wang's elder brother Mi died young. His younger brother Wenxi also died some time back and had a wife, Madam [illegible]. His elder sister, the wife of Mr. Li, survives.

Mr. Wang's taboo name is Cheng. He was calm with others and promoted harmony [illegible] established his family. He delighted in *The Book of Rites* and esteemed *The Book of Songs* and attained the ultimate way of being generous. It was unexpected that he encountered hardships and his life was destined to end. He died of illness at thirty-eight.

His wife, Madam [illegible], survives him. She cultivated the three followings in her youth, and her four virtues are complete. All kin are pleased with her motherly behavior, and her relatives value her wifely conduct. He had three sons: the eldest one is Yonghe, followed by Boy Five and Boy Three. Yonghe is incorruptible and ambitious, has extraordinary virtues, esteems righteousness, disregard wealth, and puts others before himself. [Yonghe's wife], daughter-in-law Madam Li, fully understands the etiquette of the inner chambers and follows and illuminates the wifely way. She manages the ancestral sacrifices devotedly and serves food to parents-in-law diligently. Mr. Wang had four beloved daughters: the wives of Mr. Yuan, Mr. Zhu, Mr. Li, and Xiaowoer. His niece is the wife of Mr. Yang. When they were little, they all learned needlework [illegible]. And, after they grew up, they served the ancestors and made them happy. The grandsons are Wenglian and Hanliu.

The son Yonghe is grateful for the kindness of his mother's diligent care and sighs with the loneliness of children who lose their parents. Therefore, he chose an auspicious site where an ox rested. In the second (renwu) year of the Qingli reign period [1042], on the tenth (jiashen) day of the second (yihai) month, he buried [Wang Cheng] about five li west of the prefecture and to the west of the ancestors' grave. It is in accordance with ritual to bury in a grave properly. At the time of the burial, clouds blocked the sun, and old grass was covered with frost. They sighed with grief, filled with sorrow.

The rhymed elegy reads:

Alas, Mr. Wang! He was well known in Luzhou.
Human life is transient, as difficult to preserve as [the light] of a
    candle in the wind.
All the relatives were mournful as he was buried under a desolate
    mound.
The gate of the tomb was permanently closed and will remain
    closed for thousands of years.

Considering that changes happen from generation to generation, and hills made of earth and stone get flattened, [Mr. Wang's descendants] had a stone inscribed to record the facts of his life.

Source: Peking University Library rubbing, D302:8365.

Funerary Epitaph for Chen Hou

Written by Meng Ruwei, candidate for the Presented Scholar examinations

Calligraphy by Court Gentleman for Instruction, newly appointed magistrate of Xihe County in Fenzhou, Deng Junmin

Heading in seal script by Gentleman for Loyal Defense Li Fengxian

Hou's taboo name is Li, and his courtesy name is Chizhong. He was a person from Changzi County of Longde Commandery. His great-grandfather's taboo name was Feng, grandfather's taboo name was Bao, and father's taboo name was Zhong'an. None of them held office. The family owned fertile farmlands and were locally prominent for generations. When a young man, Mr. Chen's father served as a clerk in the Military Commission. Hou was born in Daizhou and lost his father in less than one month. His mother, Madam Liu, returned home carrying him on her back. As he grew up, he proved to be quite intelligent and intent on learning. His uncles set him to work at business jobs, which was not his preference. However, he was a clever strategist and always made substantial profits from his schemes. Later on, he established a separate household from his uncles. He concentrated on business and made his family increasingly wealthy. He supported his widowed mother with extreme filial piety and did his best to obey her. He managed his household well: servants did not cross the middle gate [to maintain the separation of the inner and outer quarters]; even female neighbors were not allowed in without good reason. Maids and servants feared [his strict rules] and did not dare to act deceptively or offensively. His strict regulation of the inner quarters became a model praised by local gentlemen.

One day, Chen Hou suddenly got sick. After he recovered, he took an interest in medicine and learned the basic principles. He accumulated medicinal herbs at home in order to give them to the sick. Impoverished villagers especially relied on his gifts. He himself was careful, prudent, open-minded, and generous. He considered money lightly and valued righteousness, and sponsored impoverished visitors without hesitation. He treated friends sincerely, and the friendships got stronger as time went on. Because he truly liked virtuous and kind people, his friends were all scholars of integrity. Throughout his lifetime, he never failed to keep a promise. During seasonal festivals, he always invited guests and friends and offered them food and drink all day. All the food he presented was refined and clean. Just when he was planning on inviting scholars to tutor his son in order to glorify his family, he became sick and passed away on the eleventh day of the tenth month in the fifth year of the Xuanhe reign period [1123], at the age of forty-nine.

After Mr. Chen's first wife, Madam Wang, passed away, he married Madam Li, who gave birth to two sons. The sons are too young to have formal names. He had two daughters. The older one has not married, and the younger one is married to Meng Guochang, a Presented Scholar (*jinshi*) degree holder. Mr. Chen's mother is still alive. She patted his coffin and wailed for her son, then collapsed because of her extreme grief. Those who witnessed it could not refrain from shedding tears. His sons played by the bed [where he lay], too young to understand the sorrow of losing their father. On the *renshen* day in the eleventh month of the year, he was buried in the plain of Xihan Village. Hou's son-in-law, Meng Changguo, is my nephew. He begged me to write Hou's epitaph. The rhymed elegy reads:

This person was worth the title of a kind man and should have
lived long.
How could his life have ended so quickly? Heaven really is hard
to understand!

He had sons, who will continue the family line and perform the
ancestral sacrifices.

Hou's peaceful return to the dark chamber is not mournful.

Carved by Ren Kuang.

Source: Shen Xiufu 申修福 and Liu Zemin 劉澤民, eds., *San Jin shike daquan: Changzhi shi Changzi xian juan* 三晉石刻大全: 長治市長子縣卷 (Taiyuan: San Jin chubanshe, 2013), 49.

Notes

1. The "three followings" (a woman was to obey her father as a daughter, her husband as a wife, and her sons in widowhood) and "four virtues" (wifely virtue, wifely speech, wifely manner, and wifely work) are the orthodox definition of women's virtue prescribed in the Confucian classics.
2. Among Mr. Liang's sons and daughters-in-law, only the oldest son and his wife are praised for their virtues in Mr. Liang's epitaph. The couple likely took charge of Mr. Liang's burial and commissioned his epitaph. The commendation of the eldest son and daughter-in-law is seen in a number of early and mid–Northern Song Luzhou epitaphs.
3. In the Song dynasty, children and less-educated people usually had no official names and were referred to in accordance with the order of their births in the family. Therefore, in Song Luzhou epitaphs, many names are simply combinations of family name and number. In some cases, kinship titles such as brother, sister, boy, and girl, are added to indicate a person's sex.
4. Divination was commonly practiced in medieval China to help people choose an auspicious burial place and date, which supposedly would benefit the deceased's family.

Further Reading

Hartwell, Robert. "Demographic, Political, and Social Transformations of China, 750–1550." *Harvard Journal of Asiatic Studies* 42.2 (1982): 365–442.

Xu, Man. "Ancestors, Spouses, and Descendants: The Transformation of Epitaph Writing in Song Luzhou." *Journal of Song-Yuan Studies* 46 (2016): 119–68.

———. "China's Local Elites in Transition: Seventh- to Twelfth-Century Epitaphs Excavated in Luzhou." *Asia Major,* 3rd ser., 30.1 (2017): 59–107.

A Friend and Political Ally

Funerary Inscription for Mr. Culai 徂徠 (Shi Jie 石介, 1005–1045),
by Ouyang Xiu 歐陽修 (1007–1072)

TRANSLATED BY CONG ELLEN ZHANG

Authored by Ouyang Xiu, one of the most celebrated epitaph writers
in Chinese history, Shi Jie's funerary biography allows us to observe a
controversial political figure and teacher-thinker in action. The text
also reveals the interplay of politics and literature at a time of factionalism and major social and cultural change.

THE ELEVENTH CENTURY WAS A TIME OF LARGE POLITICAL,
intellectual, social, and cultural transformations. Among the most important changes were the expansion of the civil service examination system,
the growing influence of the literati or scholar-official elite, and the
resurgence of Confucian scholarship. Instituted in the late sixth century
to counteract the power of the great families and military nobility, the
examination system proved tremendously successful in attracting the
most talented, erudite, and conscientious men into civil service. Steeped
in Confucian learning, Northern Song scholar-bureaucrats responded
vigorously to what they perceived to be the most urgent issues of the day.
These ranged from ineffective national defense and inadequacies in the
education and recruitment systems to the state's role in managing the
economy and Buddhist and Daoist influence in culture and society. Their

enduring efforts to articulate and solve these and other problems were manifested in major reform initiatives, making the Northern Song a period of unprecedented political activism and severe factionalism. In the intellectual realm, Song thinkers joined their late Tang predecessors (the most prominent of whom was Han Yu, 768–824) in advocating the centrality of Confucian ideology. Their creative appropriation of the Classics gave Confucian thought new meanings, new structure, and a new textual basis, resulting in the establishment of a "new" Confucian philosophy, the Learning of the Way or the Learning of the Principle, better known in the West as Neo-Confucianism.

Shi Jie's (1005–1045) life and career illustrate these developments in uncanny ways. From Yanzhou in modern-day Shandong, the Shis rose above their rank of ordinary local landholders through success in the examinations. In 1012, Shi Bing, Shi Jie's father, became the first in the family to receive the *jinshi* (Presented Scholar) degree, the highest and most prestigious civil service examination degree. He was followed by Shi Jie less than two decades later in 1030. Although mainly occupying low-ranking positions, the father and son elevated the Shi clan with their public service records and scholarly credentials, making it a renowned scholar-official family of the Northern Song. Shi Jie was a prolific poet and essayist but was probably best known by his contemporaries and later generations for his active involvement in the court politics of the 1040s and the role he played in the Confucian revival movement. Shi Jie lived only to his mid-forties but enjoyed national repute as an influential teacher, accomplished Confucian philosopher, and unwavering supporter of the Qingli Reform (1043–1045), led by Fan Zhongyan (989–1052), Han Qi (1008–1075), Ouyang Xiu (1007–1072), and others.

"Funerary Inscription for Mr. Culai," by Ouyang Xiu, highlights Shi Jie's achievements in these three areas, characterizing him as a knowledgeable and courageous person as well as a dedicated and principled intellectual. Ouyang highlights Shi's vision of a society in which the emperor models himself after the ancient sages, and the common people behave just as the ancient sages' subjects did. To realize his goal, Shi called for all educated men to follow the words and deeds of the sage kings, Confucius (551–479 BCE) and Mencius (372–289 BCE), and their followers, most notably Yang Xiong (53 BCE–18 CE) of the Han and Han Yu of the Tang. Just like his fellow Confucians in earlier periods, Shi Jie elaborated in his writing on the meanings of humaneness and righteousness, core concepts in Confucianism. He condemned Buddhism and Daoism as "strange and faulty" and criticized the popular Xikun-style poetry and parallel prose for hindering the propagation of the way of the sages. In condemning these three trends, Ouyang states, Shi proved himself a true follower of Han Yu. To Shi Jie, as to Han Yu, a revival of Confucianism meant the elimination of these three "evils." In Ouyang's portrayal, not only did Shi Jie secure Han Yu's place in the genealogy of the Confucian school, but Shi also made himself a crucial part of the Confucian revival in his day.

In addition to distinguishing Shi Jie as an important thinker, Ouyang commends Shi for practicing what he preached. Long before he became a government official, Shi had shown great concern for the "worries and sufferings of the world," alluding to the Confucian commitment to improving the well-being of the state as well as that of the general populace. Both as a scholar and as a filial son, Shi Jie vigorously promoted Confucian family rituals and was keen on performing death and ancestral worship rites. He displayed profound grief on the deaths of his parents. While in mourning, Shi managed a massive burial project, laying to rest over seventy Shi men and women from five generations in his native place. Above all, through his founding of and active involvement in the Taishan (Mount Tai) and Culai Academies in his native region in the 1030s, Shi Jie emerged a key player in the formation of the Confucian curriculum in the early Northern Song. Along with Sun Fu (992–1057), one of the most prominent educators of the time, Shi turned the academies into leading institutions of Confucian scholarship. When Shi and Sun moved to the Imperial University in the capital in 1042, their large following did as well. In fact, Ouyang points out, it was not until Shi's tenure there that the Imperial University began to flourish.

In Ouyang Xiu's representation, Shi Jie was an outspoken and uncompromising person, to the extent that he had to defend himself against charges of being "a fool or a madman." Ouyang especially singles out the unusual courage that Shi manifested during the Qingli Reform, which marked the beginning of fierce political struggle in the Northern Song. More specifically, the hostilities against Shi Jie began with the circulation of his famous "Poem on the Sagacious Virtues of the Qingli Reign," dated 1043. In this long poem, Shi lauded Emperor Renzong (r. 1022–1063) for promoting talented and virtuous men, the leaders of the reform, to important positions, labeling the former powerful grand councilor as the "great evil." For exhibiting "little restraint" in criticizing what the reformers called "wicked" and "petty" men, Shi Jie endured slander and denunciation from political opponents, who wanted "nothing less than to drive Mr. Shi to his death." Shi's poem, by naming names, escalated factional strife between the reformers and their opponents. Shi Jie died in 1045, so he did not go through exile or demotion like his fellow reformers when the emperor withdrew his support of the reform programs. His enemies nonetheless attempted to incriminate him by claiming that Shi had faked his own death and demanding that his coffin be opened for confirmation. The complications surrounding Shi's death partially explains the long delay in his burial.

"Funerary Inscription for Mr. Culai" not only allows us to appreciate the life of an outstanding scholar and a fearless and controversial political figure, but also demonstrates the way funerary biographers incorporated politically sensitive material. To better understand Ouyang's rendering of Shi Jie's active participation in the Qingli Reform, it is important to note the relationship between the two men. Hailing from Jiangxi in south China, Ouyang had much in common with Shi Jie. Just like the Shis, the Ouyang family rose in the early Northern Song, with Ouyang Guan, Ouyang Xiu's father, being the first in the family to earn the Presented Scholar degree (in 1000). Ouyang Xiu passed the examination in the same year (1030) as Shi Jie, but there is no indication that the two immediately began to associate with each other. Most important, Ouyang Xiu was a leading figure in the Qingli Reform. In addition to participating in policy-making and court debates, Ouyang authored the famous "Discourse on Factions," in which he identified the reformers as superior men who selflessly served the public good and the antireformers as petty, wicked, and self-serving.

Given the similarities in their backgrounds and political stances, it was only natural that Ouyang showed no reservations in offering his eye-witness account of Shi Jie's role in the evolution of factionalism in the mid-1040s. When Shi died at the height of partisan clashes, Ouyang must have known full well that it was going to be quite some time before Shi would be laid to rest and his reputation cleared. In fact, any attempt to commemorate Shi Jie might be controversial and cause trouble for the eulogizers. Ouyang Xiu nonetheless composed a long poem in 1046 to mourn the loss of a close friend and political ally. The poem opens with a declaration that Shi's name and reputation would remain as towering as the mountains in his hometown. This is followed by a detailed account of Shi's main scholarly achievements and political activities. Ouyang shows no attempt to shy away from the controversies that Shi created and the accusations against him.[1] Given the tense atmosphere of the time and the ongoing rumor about Shi Jie's fake death, this was a truly bold gesture on Ouyang's part.

What makes Shi Jie's funerary biography especially interesting is that, not only was Ouyang Xiu one of the most celebrated essayists, poets, statesmen, historians, and calligraphers in Chinese history, but he was also the most highly sought-after epitaph writer of his time.[2] Compared to many Song funerary biographies that ran thousands of words long, Ouyang's work was normally between a few hundred and a few thousand characters. His epitaph for Shi Jie, at about 1,200 words, is of average length and, in many ways, a typical piece for a scholar-official by Song standards. Ouyang, just like other epitaph writers, celebrated Shi Jie's moral char-acter, examination success, scholarly credentials, literary achievements, and official career. He explained the circumstances under which he was asked to compose Shi's epitaph, included the names of the requesters, and specified the times of Shi's death and burial. All conformed to conven-tional Song practices.

In several other respects, "Funerary Inscription for Mr. Culai" is atypical. First, except for references to Shi's role in the evolution of the Imperial University, Ouyang did not at all mention Shi's administrative abilities and accomplishments, a routine component of Song epitaphs for office-holding men. Second, Ouyang composed Shi Jie's epitaph twenty-one years after Shi's death and long after the end of the Qingli Reform. The delay in Shi Jie's burial afforded Ouyang a chance to write about one of the most important events for him and many others in his generation. In this sense, "Funerary Inscription for Mr. Culai" is not only a celebration of Shi Jie's life, but also a reappraisal of a long-gone era. Last but not least, uncharacteristic of epitaph-writing practices of his time, Ouyang included scant information about Shi Jie's ancestry, his wives and children, and his children's marriages. This was very likely because Shi himself had authored a family genealogy, to which Ouyang would have had access. In the end, Ouyang must have chosen not to repeat what Shi had already detailed in his family history. It would have been interesting for readers of this epitaph to know, however, that the Shis had lived in Yanzhou for generations and remained a large clan; Shi Jie's father married five times; Shi Jie had to resort to borrowing large sums of money to conduct the massive burial of family members; additionally, he had two commemorative structures erected at the family graveyard. In the accounts he wrote to mark the burials, Shi Jie urged later generations to honor their ancestors by living virtuous lives and performing sacrificial offerings with diligence.

Funerary Inscription for Mr. Culai

Mr. Culai's family name is Shi, his name is Jie, and his courtesy name is Shoudao [Defending the Way]. He was a native of Fengfu County in Yanzhou [Shandong]. Culai is the name of a mountain in eastern Lu [in southwestern Shandong]. Mr. Shi did not become known as Mr. Culai because he had resided in the mountains as a recluse. Mr. Shi had occupied positions at the court, yet the people of Lu did not use his official ranks to address him. Instead, they honored his virtue. Because Culai was a revered site in Lu and Mr. Shi was someone they esteemed, the people in Lu juxtaposed the name of the mountains he had resided in with his fame as a virtuous person. That Mr. Shi became known as Mr. Culai echoed the wish of the people of Lu.

Mr. Shi's appearance was dignified, and his disposition impeccable. His learning was solid and his aspirations high. Even before he entered officialdom, he did not ignore the distresses of the world [which were the responsibilities of court officials]. He once said that "in any time period one can accomplish anything if one tries. If one does not occupy an official position, he should practice what he preaches. If my ideas are adopted [by the government], their effect will benefit the entire realm. [If that happens,] people do not need to know that those ideas and benefits came from me. If my ideas are not embraced, or, worse, if I am blamed for having them, I will not regret it even if I die."

When Mr. Shi became indignant about something, he would compose essays in which he would elaborate on the successes and failures of governing in the past and present. He had little restraint in criticizing contemporary problems and distinguishing virtue from folly, good from evil, and right from wrong. People were rather intimidated by his writings. As a result, there was an uproar of slander and denunciation against him. Petty men especially envied and hated him. They collaborated with each other, wanting nothing less than to drive Mr. Shi to his death. Mr. Shi remained unruffled and was neither baffled nor deterred by his enemies. He said, "This has always been my way. I am more courageous than Mencius [372–289 BCE]."[3] Unfortunately, he fell ill and died [in 1045].

After his passing, the wicked who wished to slander certain high-ranking officials [the reformers] for causing grave disasters used Mr. Shi to begin their attacks. They spread rumors that Mr. Shi had faked his demise and actually fled north to the Kitan Liao and requested that Mr. Shi's coffin be opened in order to verify that he was indeed dead. Owing to His Majesty's humaneness and august wisdom, the emperor recognized the falsity of the accusations. In the end, Mr. Shi's coffin was not opened. His wife and children were subsequently spared [further humiliation].

The Shis had been farmers for generations. His father, taboo name Bing, was the first to elevate the family through office-holding and reached the rank of Erudite of the Court of Imperial Sacrifices. At the age of twenty-six, Mr. Shi earned the Presented Scholar degree in the top group and was appointed surveillance administrative assistant in Yunzhou [Shandong] and regency administrative assistant in the Southern Capital [Shangqiu, Henan]. [While serving there,] he was recommended by the Censorate to be promoted to the rank of controller-general. Before his arrival at the capital, he submitted a memorial on amnesties. For this reason, his summons to the capital for reappointment was rescinded. When he fulfilled his tenure in the Southern Capital, he was promoted to be the prefectural secretary of a certain commandery. He later went to Sichuan in his father's stead, serving as military administrative assistant of Jiazhou. He was relieved of official duties owing to his parents' deaths. While mourning with utmost diligence, he worked in the field next to Mount Culai and laid to rest seventy family members from five generations who had not been [permanently] buried.

Upon completion of the mourning period, Mr. Shi was summoned to be a lecturer at the Directorate of Education. At the time, military campaigns against Li Yuanhao [1003–1048] [founder of the Tangut Xia state] were at a stalemate. The country was hard-pressed [and ready for change]. The emperor was energetic and eager to boost the dynasty's power and promote its virtue. [To realize his goal,] he replaced a few high-ranking officials and installed additional remonstrance officials and censors as ways to demonstrate his eagerness to achieve order. Mr. Shi was overjoyed and said: "This is a great event. It is my duty to extol [His Majesty's conduct]. How could I help by doing nothing?" He subsequently composed the "Poem on the Sagacious Virtue of the Qingli Reign." In this poem of hundreds of characters in length, Mr. Shi passed judgments on high-ranking officials and differentiated the wicked from the upright. Once the poem was circulated, Mr. Shi's mentor and friend Sun Fu of the Mount Tai Academy said to him: "[One day you will see] that this was the beginning of your misfortunes." The evil men who later caused the outrageous calamities were precisely the ones that the poem condemned.

Both when he lived a leisurely life at Mount Culai and during his service in the Southern Capital, Mr. Shi taught the Confucian classics. By the time he was at the Imperial University, he increasingly considered himself a teacher of the Way and attracted a very large number of disciples. The Imperial University began to flourish with Mr. Shi's appointment there.

Mr. Shi's writing was compiled in two collections of varying lengths. His criticism of Buddhism, Daoism, and contemporary literary styles can be found in "On Strange Writing" and "On the Central Kingdom." He was of the opinion that only after the elimination of the three evils was there hope for real progress to be made. His warnings about evil officials, eunuchs, and palace women were expressed in "The Mirror of the Tang," in which he said, "I did not write this to warn just one generation." Other matters that pleased, angered, or saddened him were all reflected in his work. His writing was eloquent and powerful, and his worries and concerns were profound.

Mr. Shi said: "To study is to learn to be humane and righteous. To be humane requires one to be eager to benefit the myriad things; to be righteous entails being resolute. Only those who are of utmost loyalty and exceptional resolve in their beliefs can put it into practice." Mr. Shi applied these principles to himself and taught them to others. Not a day went by that he did not recite the words and deeds of Yao, Shun, Yu, Kings Tang, Wen, and Wu, the Duke of Zhou, Confucius, Mencius, Yang Xiong, and Han Yu.[4] Along with the scholars of the world, Mr. Shi aspired to be the disciple of the Duke of Zhou and Confucius. Not even for a day did he forget his ambition to inspire the king to be just like Yao and Shun and the people just like the subjects of Yao and Shun, to the extent that his commitment offended and shocked many in the world. When people laughed at him, he would respond: "I am not a fool or a madman." For this reason, gentlemen who observed his actions trusted his words. They understood his intentions and were sympathetic with his [unfulfilled] aspirations.

After serving as lecturer at the Imperial University for over a year, Mr. Shi was recommended to the emperor by Mr. Du Yan [978–1057] and was appointed to be the Companion of the Heir Apparent. Upon further recommendation from the current grand councilor Mr. Han [Qi, 1008–1075], Mr. Shi became a member of the Academy of Scholar Worthies. A year after that, he left the Imperial University and was appointed controller-general of Puzhou [in Shandong]. He was at Culai waiting to assume his office when he died at home at the age of forty-one in the seventh month of the fifth year of the Qingli reign period [1045]. His friend Ouyang Xiu of Luling [Jiangxi] eulogized him with a poem, which said that, once people stopped slandering him, Mr. Shi's Way would shine forth.

In the wake of Mr. Shi's death, his wife and sons were reduced to poverty, unable to provide for themselves. The current grand councilor Mr. Han and Mr. Fu Bi of Heyang [Henan] used their salaries to purchase land to support Mr. Shi's family. It was not until twenty-one years after Mr. Shi's passing [1066] that his family made plans to bury him in such and such place. Before interring him, his son, Shi'ne, and his disciples, Jiang Qian, Du Mo, Xu Dun, and others, came to inform me of the burial and said: "The evil has stopped slandering Mr. Shi. It is now time to promote his reputation. Could we ask you to write an epitaph for him?" I said: "Did I not say in my poem that 'your way will certainly endure'? Why do you need an epitaph from me?" Dun and the others said, "This is nonetheless the wish of the people of Lu." I therefore compose the following rhymed elegy:

> The mountains at Culai,
> And your virtue,
> Are what the people of Lu look up to;
> The water at the Wen River,
> And your path,
> Will run ever far and long.
> The hardships of practicing the Way,
> Had agonized even Confucius and Mencius.
> What you have achieved in this one life,
> Will enlighten tens of thousands of generations.
> You said, "This is perhaps my fate,

What did it matter who the wicked were?"
All the sages in ancient times suffered vilification.
Alas! Although you were disparaged, what harm did that do?

Source: Zeng Zaozhuang 曾棗莊 and Liu Lin 劉琳, eds., *Quan Song wen* 全宋文 (Shanghai: Shanghai cishu chubanshe, 2006), 35:755.367–69.

Notes

1. Fu Xuancong, Ni Qixin, Sun Qinshan, Chen Xin, and Xu Yiming, eds., *Quan Song shi* 全宋詩 (Beijing: Beijing daxue chubanshe, 1991), 6:284.3604.
2. Ronald Egan, *The Literary Works of Ou-yang Hsiu (1007–72)* (Cambridge, UK: Cambridge University Press, 1984).
3. Mencius was the second most important Confucian scholar, after Confucius.
4. This list includes the most celebrated figures in the Confucian tradition, from the ancient sage kings, Yao, Shun, and Yu, through founding figures of the Shang and Zhou dynasties, and Confucius and his followers in subsequent centuries, up to the Tang.

Further Reading

Bol, Peter. *Neo-Confucianism in History.* Cambridge, MA: Harvard University Asia Center, 2010.

Chaffee, John W. *The Thorny Gates of Learning in Sung China: A Social History of Examinations.* Cambridge, UK: Cambridge University Press, 1985.

Levine, Ari. *Divided by a Common Language: Factional Conflict in Late Northern Song China.* Honolulu: University of Hawai'i Press, 2008.

Kuhn, Dieter. *The Age of Confucian Rule: The Song Transformation of China.* Cambridge, MA: Belknap Press, 2009.

Zhang, Cong Ellen. "Bureaucratic Politics and Commemorative Biography: The Epitaphs of Fan Zhongyan." In *State Power in China, 900–1400,* edited by Patricia Ebrey and Paul Jakov Smith, 192–216. Seattle: University of Washington Press, 2016.

Preserving a Father's Memory

Funerary Inscription for Chao Juncheng 晁君成 (1029–1075),
by Huang Tingjian 黄庭堅 (1045–1105)

TRANSLATED BY CONG ELLEN ZHANG

This epitaph shows two sides of the great effort made by sons to persuade famous writers to write their parents' funerary biographies. On the one hand, securing such an epitaph perpetuated their parents' legacy; on the other, it added to their own fame as exemplars of filial piety.

SINCE ANCIENT TIMES, THE CONFUCIAN CLASSICS OFFERED detailed guidelines regarding a son's filial obligations toward his parents. The son was instructed to devote himself to his parents' physical and emotional well-being. At the time of their deaths, he was expected to perform the Three-Year Rites, during which he wore coarse mourning clothes, lived in isolation, and deprived himself of material comfort. Among a mourning son's most sacred duties was to give his parents a proper burial, which would effectively transform them into ancestors. After completion of the burial rituals, the son would perform seasonal sacrifices at shrines and graveyards every year, aiming to perpetuate ancestral memory as well as reinforce family unity.

These classical prescriptions aside, actual filial practice varied greatly over the course of Chinese history. Starting from the second half of the

Tang dynasty, epitaph writing was gradually recognized as a new form of filial expression. By the eleventh century, securing an epitaph for one's parents from a renowned writer became a major preoccupation of Song elite men, and sons were routinely commended for their dedication to this cause. Many attempted to move the prospective epitaph writer with a public display of extreme grief at their loss. Others were praised for their willingness to wait for months, even years, for the completed epitaph.

Most of the epitaph requests were made through written correspondence. In 1084, the Northern Song scholar-official Chao Buzhi (1053–1100) wrote to his good friend Huang Tingjian (1045–1105). One purpose of the letter was to inform Huang that he was laying his father, Chao Juncheng (1029–1075), to rest later that year and to ask Huang to author his father's epitaph. Chao Buzhi enclosed with his letter his father's record of conduct (*xingzhuang*), prepared by a certain Du Chun.[1] Du's writing does not survive. Based on similar extant texts, it is reasonable to assume that Du's work provided all the necessary information that Huang Tingjian would have needed to write Chao Juncheng's epitaph.

At over six hundred words, Chao Buzhi's letter is among the longest epitaph requests that have survived from Chinese history. It is, however, more than a simple request for service. Chao Buzhi also wanted to supplement his father's record of conduct. The bulk of the document depicts Juncheng as a caring and respected local official, talented writer, generous friend, and devoted son and brother. Much of Chao's supplemental information found its way into Chao Juncheng's epitaph. Seen from this perspective, Chao's letter was as useful as Du's record of conduct for the composition of Juncheng's funerary inscription.

Chao Buzhi's letter offers a starting point to think about the role a son could play in defining his parents' legacy. Chao Buzhi took it for granted that his father "must be remembered by posterity" through a funerary biography. This makes us wonder: if he was so keen on preserving his father's memory, why did he not personally author his father's epitaph? After all, Chao was a prolific epitaph writer, with forty-eight funerary inscriptions extant. His decision, however, was nothing out of the ordinary. To put it simply, although the majority of Northern Song epitaph writers identified themselves as friends, relatives, and acquaintances of the family, only a few dozen of them authored the funerary biographies of their own wives and parents. Even the most accomplished writers would compete to commission the most prominent political or literary figures for this task. This common practice was the result of several considerations: with the passing of a parent, a son was expected to focus on mourning; he might be too emotionally overwhelmed or physically emaciated to write; it would be more appropriate for a relative or friend to praise the deceased, especially because, as commemorative literature, epitaphs often used hyperbolic language; the more famous the epitaph writer was, the better the chance of the epitaph's survival and transmission; and, last but not least, Song epitaphs routinely included detailed information about the subject's descendants and their accomplishments. The son who was responsible for obtaining his parent's epitaph often ended up occupying a prominent place in it.

Despite Chao Buzhi's determination to perpetuate his father's name, Chao Juncheng was not a particularly noteworthy person. He was not from the most successful branch of the Chao clan, which continuously produced examination degree holders and high-ranking officials throughout the Northern Song, nor did he stand out in his generation of Chao men for his literary talent or official service. As far as we know, Chao Juncheng only served in two local positions in south China. When he died in 1075, his only son, Buzhi, was twenty-three and said to have been "too poor to hold a timely burial." Had Buzhi conducted a prompt funeral, he would not have been in the position to recruit a famed epitaph writer.

In the nine years between his father's death and the planned burial, Chao Buzhi earned the *jinshi* (Presented Scholar) degree (in 1079) and established himself as a major poet and essayist. This afforded him the right connections to perpetuate his father's reputation. Du Chun, as Chao Juncheng's old friend and Buzhi's father-in-law as well as a high-ranking official, seemed to be the ideal person to prepare the record of conduct. However, it was Buzhi's close relationship with Su Shi (1037–1101) and Huang Tingjian, two literary giants of the day, that eventually transformed Chao Juncheng from someone unknown to a person of repute.

At Chao Buzhi's request, Su authored a preface to Chao Juncheng's poetry collection. Su's comments were subsequently quoted in Chao's letter and Huang's epitaph for Juncheng. Next, Chao turned to Huang Tingjian for his father's epitaph. Huang and Chao had known each other for several years; in fact, since Huang had associated with Chao's uncles, one could say that Huang was a family friend. What further validated Huang's suitability was his reputation as a highly sought-after epitaph writer—Huang penned sixty-two epitaphs and a large number of other types of funerary writings.

In his letter to Huang, Chao readily acknowledged that, because Juncheng "did not desire to be known by others, few had heard of him," making it all the more important to make his deeds known posthumously.[2] Having been an admirer of Huang's work and character, Chao was convinced that "no one would be more capable than you of elevating my father's hidden virtues and pleasing him in death. This is why I have disregarded my failings [in delaying his burial] and taken the liberty of making such a request of you. If, out of sympathy for me, you would generously agree to my entreaty, I would feel most fortunate." To be emphatic, Chao added, "Weeping, I implore you to show pity on me."[3] Given the friendship between the two, Chao would have had no reason to worry that Huang might decline his petition. He nonetheless followed convention, as filial sons normally did when approaching a potential epitaph writer.

Chao Buzhi's initiative assured that his father would be remembered in the way that he wanted. Huang Tingjian's funerary biography for Chao Juncheng, however, does not stop at extolling the deceased. The same text also elevates Chao Buzhi, the son. Specifically, Huang comments, "Buzhi loves learning and is dedicated to important things. His writing captures the style of Qin and Han times. There is hope that he will become an influential writer of the age. Given Buzhi's talent, is it not time for Juncheng's posterity to prosper?" Through highlighting Buzhi's potential to advance his family, Huang Tingjian makes him a filial son and worthy descendant. One thing that Huang conveniently downplays is the long delay in Chao Juncheng's burial, even though, for this failure, Chao Buzhi confessed his own feelings of guilt.

Funerary Inscription for Chao Juncheng

Mr. Chao Juncheng waited on his parents with filial devotion and respect. No one could find fault with what his brothers had to say about him. In associating with others, he was reasonable and affable. Yet he was principled, so awe-inspiring. He loved to entertain guests and never abstained from wine. He especially took delight in roaming around mountains, forests, and rivers. It was truly his lifetime wish to live this way. He was not focused on making a living or on his fortune in government service. He participated in the examinations at twenty-five and was appointed to an official position. Having spent twenty-three years in officialdom, he reached the rank of assistant editorial director before dying at the age of forty-seven.

Juncheng lived a reclusive life. When he resided at home, he never expressed interest in becoming an official. Yet, as an official, he was extremely responsible. Whenever anything inconvenienced the local people, he would memorialize the matter to the court with much vigor. When he was the magistrate of Shangyu [Zhejiang] and resigned because of mourning obligations, people stopped his boat from leaving for days. When a court inspector entrusted him with a certain matter and ordered him to spy on his colleagues, Juncheng did not violate the law or deceive his colleagues. He did his best to fulfill his duty yet refused to be used as a weapon against others. Because he behaved this way in office, he failed to advance in his career.

When Juncheng was young, he presented his writing to Mr. Song Qi [998–1061], who praised and was fond of his work. Late in his life, Juncheng particularly loved writing poetry and would often produce extraordinary compositions to display his talent. He would use poetry to express what he had learned from observing the successes and failures of the ancients, the ways of the world, and his own achievements. In the *yimao* year [1075] during the Xining reign period [1068–1077], he was living in the capital. Sick in the Zhaode Ward, he would groan in pain but continue to compose poems. His son, Buzhi, wrote them down by the side of his bed. By the end, he had completed about forty poems.

Su Shi (courtesy name Zizhan) from Sichuan remarked that Juncheng's poems are "pure, profound, deep, and calm, just like Juncheng the person." Du Chun (courtesy name Xiaoxi) of Puyang [Henan] wrote in Juncheng's record of conduct, "Of those who mourned Juncheng, none was not extremely saddened." Su and Du are both venerable elders. Zizhan's name is known to the whole world. Xiaoxi is a principled person. In associating with his brothers and friends, Juncheng achieved what the ancients had failed to overcome. Buzhi loves learning and is dedicated to important things. His writing captures the style of Qin and Han times. There is hope that he will become an influential writer of the age. Given Buzhi's talent, is it not time for Juncheng's posterity to prosper? I have therefore recounted his ancestry, life experiences, marriage, and official service as records for later generations. The inscribed poem is meant to commend his aspirations, not lament his misfortunes.

Juncheng is Mr. Chao's courtesy name. His taboo name is such and such [Duanyou, Upright and Friendly]. The Chaos were a clan of ancient origin, but the family declined in the middle. Of the more recent ancestors was Jiong, who served a certain emperor [Emperor Renzong, r. 1023–1063] as a Hanlin Academician Recipient of Edicts. Retiring at the rank of Junior Guardian of the Heir Apparent, he was given the posthumous title of Wenyuan [Cultured and Great]. His son was a grand councilor in Kaifeng. From then on, the Chaos began to distinguish themselves. Juncheng's great-grandfather's taboo name is Di, and he was granted the honorary title of vice-director in the Ministry of Punishment. His grandfather's taboo name is Zongjian, and he received the honorary title of minister of personnel. His father's taboo name is Zhongyan, and he reached the rank of vice-director in the Bureau of Provisions. Juncheng's great-grandfather was Jiong's older brother. Juncheng's wife, Madam Yang, gave birth to one son, Buzhi. Among their daughters, one has married an official, Zhang Yuanbi, and three others are married to Presented Scholar examination candidates Chai Zhu, Jia Shuo, and Chen Qi. The remaining three young daughters are not married yet. Buzhi is planning to have Juncheng buried at Lüyuan in Rencheng of Jizhou in the tenth month of the *jiazi* year in the Yuanfeng reign period [1084]. The rhymed elegy reads:

You did not have to bathe in snow to become striking and clear,
And had never fallen to become filthy.
In mountains and forests and at rivers and lakes,
You had fish and birds as companions.
In large cities,
You traveled along with prominent officials.
Untainted in conduct,
People said you were foolish.
Arguing with others,
People said you were wrong.
Those that others discarded,
You pursued.
When others rushed,
You took it slow.
You remained content when experiencing ups and downs,
Not deterred by the allotted life span.
Your brilliance will endure,
Suddenly you passed away; nothing can be done.
The Yellow River is muddy, and the Ji River clear,
Rencheng is a beautiful city.
Riding on wind, you reach the clouds,
And love roaming as much as when you were alive.
Dig the grave deep in the middle,
Widen it on the four sides.
So as to place your coffin,
Without damaging it.
Planting pine and cypress trees to flourish,
Face to face with posterity.

Source: Zeng Zaozhuang 曾棗莊 and Liu Lin 劉琳, eds., *Quan Song wen* 全宋文 (Shanghai: Shanghai cishu chubanshe, 2006), 108:2335.70–71.

Notes

1. Chao Buzhi, in Zeng Zaozhuang 曾棗莊 and Liu Lin 劉琳, eds., *Quan Song wen* 全宋文(Shanghai: Shanghai cishu chubanshe, 2006), 126:2718.41–42.
2. *Quan Song wen*, 126:2718.40.
3. *Quan Song wen*, 126:2718.41–42.

Further Reading

Brown, Miranda. *The Politics of Mourning in Early China*. Albany: State University of New York Press, 2007.

Choi, Mihwa. *Death Rituals and Politics in Northern Song China*. Oxford: Oxford University Press, 2017.

Knapp, Keith N. *Selfless Offspring*: *Filial Children and the Social Order in Medieval China*. Honolulu: University of Hawai'i Press, 2005.

Zhang, Cong Ellen. "A Family of Filial Exemplars: The Baos of Luzhou." *Journal of Chinese Literature and Culture* 4.2 (2017): 360–82.

A Gentleman without Office

Epitaph for Scholar Residing at Home Wei Xiongfei 魏雄飛
(1130–1207), by Wei Liaoweng 魏了翁 (1178–1237)

TRANSLATED BY MARK HALPERIN

This epitaph for a non–office holder gives the reader a feel for village
life in Southern Song China. The eulogist presents a hodgepodge
of observations to produce a complex picture of a "gentleman in
residence."

RURAL LIFE IN THE SONG DYNASTY FEATURED NEW, INTENSE
arenas of competition and cooperation. First, increasing numbers of men
sought a Confucian education and took the civil service examinations,
deeply aware that success even at its lowest levels could transform their
own and their relatives' social standing. Second, the economy's commercialization led to greater prosperity but also increased litigation, as commercial disputes proliferated. Some counties and prefectures, in fact, won
reputations as being difficult to govern because of the readiness with
which their residents sued each other. Third, partly in response to such
pressures, Chinese families developed new structures to strengthen kinship ties. Elite men wrote genealogies, circulated family management
manuals, and wrote guides to kin-based rituals. No set of rituals carried
greater importance than those concerning proper burial, mourning, and
worship of the ancestral dead. These performances constituted the central

means through which close kin expressed filial devotion and maintained cohesion as a social group.

These rituals formed part of a larger, vital Confucian concept called *li*, translated here as "proper conduct." Narrowly conceived, *li* referred to the correct practice of rites of passage such as weddings and funerals, as well as seasonal ancestral offerings. Broadly conceived, *li* encompassed rules of interaction among different generations, genders, and social strata, prescribing matters such as personal address, dress, and even food presentation. Strict adherence to *li* ranked among the most important ways that true Confucian gentlemen and their families distinguished themselves from the rest of society and demonstrated their allegiance to China's elite cultural heritage.

Most Chinese funerary epitaphs relate the lives of men who worked for the government. At times, however, writers found other worthy subjects, including virtuous women, eminent Buddhist and Daoist clergy, and men who did not serve the state. Epitaphs that fall into the final category often called the deceased a "scholar residing at home" (*chushi*). Eulogists, lacking the usual raw material of office titles, meritorious service, and memoranda, looked elsewhere for reasons to commend the departed. A *chushi* might win praise for his Confucian learning, his generosity to the needy, his skills in dispute mediation, his filial piety, or perhaps simply for his distinctive character, which made him a memorable figure who warranted an epitaph from a respected man. Writers sometimes knew their subjects, as relatives or neighbors, and sometimes did not. These descriptions of people doing good tend to have a generic feel, but on occasion they include striking anecdotes in which the subject starkly contrasts with his neighbors, who might exhibit such vices as sloth, avarice, greed, litigiousness, and even affinity for Buddhist practices. In sum, epitaphs for *chushi* can give readers today a richer feel for life in village China than do works composed for politically successful men.

Wei Liaoweng (1178–1237) ranks among the great Confucian stalwarts of the late Southern Song dynasty. He was a native of Pujiang in present-day western Sichuan. Western Sichuan during Wei's lifetime was one of the empire's more prosperous and cultured regions, but the area lay distant from the capital, and its literati did not receive their fair share of civil service examination degrees. Wei, however, passed the *jinshi* examinations in 1199, which made him a local favorite son. His initial government appointments were in Sichuan, but in 1202 the court called him to the capital, where he eventually served at the Palace Library. An outspoken man, Wei criticized the powerful court official Han Tuozhou (1152–1207) and his war plans against the neighboring Jin dynasty. Soon after, he became a foe of the powerful grand councilor Shi Miyuan (1164–1233). As a result, Wei requested to return to Sichuan in 1205 and for the next many years mostly served in local positions, distinguishing himself by his promotion of schools and fortification of military defenses. He founded a Neo-Confucian academy, which attracted many scholars from the area. Recalled to the capital in 1222, his attacks on administrative abuses and Emperor Lizong's (r. 1224–1265) succession won him many enemies and led to demotion and another exile in Sichuan until Shi Miyuan's death. In 1233, the court again sent for him, and Wei spent his final years mostly at the capital. He left behind one of the largest collections of literary works from the late Southern Song and compiled many commentaries on the Confucian canon. Like most Southern Song Neo-Confucians, Wei met mostly frustration in his political career and owes his posthumous fame to his scholarly achievements.

Wei Liaoweng composed over one hundred epitaphs. He probably wrote Wei Xiongfei's in the latter part of 1210, when he was serving as prefect of Meizhou, which borders Qiongzhou, the Wei family ancestral home and Xiongfei's place of death. During his long service in Sichuan, Wei Liaoweng wrote many epitaphs for his relatives. Unlike his other epitaphs for relatives, Xiongfei's notably does not clarify his kinship ties to the deceased. The text reports that Wei Xiongfei died in 1207, but the next of kin did not bury him until more than three years had passed. In a similar case, the Wei family only belatedly interred Wei Liaoweng's paternal grandmother, but Wei in his epitaph for her specifies the geomantic rationales for their delay. Here, however, he gives no explanation.

This inscription warrants attention for several reasons and raises questions about the epitaph genre itself. First, Wei's epitaphs usually begin by discussing the deceased. In other cases, Wei details how he came to know the deceased or supplies pertinent recent historical background.

This text is very different. Wei starts with an extensive citation from a biography in a dynastic history written over a thousand years earlier of someone who had no direct ties to Wei's family. Second, when the epitaph finally turns to its subject, Wei presents readers with a hodgepodge of observations and produces an unusually complex picture. On the one hand, Wei Xiongfei works hard, takes care of his family, and delights in seeing and learning about good deeds. On the other hand, he has a litigious side and fails to discriminate when choosing his friends and associates, which violates Confucius's instruction that one should not make friends with people of lesser moral worth. This aspect of Xiongfei troubles Wei Liaoweng, leading him to start his inscription with a similar example from the Han dynastic history and then to return to the point later. In addition, he presents himself as initially reluctant to compose the work, relenting only after Xiongfei's son cites noteworthy past epitaphs. Some writers voiced such reluctance as a gesture of Confucian modesty. Wei, however, did so in only one other text. In addition, the men cited in those previous epitaphs held high official posts and thus differed greatly from Wei Xiongfei, which makes the appeal seem incongruous. Finally, the concluding rhymed elegy was nominally the most important part of the epitaph. In these sections, writers turned their subjects' lives into poetry and sometimes versified at great length. In this case, however, the elegy is brief and generic, lacking any specific references to Wei Xiongfei's own distinctive life.

Wei Liaoweng's epitaph presents readers today with many questions. Why was Wei Xiongfei unable to continue his studies? What sort of "disasters" did he experience? What "troubled" him and what caused him to change his conduct? Did reading Buddhist books change him? What, in particular, so upset Wei Liaoweng about his ancestor's mixed company, which led the writer to emphasize this aspect of Wei Xiongfei's life? Why does Wei Liaoweng present himself as requiring pressure from relatives before writing the epitaph? Whatever his faults, Wei Xiongfei belongs to the ranks of the Wei ancestors, receiving presumably his due ritual offerings at periodic intervals. Wei Liaoweng's reluctance, from our perspective, does the writer little credit. Why does he refer to these particular texts, written by famous scholar-officials but for men whose lives in government and at court differed enormously from that of Wei Xiongfei? All epitaphs, and biographies in general, inevitably leave their mysteries. Wei Liaoweng's epitaph stands apart, however, in its clear demonstration that, whatever the generic constraints placed on men as they composed such texts, some writers on some occasions took liberties to ignore those constraints and compose as they saw fit.

Funerary Biography of Gentleman Residing at Home Mr. Wei Xiongfei

In the Han dynasty, there was Yuan Juxian [fl. first century CE], a powerful local man in Gukou [Shaanxi].[1] All sorts of worthies and riff-raff filled his gate and courtyard. Someone chided him, saying, "You started out as the heir of a high official with a salary of two thousand bushels of grain. As an adult, you bound up your hair and cultivated yourself. How then do you indulge yourself and become a wandering knight sort of person?" Juxian had no way to respond and then compared himself with the widows of various families.[2] He further said, "I know that [my way of life] does not accord with proper conduct, but I cannot return to my earlier proper ways." Alas—such words! It is the utmost nonsense. When gentlemen are only servants to their passions and are confused by external matters, it is only that they worry that others do not know about them, and that is all. Once others know of their fame, then these men are quickly over these difficulties. Yet how can there be those who cannot return to proper conduct?

The taboo name of our clan patriarch Zhongju is Xiongfei. When he was young, he also covered the hamlet with his energy. He had packed his books and studied with Li Jingyi (courtesy name Chuncui) of Linqiong [Sichuan] but, owing to a disaster in the family, he could not finish his studies. He resided in Nandao in Linqiong. The place was known for its winding roads. The residents were few, and livelihoods were meager. Farmers plowed, and merchants did business. They gathered and accumulated bit by bit, and their incomes barely provided for the New Year's offerings.

Mr. Wei as a result moved to Pujiang [Sichuan]. After a long time, he followed its customs. He bought a wine shop and summoned workers to do odd jobs. When he raised his head and clapped his hands, matters were carried out with dispatch. If there was the slightest trouble, he inevitably put forth a complaint before the county magistrate and would not stop until he had obtained what he considered to be fair and proper. After a long period of disasters, he was distressed in mind and perplexed in his thoughts. Thereupon Mr. Wei became a person who restrained wanton and violent sorts and obeyed the authorities. He relieved his township neighbors of their troubles and made his in-laws harmonious and mild. When the harvest experienced massive crop failure, he released grain to feed the hungry. As for those who were unfortunate and were punished by the law, he complained in court against such injustices until they were fixed. Among the clan descendants, there were orphans, and three generations of ancestors remained temporarily buried.[3] Mr. Wei assembled the clan and gave money for funeral expenses. He managed the encoffining and burial matters for all of them.

. In later years, he especially liked Buddhist books. With his big eyebrows and cane carved with a hawk's likeness, he was unrestrained all the time. His conversation did not touch on family business. If he heard of other people's good deeds, he would immediately praise them as if praising his own children. My uncle Xiangfu and I participated in the examinations. When we succeeded, Mr. Wei was so delighted that he forgot to eat. Henceforth, he increasingly urged his sons and grandsons to do good. He deeply improved himself, successfully returning to true devotion and generosity. That said, although he could not return to proper conduct, just as Yuan Juxian could not in the past, there certainly is no debate about whether or not he was a worthy person.

Mr. Wei lived until he was seventy-eight years old and died at his home on the *bingzi* day of the seventh month, the third year of the Kaixi reign period [1207]. His great-grandfather was so and so, his grandfather so and so, his father so and so, and his mother so and so.

He married Madam Wang of the same hamlet. She died on the *renyin* day of the seventh month, the fourth year of the Chunxi reign period [1177]. They had three sons: Yizhi, Xunzhi, and Shenzhi. As for his daughters, the eldest married Guo Yisun, the next Wen Gui, and the third Zhang Youli. His grandchildren on both sides came to ten boys and girls.

Yizhi was going to bury Mr. Wei and his wife on the [missing character] day of the eleventh month, the third year of the Jiading reign period [1210], on Mount Zhen in Kuangli hamlet in Qinde District (Sichuan). Ahead of time, he entrusted writing the inscription to me. I was profoundly grieved and demurred that I could not compose the text. He then said, "Liu Liuzhou [Liu Zongyuan, 773–819] praised Lu Yuanchong [d. 805] and Ouyang Wenzhong [Ouyang Xiu, 1007–1072] wrote an inscription for Du Weichang [Du Qi, 1005–1050]. In both cases they extended their grief and reached many others. That so, how can you refuse with respect to your kinsman?" I then gathered what as a youngster I had learned from my father and uncles and related it in order. I further attach a rhymed elegy that reads:

> On and on, he galloped his horse,
>   he rides home, he gallops.
> Yet the lord returned to it
>   happy among the mulberries and elms.
> In the field and house,
>   we plow and reside.
> Millet and rice wine,
>   we strain it, we buy it.
> Uncultivated was that Nandao
>   Thereupon he initiated its beginning.
> Its roots were rich, its fruits were fine
>   —the necessities of later generations.

Source: Zeng Zaozhuang 曾棗莊 and Liu Lin 劉琳, eds., *Quan Song wen* 全宋文 (Shanghai: Shanghai cishu chubanshe, 2006), 311:92–93.

Notes

1. Yuan numbered among the social type of "wandering knights," generous, violent, self-appointed strongmen who settled injustices and often ran afoul of state law. Yuan eventually was executed by the Han state.
2. In his biography, Yuan refers to women who begin with intentions of chastity but fall victim to seduction or rape at the hands of men, and then lead promiscuous lives.
3. That is, the dead had received simple coffins but had not been interred, presumably because the next of kin had lacked the means to supply formal coffins and secure auspicious burial sites.

Further Reading

Ebrey, Patricia Buckley. *Family and Property in Sung China: Yüan Ts'ai's "Precepts for Social Life."* Princeton, NJ: Princeton University Press, 1984.

Egan, Ronald. *The Literary Works of Ou-yang Hsiu (1007–72).* Cambridge, UK: Cambridge University Press, 1984.

Halperin, Mark. *Out of the Cloister: Literati Perspectives on Buddhism in Sung China, 960–1279.* Cambridge, MA: Harvard University Asia Center, 2006.

McKnight, Brian E., and James T. C. Liu, trans. *The Enlightened Judgments Ch'ing-ming Chi: The Sung Dynasty Collection.* Albany: State University of New York Press, 1999.

13

Wives and In-Laws

Funerary Inscription for [My Father-in-Law] Mr. Zou of Fengcheng (Zou Yilong 鄒一龍, 1204–1255) and Funerary Inscription for [My Wife] Madam Plum Mansion (Zou Miaozhuang 鄒妙莊, 1230–1257), by Yao Mian 姚勉 (1216–1262)

TRANSLATED BY BEVERLY BOSSLER

These two funerary inscriptions provide a rare glimpse into the private and emotional life of a Song scholar and his family. In addition to rich details about his marriages, his wives' literary skills and spirit, and his and his in-laws' households, they convey with unusual frankness the personalities of the author and his subjects.

THROUGHOUT CHINA'S IMPERIAL PERIOD, FAMILY AND KINSHIP relationships were important aspects of social life. Although Confucian ideology tended to stress the importance of relationships among kinsmen related through the male line, in practice marital connections were also recognized as critical for the long-term success of individuals and families. Fathers-in-law could provide valuable guidance and advantages to sons-in-law. Conversely, having a talented son-in-law not only could help ensure that one's daughter and her children would be well taken care of, but also increased the chances that one's sons and their children could count on assistance from their sister's or aunt's family. Meanwhile, since sons usually brought their wives to their parents' home to live, a good daughter-in-law helped assure that the household would be harmonious, the family budget well managed, and the next generation well brought up. For these reasons, Chinese parents took very seriously the duty of choosing marital partners for their children.

The two funerary inscriptions translated here highlight this point. They were written by the late Song scholar-official Yao Mian (1216–1262) and record the lives and deaths of Yao's father-in-law, Zou Yilong (1204–1255), and the latter's two daughters, Zou Miaoshan (1228–1249) and Zou Miaozhuang (1230–1257), who successively became Yao's wives. Both inscriptions stress Zou Yilong's steadfast belief—based on his appraisal of Yao Mian's physiognomy—that Yao would eventually become a successful official.

The inscriptions also describe in some detail the circumstances of the two households and convey something of the two women's personalities, literary skills, and spirit. Funerary inscriptions in general are among our best sources for information about women and family life, and Yao Mian's unusual frankness makes these two texts particularly revealing. Finally, the two inscriptions also inadvertently expose many aspects of Yao Mian's own personality: his pride in his own talent, his desire for official recognition, his fascination with the occult, and his struggle to make sense of a world that was beginning to crumble around him. Together, they provide us with a rare glimpse into the private and emotional life of a Song scholar and his family.

Yao Mian, Mr. Snowy Slope, is a fascinating and ultimately somewhat tragic figure. He was born in 1216 into a literati family that was apparently down at heel. Two of Yao Mian's ancestors had held degrees in the early twelfth century, but there is no evidence of office holding or degrees in the intervening century. Yao Mian's father, the son of a concubine, seems to have lived the life of a local gentleman, and Yao Mian himself was clearly well educated, but his writings (including the inscription for his father-in-law) stress the family's poverty. Yao began taking the local examinations at the young age of fifteen but did not see real success until the age of thirty-seven, when he won the honor of the top ranking in the examination of 1253. His career progress was stalled, however, by the death of his father less than a month after he returned from the examinations:

Chinese mourning laws stipulated that sons withdraw from office for nearly three years after the death of a parent. Only after emerging from mourning in 1256 was Yao Mian, now forty, truly able to begin his official career; but, before he even reached the court to take up his new position, the outbreak of a fierce factional conflict sent him back into retirement. In 1260, he was finally once again awarded office, but after only eight months at court he managed to offend those in power and was dismissed. Back in the countryside, he lived for less than two more years before dying of illness in 1262.

Outside of what Yao Mian tells us in these funerary inscriptions, we know almost nothing about his in-laws, the Zou family of Fengcheng County (Jiangxi). Yao Mian does reveal, however (indeed, he makes a major point of it in both inscriptions), that the Zous also intermarried with a Li family, also of Fengcheng, that had a more prominent office-holding background. Yao's wives' maternal grandfather, one Li Shuji, had served as a county magistrate. Moreover, Shuji's older brother Li Xiuji had served as a mid-ranked official. Li Xiuji's son, Li Yishan (a first cousin of Yao Mian's mother-in-law), did even better, attaining prefectural- and circuit-level offices. From this we can infer that the Zous, though without a history of office holding themselves, were (or had once been) sufficiently wealthy and powerful to be attractive marriage partners to office-holding families in their local area.

The vicissitudes of Yao Mian's ill-fated career were interspersed with family tragedies: both are outlined in great detail in these two inscriptions, filling in details of Yao Mian's personal as well as professional biography. As Yao tells it, he was a sorry marriage prospect—and the fact that he was already twenty-nine and had never married when his prospective father-in-law first considered him as a son-in-law gives some credence to this assessment. Although Yao Mian had earned some reputation for his skill as a writer, he was poor and had been unsuccessful at the examinations. We are told that, during a surreptitious visit to Yao Mian's house with a group of neighbors, the prospective father-in-law, Zou Yilong, was deeply impressed with Yao Mian's auspicious physiognomy. Zou insisted, against the opposition of many members of his family, that Yao would surely become successful and resolved to marry his daughter to him.[1] The marriage took place a few years later, in 1248 (even though in the interim Yao Mian had twice failed examination attempts). Unfortunately, barely a year into their marriage, Yao Mian's wife died shortly after childbirth. (The child, a girl, died a year later.) Yao initially proposed that the families renew the connection by allowing him to marry his first wife's younger sister, but he was roundly rebuffed. Yao portrays his father-in-law as keeping the faith during this period by refusing to negotiate a different marriage for his younger daughter, but it was not until five years later, and only after Yao Mian finally achieved examination success, that a new betrothal was arranged. This time, in Yao's view, it was he who kept the faith: he explicitly portrays himself as repaying his father-in-law's confidence in him by not seeking a connection elsewhere. Presumably, having become a top-ranked degree holder would have greatly enhanced Yao Mian's attractiveness on the marriage market.

The couple were to have been married later that year, but Yao Mian's own father's death in the fall of 1253 caused the marriage to be postponed, so it was not until early 1256 that Yao Mian welcomed this second Zou bride to his home. (Strikingly, although Yao Mian glosses over the fact, the marriage took place only three months after Zou Yilong's own death in the eleventh month of 1255—by ritual, his wife should have mourned her father for a full year.) Like the first, Yao's second marriage was ill-fated: like her sister, Yao's second wife died not much more than a year after their marriage, shortly after giving birth to a child, this time a stillborn son.

In addition to the details they provide about Yao Mian's life, the two inscriptions are notable for the way they portray their actual subjects. The main theme of the inscription for Yao Mian's father-in-law is the latter's ability to "know people," especially as revealed in his unwavering faith in Yao Mian's talent. This theme carries through the entire inscription and even dominates the rhymed elegy at the end. The theme is enhanced by the emphasis on Zou Yilong's interest in and support for scholarship and scholars. We are told that he treated visiting scholars with deference and honor, feeding them lavishly and conferring rich gifts upon them. He employed tutors to instruct his sons and listened rapt to their lessons.

Although Yao Mian does not say so outright, and indeed he defends Zou Yilong's attitude, his account hints that Zou may have been spending more on entertaining scholars than he could really afford. We see this in the observation that others ridiculed Zou for not focusing on making a living and also, obliquely, in the fact that Zou failed to arrange marriages for his two sons and a remaining daughter. Although Yao excuses this failure as a result of Zou's commendable fastidiousness in choosing marriage partners, it may also reflect a decline in the family's circumstances.

The inscription for Yao's second wife, Zou Miaozhuang (which also describes his first wife, Miaoshan), is unusual in its level of detail. It contains all the usual tropes seen in women's funerary inscriptions: Miaoshan was content in poverty, filial to her father-in-law, and understood *The Analects* and *The Mencius*; Miaozhuang was filial in performing the ancestral sacrifices, treated superiors and inferiors appropriately, and treated a concubine's son as her own. Both women supported Yao in his studies, managed the family well, and used their dowries to help the Yao family. But, as is frequently the case in the (rather rare) funerary inscriptions composed by men for their own wives, we also get glimpses of more personal interactions. Yao Mian stresses both wives' literacy, including their ability to write poetry (though he is at pains to assure us that they were both circumspect about doing so—women's poetry writing was regarded with some suspicion in this period because it was associated with courtesans and the pleasure quarters). He refers to his wives by their literary names, Miaoshan as "Bamboo Hall" and Miaozhuang as "Plum Mansion." He relates that Miaoshan once spontaneously came up with a brilliant—and teasing—line of poetry to match one he had assigned to her younger brother. He likewise paints a vivid scene of Miaozhuang leaving a wall poem—which he quotes—at the top of a mountain. He observes that Miaozhuang loved natural scenery and reveals that they enjoyed several outings together; he mourns that she did not live to visit Mount Lu, where he had once promised to take her. He also makes quite an issue of her equanimity when he decided en route not to take up his position in the capital. He describes how she exchanged her "gold and pearl" headdress for a simple hairpin and credits her with the inspiring sentiment "I'd rather be the wife of a virtuous man, not just the wife of a high-ranking man."

Yao's account of his wives also reveals aspects of family interaction that are seldom described in funerary inscriptions. He stresses that Miaozhuang did not set up a kitchen separate from the rest of the household, hinting that his new status as an official might have made such a separation natural.[2] He describes her drinking with her sisters-in-law rather than with him. He also explains that after Miaoshan's death he had a concubine who gave birth to a son, whom Yao Mian formally legitimized as his heir. He praises Miaozhuang not only for treating this son as her own, but for offering to give up her own unborn child to be adopted as the heir of Yao's childless elder brother. Finally, he stresses that, before he left to take up office, she insisted that, "now that you are an official," they should manage the weddings of his siblings as well as the burial and reburial of her father and grandfather. One gets the impression that Yao's new position put the family in a financial position to carry out rituals they had formerly been unable to afford.

But, however much these inscriptions reveal of social and family life, they are even more revealing of Yao Mian's own personality and foibles. They lay bare his confidence, not to say arrogance, in his own brilliance. This is evident both in his emphasis on his father-in-law's ability to recognize his talent and in his assertions that, in eulogizing his father-in-law and his wives, he is assuring their immortality. The funerary inscriptions also display Yao Mian's near obsession with omens and signs. He is fascinated by the fact that his second wife's birthday coincided with his first wife's death day and with the notion that she and her sister might have been "one person with two lives"—a notion that he sees borne out in the fact that both were married to him for a year and both died of complications in childbirth. His anxiety about omens is also evident in his concern about Miaozhuang's cryptic deathbed words, warning him about taking up office. Finally, the inscriptions expose a certain defensiveness or insecurity that lurked underneath Yao Mian's arrogance. That insecurity is evident in his insistence on his own "righteousness" in maintaining his marital connection to the Zous (buttressed by his express vow never to take another wife after his second wife died). It is even more palpable in the final few lines of his inscription for his wife, where he appears to be trying to shore up his own moral principles:

"For me to associate with immoral people, obtain high rank and wealth by unrighteous means, be cursed and ridiculed by the world, changing this for that—not only would my father-in-law not want this; my two wives would also not want it."

Funerary Inscription for Mr. Zou of Fengcheng

Originally, before I passed the examinations, my house was no more than four standing walls, and the sounds of reading mixed with the sounds of stomachs growling. Those who passed by averted their eyes; who would have given his child as a wife to such a household? In the tenth month of the winter of 1245, suddenly one morning several guests arrived. I invited them in, not knowing that one of those among them was Mr. Zou. Several days later, a go-between brought a letter and said,

> Mr. Zou of Fengcheng has a daughter whom he is unwilling to marry to an ordinary boy; he wants to select a famous scholar as a son-in-law. The other day he secretly came by. Seeing you, he was delighted, feeling that, even without your writings, on the basis of your physiognomy alone you ought to become wealthy and high-ranking: he is determined to make you his son-in-law. There was a naysayer who said, "Although Yao is a scholar, he is poor. His house has only a few rooms and is dilapidated. The tiles don't cover the rafters, sun and sky are daily visible; the winds come in the sides, and the rain comes in above: what kind of place is that for your daughter?" Mr. Zou laughed at him saying, "As for this fellow, even if he had no rooms at all, he could still be my son-in-law; how much more so when he has rafters! There will soon be an edict seeking scholars [to take the examinations]; this fellow will be recommended and will pass!" Since Mr. Zou feels this way, what do you think?

At that time, when my late father heard this, he regarded Zou as highly virtuous and so agreed to the betrothal. The following year, in

1246, I took the local examinations but was not chosen; in 1247, I went to the Imperial University and again did not pass. Everyone laughed that Mr. Zou had made a big mistake, but he did not change his opinion. In 1248, I finally was able to receive his daughter as my wife. In 1249, unfortunately, she passed away. Those who ridiculed Mr. Zou's mistake were even more raucous, but he still ignored them. After another five years, in 1253, I was in fact named the top-ranked degree holder [by the emperor] at the Jiying Palace. At the time, Mr. Zou still kept back his second daughter from marrying, waiting for me to make a name for myself so as to continue the marriage alliance. I also felt that Mr. Zou was someone who truly understood me, and I did not dare to contravene virtue and righteousness [by seeking a bride elsewhere]. And so we continued the connection. Those who had formerly laughed finally stopped, all persuaded that Mr. Zou had the vision to "recognize the talent of people." I had just managed to achieve a small emolument and looked forward to serving the two families' patriarchs as they traveled the world with me in office. Alas, who knew that I could be so unfilial and unlucky that, only a month after my return from the capital, my late father abandoned me [i.e., died], and, in less than two years, my wife's father also abandoned me?! In my grief, I have not forgotten that I never paid back his great kindness: if I do not write an inscription for him, his true nature will never be known.

Mr. Zou's taboo name is Yilong; his courtesy name is Boxiang. For generations, his family were people from East Lake in Fengcheng County in Yuzhang [Nanchang, Jiangxi]; later they moved to Zoushe Village. His great-grandfather so-and-so, grandfather so-and-so, and father so-and-so were all virtuous but not well known. Mr. Zou was unassuming and honest, sincere and reliable. When young, he studied diligently and served his parents with filiality. As an older brother, he was friendly, always choosing the inferior fields and houses for himself, while leaving the fancy and fertile ones to his younger brother. In his village, he treated even farmers and old countrymen with courtesy. He had no conflicts with people, he loved the good, and he was insistent about righteousness, always harming his own interests to help others. Among his relatives by marriage, there was once someone who ran into trouble with a lawsuit; Mr. Zou mortgaged land to save him. When in the end the loan was never paid back, Mr. Zou did not ask about it.

When others were perverse and unreasonable, he would always reflect on his [own behavior]; "when others offended against him, he did not dispute with them."[3] But he resolutely detested evil; if a man violated morality, he would never associate with him, regarding him as an enemy. Even if such a person invited him to socialize, he would not go. Whenever scholars arrived, he loved them like his own parents, walking backwards to welcome them, pressing them to stay for several days. He would treat them to banquets and entertainment, and, when they left, he plied them with parting gifts. Other people's gates might be deserted, but outside Mr. Zou's every day there were tracks from the carriages of venerables. By nature, he did not like to drink, but he enjoyed setting out wine and delicacies to feast his guests. His yearly income was just sufficient to provide accommodation for guests. As a result, the family did not accumulate any wealth. People laughed at Mr. Zou for not working to make a living or devoting his efforts to stockpiling goods, but he in return scorned their slavish devotion to money and grain.

Mr. Zou took delight in teaching his sons; he selected famous teachers and housed them at his home, having them live together with his sons day and night, chanting sonorously into the night, leading them till first light. Mr. Zou would sit among them, listening no differently than if it had been the music of strings and flutes, never once appearing tired or bored. He enjoyed scholars and loved books, for his original nature was like this. He was unwilling to marry his daughters to commonplace men, nor did he take it lightly when taking in wives for his sons. Because of this, on the day he passed away, his two sons were both unmarried, and his youngest daughter did not yet have a spouse.

Mr. Zou initially married a woman surnamed Chen, who died young. He remarried a woman surnamed Li, the granddaughter of Mr. Bamboo Grove [Li Xiyue], the daughter of Shuji, magistrate of Wugang, and the elder cousin of the current intendant of Huaidong

Judicial Commission, Aide to the Office of Imperial Affairs Li Yishan. Madam Li died twenty years before Mr. Zou. My wife and Mr. Zou's eldest son were her birth children. His third wife was surnamed Zhou; all his wives were from scholarly families.

Mr. Zou was born on the *xinsi* day of the seventh month of 1204; he died on the *jiawu* day of the eleventh month of 1255: he was only fifty-two. Initially, he suffered from hemorrhoids; that was followed by shortness of breath. He knew he could not be cured, so he refused medicine and would not take it. When he was on the point of death, he said nothing selfish but merely admonished his sons to study and instructed me and the teacher to rebury his father and teach his sons, and that was all. Other questions he did not answer but commanded his family members to leave, saying, "I will not die in the hands of women."[4] When his face and hair had been washed, he straightened his pillow and covers, and passed away at home. Those who heard of it all sighed mournfully. Alas! To find someone like Mr. Zou, one must look to the ancients; one does not see many like him today. In the face of ridicule, he selected a poor scholar as a son-in-law not once but twice. Although I was unable to repay him with generous gifts, at least I can write about his life [lit. "affairs"]. Although Heaven would not lend him long life, to die and still be spoken of constitutes a kind of longevity. All the more in that what he accumulated is long-lasting; later his name will no doubt flourish.

Mr. Zou had two sons, Chengda and Keda. There were three girls: Miaoshan and Miaozhuang were the two who married me; Miaoduan is unmarried. In 1256, just a year after Mr. Zou's death and before his grave site had even been divined, through the mistaken benevolence of the emperor, I received a summons to court.[5] Although I had not been able to support my parents with my emolument, I could not bear to refuse office; but, thinking of the fact that Mr. Zou remained unburied, I did not dare to turn my back on what he had requested of me. Just a fortnight after the reburial of Mr. Zou's father, on the *geng-shen* day of the tenth month, I was able with the two orphans to carry out the funeral, burying Mr. Zou in Chestnut Field in Gui'de District, next to the grave of his father, also at Leqiu. We set up a stele on the path to his grave, to inform his descendants.

The rhymed elegy reads:

Alas, this place is the chamber of Mr. Zou;
Throughout his lifetime, he always loved scholars.
He instructed his sons in the Classics, his will deep and sincere
But the affair of selecting a son-in-law is most worthy of
 recording.
Sons-in-law like this are not rare in the world,
But recognizing his potential before it was acknowledged—that
 is very rare.
Heaven was stingy with his years, people exclaimed in shock;
But the fortune he earned by accumulating good must still have
 surplus.
Among the mountains, lofty and high is the cottage by his tomb
When passing by the grave of the virtuous, you ought to step
 down from your carriage.

Source: Zeng Zaozhuang 曾棗莊 and Liu Lin 劉琳, eds., *Quan Song wen* 全宋文 (Shanghai: Shanghai cishu chubanshe, 2006), 352:8143.145–47.

Funerary Inscription for Madam Plum Mansion

Madam Plum Mansion, née Zou, had the taboo name Miaozhuang; her courtesy name was Meiwen. She was a person of Zoushe Village in the Xingren District of Fengcheng County and the wife of Mr. Snowy Slope Yao of Gao'an [Jiangxi]. Her great-grandfather had the taboo name so-and-so, her grandfather, so-and-so. Her father, Master Spring Valley, had the taboo name so-and-so; his courtesy name was Boxiang.[6] Her mother, surnamed Li, was the daughter of Li Shuji, the magistrate of Wugang; the niece of Li Xiuji, the military commissioner of Yongguan; and the elder cousin of Li Yishan, the judicial commissioner of Huaidong Circuit. I had previously married her elder sister, whose taboo name was Miaoshan and courtesy name Meishao; she was also regulated and kind, pure and obedient. Miaoshan was born in the *shen* hour [3:00 to 5:00 p.m.] of the first day of the tenth month of 1228. At age nine, she lost her mother; she was able to manage family affairs and rear her younger brothers and sisters into adulthood. At the age of twenty-one, she was married to me. At the time I was very poor, and no one was willing to let his child marry me; only my father-in-law was willing to give me his daughter. The more his family members protested, the less he would listen, and in the end the marriage was agreed to. When Madam Bamboo Hall [that is, Miaoshan] married me, she was able to be content in poverty. She served my father with extreme filiality and dispersed the contents of her dowry to provide for my paternal relatives. When guests arrived, without any urging the food and drink were supplied. She was quiet and serious, of few words, and thoroughly understood *The Classic of Filial Piety*, *The Analects*, and *The Mencius*. At night, she would read books with me, not falling asleep until daylight. Although I was poor, Bamboo Hall was good at managing the family, making it so we were not in want and encouraging me to study: all my relatives and neighbors greatly esteemed her. Unfortunately, after nearly a year, in the fifth month of 1249, she gave birth to our daughter, Rong, and only twenty days later, on the first day of the sixth month, she passed away. The next year, Rong also died.

Grateful that my father-in-law had understood me, I did not dare to forget righteousness and could not bear to marry elsewhere. Once I was out of mourning, I sought to continue the connection [by taking another bride from their family]. My in-laws were clamorous in opposition, and Madam Plum Mansion was also angry that I had made such a request. Only my father-in-law loved me in his heart and in the end did not permit madam to become engaged to anyone else. In the interim, others asked to marry her, but in the end the negotiations always broke down. After five years, in 1253, I faced the grand palace [at the highest level of the examinations], and the emperor personally awarded me first rank. Grateful, I could not bear to turn my back on my father-in-law and once again asked my father to seek an alliance; only then did the family agree. Madam also agreed, saying, "This is someone who does not change his relationships or his wife," and we were to be married that winter. In the event, in the eleventh month my late father died, and so the wedding did not take place. In the second month of 1256, I was able to [complete the wedding ceremony] by bringing her to my house.

Madam Plum Mansion was virtuous like Madam Bamboo Hall and was also clever and perceptive, forthright and decorous. Regretting that she had not been able to take care of her father- and mother-in-law, she scrupulously and respectfully carried out the seasonal sacrifices. She served the elders with extreme politeness and nurtured her juniors with great grace. My former wife had no sons, and after her death my concubine Madam Huang gave birth to my son Yuanfu, whose birth I reported to the temple, establishing him as my lawful heir. When Madam Plum Mansion married me, she loved Yuanfu truly like he was her sister's and her own son; in sewing clothing and shoes for him, she was not the slightest bit remiss. She personally instructed him in reading; she said that her father had chosen a scholar for a son-in-law specifically to have someone to instruct his sons. She invited a famous scholar to instruct her two younger brothers and had Yuanfu study with them.

Madam did not set up a private kitchen, and, if we had wine, she would always drink together with the sisters-in-law and have me drink outside with the younger males and guests; almost never did we share a flask ourselves. She upheld both principle and righteousness, and, if she made a mistake, she would invariably correct it. If I sometimes became angry at the servants, she would always admonish me, saying, "[A gentleman] controls his anger and suppresses his desires."[7] If I raised some selfish thought, she would always admonish me, saying, "Restrain oneself and return to the rites."[8] From morning to night, I relied on her help. She loved goodness and took pleasure in righteousness, cared little for wealth, and always helped those in distress. When she first married me, my female younger cousin and step-brothers were all unmarried. She said, "As you are about to take up office, you cannot have uncompleted marriages," and she busied herself choosing affines. Hearing that the orphaned daughter of Administrator Zhao of Wuzhou was virtuous, she engaged her as the wife of my younger brother, and she had my younger cousin marry the degree holder Gong Sande. In the fifth month of that year, I obtained a job as a secretary in Yue. In the seventh month, due to mistaken benevolence, I received a call to office,[9] which I refused and did not accept. In the ninth month, I was appointed proofreader in the Palace Library. Madam said, "Don't be in a hurry to go; let me finish my affairs." We had to marry off my brother and cousin and bury her father and rebury her grandfather. At the end of the eleventh month, we departed. There had been four marriages and burials; in two or three months, she had managed everything in an orderly fashion, hardly ever showing a troubled expression. The betrothal gifts for the most part were her clothing and earrings, and she had no regrets. She accompanied me to the capital, but, when we were halfway there, the students of the Three Halls of the Imperial University submitted a protest to the emperor. The scholars were all driven out for their crimes, piling up and filling the road, and [my mentor] Vice Grand Councilor Mr. Longtime Studio [Cai Hang (1193–1259)] also left the court. I was terrified by what I saw and heard and became ill from worry. I did not wish to proceed but feared to disappoint Madam's intent that I should serve. Unable to go forward or back, I had no good options. Madam said, "A person entering or leaving office is like fish drinking water; they know automatically whether it is cold or warm. What doubt can you still have?! If a minister has received favor from a lord, when the lord makes mistakes, he remonstrates; if he remonstrates and the lord does not listen, he departs. Do not worry about me! If, because you speak forthrightly, you are punished, I am willing to be exiled with you to the mountainous coast; even if I die, I will have no regrets. I want to be the wife of a virtuous man; I don't want to be merely the wife of a high-ranking man." I thought her words were magnificent.

At the time, there had just been a warning that leaving office without good reason would be punished with severe exile; I feared that, if I got to court, I would not be able to speak. If I spoke beyond my office, I would already be committing a crime;[10] if I spoke and then left, my crime would be even more severe. Madam was already very pregnant, and I could not bear to burden her with a distant exile; so, using the precedent of Mr. Old-Spring Su [Su Xun (1009–1066)], I refused the invitation to office and submitted a sealed memorial, while also writing to the grand councilor. I rented a boat and returned by way of the Xin River route. Madam was pleased. The same day she cast aside her gold and pearl headdress and sent someone to buy a worked stone hairpin to stick in her hair. I asked her why, and she laughingly replied, "Hairpins of thorn and a cotton skirt are the appropriate clothing for living in obscurity!" I even more respectfully sighed at her courage.

In the first month of 1257, we reached home. She admonished me to close my door, refrain from seeing guests, and single-mindedly read books. When we had first left home, she had turned over the family affairs to my elder cousin's wife; on the day we returned, everything was as before. She led the younger sister-in-law in managing the household. Although our provisions were poor and meager, the whole house was full of life. In the third month, just when the inner quarters had become respectful and orderly, Madam died.

Before this, my elder brother had died without a son. Among the branches of the lineage, there was none who was appropriate to succeed him, so he did not have an heir. Madam had said, "Fortunately, I am pregnant. If it is a girl, I will raise her myself; if it is a boy, he can be the heir to elder brother, because Yuanfu is my son." Alas! Such words could move Heaven and Earth as well as the ancestors, yet in the end because of this pregnancy she died.[11] On the fourteenth of the third month, she was brought to childbed. As it turned out, she did give birth to a son, but he was stillborn. After another seven days, on the *bingwu* day, Madam also passed away. When her illness was already dire, she still ordered sewing to be done so as to clothe Yuanfu. Down to today, I have ordered Yuanfu not to dare to wear those clothes, storing them in a basket so that he can know his mother's virtue. On the day she died, she also warned me not to go out to serve lightly and chanted the phrase "like our great officer, Master Cui,"[12] several times. I did not understand her meaning, and, when I asked her, she did not answer. Alas! What can be done?! Madam was a niece of the Li family, and the Li family's learning came from Mr. Wengong [the eminent Neo-Confucian scholar Zhu Xi, 1130–1200]. She also was used to

hearing of the family rules that Madam Peng gave to the family of
Mr. Backwoods [Li Yishan, her mother's cousin]: she worked to emulate them and put them into practice. Daily she read several chapters
of *The Analects* and *The Mencius*, and in between she enjoyed looking
at Tang quatrains (*jue ju*). She especially loved reciting Mr. Wengong's
"Ten Poems on Wuyi Mountain." Her voice would wander from high
to low as she sang them, but she did not like what ordinary people call
"music bureau" (*yuefu*) poems.[13] Both sisters were able to compose
poetry, but both were unwilling to do so, saying, "Poetry is not the
affair of women." When Bamboo Hall [Miaoshan] was still alive, she
saw me teaching her younger brother to compose five-word couplets.
I gave him the phrase "two banks, green willow wind," and Bamboo
Hall matched it with "eight bricks, red peony days," her intent being to
refer to me.[14] I was astonished by her ability. When Plum Mansion
[Miaozhuang] and I passed by Moon Peak in Xinzhou, she loved its
strangeness and led the concubines and maidservants to scamper up.
From my vantage point behind, they looked like immortals. When she
reached the peak, she took up a brush to leave a mark for posterity and
composed a quatrain that said:

> On the half wall pacing the Heavens, the pillar leans against
>   emptiness
> Here in the human world is a Moon Palace.
> From now on it will truly seem like the moon on the horizon
> For the Moon Goddess Chang'e has come here.

She personally selected a place where the wind and rain would not
reach, and inscribed it there. If it were not for this inscription, I would
never have known that she could write poetry—she was always so
profound and reticent like this. After this, I asked her for more poetry,
but she refused.

By nature, Madam took delight in scenery, and, when we were on
the boat heading west, she said, "Although you have given up office, we
cannot give up enjoying the scenery." We climbed to Creek-Mountain
Hall, where we drank and then left. Once again, I asked her to write a

poem [on the wall], but she said, "This is a place where people come; how can I leave a woman's name and surname among them?" and in the end she would not agree. Ah! In this Madam's will is also evident. When our boat crossed Lake Boyang, she heard that from there one could go to Mount Lu; she was elated and wanted to go. I refused but promised to take her in autumn—but Madam had no more autumns! Oh, such grief!

Madam was born at the *si* hour [9:00 to 11:00 a.m.] in the year 1230, on the first day of the sixth month—the same day as Madam Bamboo Hall's death day. When she was in my household, on that day [her birthday] Yuanfu came to pay his respects; she knit her eyebrows and would not permit it. She herself often said that she suspected she and her sister were one person with two lives, and thus her sister died on the same date that she was born. Her appearance was originally quite different from that of Bamboo Hall, but, after our marriage, my family members all felt that her movements, speech, and laughter strongly resembled those of Bamboo Hall. Moreover, both of them were married to me for just a year, and both died in childbirth; this is something that cannot be fathomed.

Alas! My father-in-law bestowed the two sisters on me, and I was unable to repay him in the slightest. Then, in trying to assure my posterity, I caused his two daughters to die prematurely. Why has Heaven punished me like this?! Where is the principle that "fortune goes to the good and longevity to the benevolent"?! My father-in-law selected a son-in-law who was poor and humble: [if Heaven had] let his daughters share in the wealth and nobility of my official position, it might have been sufficient to somewhat encourage good scholars. But with their recompense like this, the good will only be frightened. Still, although this is the case, there are people whose lives are like death, and there are also people who die but are as if living. In my life between Heaven and Earth, although I had only two wives over a period of two years, and each wife died within a year, still, in that single year a hundred years of righteousness was present: I vow not to turn my back on my father-in-law's recognition of me. Moreover, I

have my son Yuanfu, so I will definitely not remarry. I will make
Yuanfu exhaust his duty as a son to repay my wife's efforts in raising
him, and I will also further establish myself and establish her two
younger brothers to ensure that in the end the Zou household will
achieve reputation and glory. My father-in-law and my two wives
although dead will be undying, even more than when they were alive.
In this way the good will ultimately be fortunate, and the benevolent
will in the end achieve longevity, and this can in turn serve to encourage improvement in shallow customs. For me to associate with
immoral people, obtain nobility and wealth by unrighteous means,
be cursed and ridiculed by the world, changing this for that—not only
would my father-in-law not want this; my two wives would also not
want it. "I desire virtue over noble rank"—these words of Plum Mansion, are they not a prescription for my entire life? They are inscribed
on my heart and will be inscribed on her grave. Her grave is in the
same graveyard as that of Bamboo Hall; she was buried on the *renshen*
day of the third month of 1258. The rhymed elegy reads:

> Husband and wife are Heaven's principle, without past and with-
>   out present.
> Who among humans does not die? What does not die is the heart.
> The elder sister was virtuous and perished prematurely; the
>   younger sister passed away in succession.
> Heaven should watch me—[I will maintain] this righteousness
>   from beginning to end.
> She did not admire her husband's high rank, desiring high rank
>   coupled with virtue.
> This phrase has savor; it can be passed down in the histories.
> Display the inscription at the path to the grave, to instruct ten
>   thousand generations.
> Chant their praises, the two virtuous females of this hamlet.

Source: Zeng Zaozhuang and Liu Lin, eds., *Quan Song wen* (Shanghai:
Shanghai cishu chubanshe, 2006), 352:8143.145–47.

Notes

1. This is a common trope in Chinese biographical literature, that of the prescient senior man who recognizes a junior man's talent before it has been publicly rewarded.
2. A separate "stove" implied a separate budget. Confucian ideology admired men who shared a family budget with their brothers regardless of their relative incomes.
3. The quotation is from Confucius's *Analects* 8.5.
4. Early Chinese texts had stipulated that men should not die with women around, so here Yao Mian is stressing that his father-in-law died in a ritually correct manner.
5. The phrase "mistaken benevolence" here is a conventional self-deprecating phrase used to describe being called to office or receiving other government honors.
6. Note that, out of respect, Yao Mian does not give his father-in-law's taboo name here.
7. This phrase is from *The Classic of Changes*, hexagram "Loss" (sun).
8. From *Analects* 12.1.
9. "Mistaken benevolence" here is a conventional, self-deprecating phrase used to describe being called to office or receiving other government honors.
10. Only officials of stipulated ranks were allowed to address the emperor; here Yao Mian expresses concern that his rank does not qualify him to remonstrate.
11. Yao Mian is saying that his wife's unselfishness (in accepting a concubine's son as her own child and offering to relinquish the child she would bear to Yao Mian's brother) should have been rewarded by Heaven, but instead she was punished.
12. From *Analects* 5.19. Cui was an officer who killed his lord, the Prince of Qi; at that point, a man named Chen Wen left the state of Qi, but he also refused to stay in other states where, he said, "they are like our great officer, Cui." What his wife was trying to convey was obscure to Yao Mian, as it is to modern readers.
13. Here Yao Mian is stressing that his wife only enjoyed morally correct poetry, not romantic and often suggestive poetry known as "music bureau" poems.
14. A common test of poetic skill was to compose a line of poetry to match an existing line. Miaozhuang here uses an obscure Tang dynasty allusion to suggest that Yao Mian's success at court had been delayed. (Specifically, "eight bricks" refers to a Tang story about people waiting in the courtyard of the prestigious Hanlin Academy until the sun's shadow had hit eight flowered bricks.)

Further Reading

Birge, Bettine. *Women, Property, and Confucian Reaction in Sung and Yüan China (960–1368)*. Cambridge, UK: Cambridge University Press, 2002.

Bossler, Beverly Jo. *Courtesans, Concubines, and the Cult of Female Fidelity: Gender and Social Change in China, 1000–1400*. Harvard-Yenching Institute monograph series. Cambridge, MA: Harvard University Asia Center, distributed by Harvard University Press, 2013.

Ebrey, Patricia Buckley. *The Inner Quarters: Marriage and the Lives of Chinese Women in the Sung Period*. Berkeley: University of California Press, 1993.

Xu, Man. *Crossing the Gate: Everyday Lives of Women in Song Fujian (960–1279)*. Albany: State University of New York Press, 2016.

A Clerk Promoted to Official
under the Mongols

Funerary Inscription for Mr. Su (Su Zhidao 蘇志道, 1261–1320),
Director of the Left and Right Offices of the Branch Secretariat
for the Lingbei Region, by Yu Ji 虞集 (1271–1348)

PATRICIA BUCKLEY EBREY

Service as a clerk was one way that men from literati families could
support themselves after the Mongol conquest of China. This epitaph
highlights the deceased's character and capabilities, while pointing
out that there was no reason for people to look down on those who
started as clerks.

MEN WHO WORKED IN GOVERNMENT OFFICES NOT AS OFFICIALS
but as their subordinates, a group generally called clerks, rarely are referred
to by their names in Chinese historical texts. Moreover, they are usually
referred to disparagingly—as individuals whom officials should keep
under close watch because of their moral inferiority. They were charged
with taking bribes, demanding illegal fees, and otherwise proving a
scourge on the population. Still, it was recognized that the government
could not be run without them, and in most government offices there
were more men in clerical posts than in ranked offices. Those who took
jobs as clerks did not have to take civil service examinations, and they

did not have to move from one place to another the way ranked officials did.

After the Mongol conquest of north China in 1234 and of south China in 1279, there was a growing need for clerks who could handle paperwork for officials who could not read or write Chinese. At the same time, under the Yuan dynasty there were fewer opportunities for literati with traditional Confucian educations to become officials, especially before the civil service examinations were reintroduced in 1315. Service as a clerk was one way men from literati families could support themselves, and it also offered a slim chance of promotion into a regular ranked position.

Su Zhidao (1261–1320), the subject of this funerary biography, is an example of a man who served as a clerk for decades before being promoted into the regular bureaucracy. The account of him written by Yu Ji (1271–1348) highlights his service as a clerk and rather defensively points out that there was no reason for people to look down on those who started as clerks. "The schedules for the transport of money and grain, the budgeting for construction, the examination of rewards and punishments, and the right terms for things are all activities that can only be done by those wielding writing brushes," we are told. Much of Su Zhidao's early career was in north China, but, after he became a ranked official, he found himself in the Jiangnan area during an investigation into a Buddhist sect suspected of sedition, the White Cloud Society, and later in Mongolia during a violent uprising and a disastrously heavy snow.

Su Zhidao's close relatives are also documented in four other inscriptions.[1] The reason for so many funerary inscriptions is that Su Zhidao's son Su Tianjue (1294–1352) rose high in the Yuan government, which allowed him to obtain posthumous offices for his ancestors, which in turn justified writing funerary biographies for them. From these sources, we know that Su Zhidao could not trace his descent back more than four generations and that his father was the earliest to gain a post of any sort. In 1214, Zhidao's great-grandfather Yuanlao fled with his family to Kaifeng (Henan) after the Mongols wreaked havoc in Hebei. When Kaifeng itself was endangered in the early 1230s, Yuanlao decided to try to return to where his ancestors were buried. The trip was fraught with danger, and they came close to death several times, but they eventually reached Zhending (Hebei), where they were able to buy land. In the chaos that accompanied the attack on Kaifeng, Yuanlao became separated from his younger brother and never saw him again. For several years, there were shortages of food, and Yuanlao, we are told, did what he could to help his community. He himself lived to the age of eighty-six, dying in 1276. He had one son, Cheng, who was twelve when they fled to Kaifeng. Undoubtedly reflecting the times, Cheng became skilled with weapons and horses. People had become accustomed to running away from local thugs, but Cheng wanted to stand up to them and would organize people to oppose them, earning his community's appreciation, we are told. As there were then no local schools, Cheng instructed his sons at home. His eldest son, Rongzu, was a diligent student, had a large number of books, and made use of his literacy, performing divinations for people and offering medical advice. He eventually held a low position in the Zhending tax office but soon gave it up to take care of his elderly grandfather.

Yu Ji, the author of the funerary biography translated below, was a well-known scholar and the author of eighty-nine funerary biographies. Su Tianjue and Yu Ji traveled in similar circles. We can feel confident that Yu Ji based his inscription on information that Su Tianjue provided. From a late Yuan source, we know that the stele written by Yu Ji was in the calligraphy of one of the most renowned of Yuan period calligraphers, Zhao Mengfu (1254–1322). The stone for this epitaph has not survived, nor, apparently, have any rubbings.

Su Zhidao's inscription documents the extension of Chinese-style administration into Mongolia. This included the transport of grain to feed the population of Karakorum and to provide relief in times of hardship for farmers who had been moved into Mongolia and for herdsmen. Su Zhidao's efforts to efficiently resupply the region seems a good example of larger processes at work. Su Zhidao's funerary biography is also valuable as one of the rare sources that look at government from the perspective of clerks. In this regard, it is interesting to notice that Su Zhidao's biography lists by name the men that he served under as clerk. It would seem that clerks who were trusted by high and important officials took pride in their relationships with their patrons.

In writing the funerary biography for Su Zhidao, Yu Ji seems to have been purposefully reticent in some places. He mentions those who had been moved to Mongolia and their success in adapting to the environment there, but he does not explicitly say that it was the Mongols who had captured them and forced them to move. The opening passage on Su's service at Karakorum after an uprising also leaves the story incomplete. Most likely the uprising is not identified because it involved members of the imperial family. It began in the sixth month of 1315, when the current emperor (Renzong/Ayurbarwada, r. 1311–1320), wanting the throne to pass to his own son rather than return to the line of his elder brother, the previous emperor (Wuzong/Khaishan, r. 1307–1311), assigned his cousin/rival Khosila a fief far from the center in distant Yunnan. When Khosila reached Yan'an (Shaanxi) and met with men who had served his father, they convinced him to try to take the throne himself, or, in other words, rebel. The uprising did not fare well, and many of his forces fled north. When they reached Karakorum, Kosila's forces seem to have wreaked quite a bit of destruction. An excavated inscription for another man who was in Karakorum in this period reports that their wives and children, family members, vehicles, clothes, implements, stores of food, horses, and cattle were all destroyed or killed by the rebels.

The organization of Su's *muzhiming* is somewhat unusual. After referring to Su Zhidao's death in 1320, Yu Ji turns to Lingbei, the province that largely corresponds with today's Mongolia, and Su Zhidao's service there beginning in 1316. This exposition takes up about 40 percent of the epitaph. It is followed by what is apparently a chronological account of Su Zhidao's career before his appointment in Lingbei, starting with his time as a clerk, with emphasis on who recommended him and the offices he served in, without giving any specific dates. Like other epitaphs, it concludes with a poetic elegy, but this one is exceptionally long.

Funerary Inscription for Mr. Su, Director of the Left and Right Offices of the Branch Secretariat for the Lingbei Region

In the second month, the *renxu* day, of the seventh year of the Yanyou reign period [1320], the Grand Master Exemplar, Director of the Left and Right Offices of the Branch Secretariat for the Lingbei Region [Mongolia], Su Zhidao (courtesy name Ningfu), died in the capital. On the day *wuchen*, his son Tianjue [1294–1352] returned his body to be buried in Zhending. In the third month, on the day *yiyou*, his body was buried north of the county seat at New Market District's New City, in sequence with his ancestors' graves. [His son] had a stone carved with the following words.

The seat of the Lingbei branch secretariat is Karakorum, established after the dynasty was founded. From the current capital, it is ten thousand *li* away on the northern border.[2] Mongol princes heavily garrison it. The grand councilor was sent there to be councilor of the branch secretariat. The staff there get good salaries, and the soldiers there get generous pay. Merchants, attracted by the possibilities of making large profits, deliver grain, cloth, and daily necessities. As a kindness to the people, legal penalties are light. Over the course of several decades, [the families moved there] have married off their children and planted crops, and now seem locally grown. They have mastered raising sheep, oxen, horses, and camels; shooting and hunting; as well as trading. At the border garrisons from Jinshan [in the west] to Chenghai, they are treated generously and have all become content and well-off, having long since forgotten the suffering of the wars and being transported there.

In winter of the *bingchen* year [1316], there suddenly was an incident in central Shaanxi, and in less than two months it had reached Karakorum. The governor did not know what to do about it; the people were shaken and afraid, and they fled in all directions. Then there was a heavy snowfall, more than ten feet deep, so that carts and houses, people and animals were crushed to death. Those not killed, not knowing how to survive, converged on Karakorum, where they begged for food, ate each other, or ended up in a pile of corpses. Before the sun went down, there were no more people on the roads.

At this time, the government staff were fearful and made excuses for not reporting in, all except for Mr. Su, who went immediately on receiving the order. He said, "This is not the time to seek the quiet life and shirk responsibilities." Once he arrived, he said, "What could be more urgent than providing relief to the starving?"

The next day, he told his superior, "The government office has diligently kept records of the stored money and grain. Before this incident, there were no great expenditures or losses, but, because of corrupt practices by the high and the low, nearly everything is gone. There is only 50,000 [*shi*] of grain.[3] Among the people, a *shi* of grain goes for around 800 strings worth of paper money. So how can they buy food [when it costs so much]? I request immediate distribution of 3 *dou* to each adult and one-sixth of that for each child."

He immediately sent a request to the court, saying: "We don't have much stored, and the common people and the soldiers are all the Son of Heaven's children. If we relieve the starving, the army will face shortages. If we just cautiously store the grain, then we will be letting the starving die. As the starving were in imminent danger, we had no choice but to act on our own authority to issue food to them. We would like to urgently recruit rich merchants and great houses to first obtain grain from the vicinity of Kaiping and Shajing [Inner Mongolia] and then set up a system for buying grain at generous prices to supply the border. It will be fortunate indeed if, by not begrudging one day's expenses, we deal with long-term worries."

The Secretariat reported this, and the emperor sent a commissioner to supervise the distribution to the starving and in addition issued this order: "Those able to deliver grain to Karakorum who get it there by the third month will get 500,000 per *shi*; by the fourth month, 450,000; by the fifth, 50,000 less, and so on. These funds will be immediately disbursed." Merchants arrived one after the other, and, in less than three years, [stored grain] was back to where it had been before. Mr. Su made this a fixed rule, used for audits as part of a double-entry system. The rule was followed by successive administrators, none daring to deviate from it.

The [Mongol] princes along the border often made excessive demands. Mr. Su used the law to turn down their requests. Angry, the princes sent someone to tell Mr. Su, "What gives you the right to treat this money as your private property?" But Mr. Su replied: "The authorities are responsible for supplying the military and do not dare use funds for other purposes. The reason we are cautious and frugal is not to benefit personally. If [you] the prince would look into it, you would find that I have done nothing wrong." The emperor's son the Prince of An agreed to this and rewarded Mr. Su with a set of clothes. The Prince of Wu also realized that Mr. Su [not owning a horse] walked everywhere and so gave him a fine horse. Mr. Su accepted it but then emptied his savings to repay its cost [to avoid any taint of corruption].

In Karakorum, because the rules prohibiting [private] brewing of wine were not strict, the practice could not be stopped. The Secretariat toughened the law and imposed the death penalty. Three days after the order was issued, a search uncovered a jug of wine. Zhao Zhongliang and four others were condemned for it. When the provincial staff wrote up the case using the new penalty, Mr. Su said it was not appropriate: "Wine cannot be made in three days, so the offense occurred before the ruling was promulgated but discovered afterwards. If we apply the later law to determine the penalty, it would be like doing that with edicts [which we all know is unfair]. We should consider this in more detail before reporting our decision and should not dare on our own to carry out the death penalty." The others disagreed, so Mr. Su alone reported the matter to the Secretariat. The Ministry of Justice concurred with his finding, and the men were found not liable for the death sentence.

People recognized Mr. Su's understanding of judicial decisions and, when they had disagreements, would call on him for advice. He said, "I do not decide government affairs." He would chase them away, but they would not go until they got a word from him.

Once Karakorum was in good order and daily business was manageable, Mr. Su would go to the Confucian temple and invite scholars familiar with the Classics to lecture. All the government officials and clerks would go to listen, not breaking up until midnight. The deceased grand councilor, posthumously titled Prince of Compliant Virtue Displaying Loyalty, had died before he finished building a Confucian temple, and it was not until Mr. Su took charge that the work was completed. The court knew of Mr. Su's accomplishments, and envoys going back and forth would convey encouragement. When the investigating censor came to the border on business, people by the hundreds would report Mr. Su's accomplishments to him, several dozens of them outstanding ones. And yet Mr. Su frequently was at odds with his colleagues. When he was departing because he was replaced, the common people lamented his departure. Soon after arriving at the capital, he died.

[Early in his career] Mr. Su was recommended on the basis of his service as a clerk by the Zhending governor, Yao Tianfu [1229–1302] of Shanxi [ca. 1295]. Once he had established a reputation, he was transferred to be clerk of the Surveillance Commission of Shanxi's Hedong Circuit.

On the basis of the recommendation of the commissioner Cheng Silian [1235–1296], he became a clerk to the investigating censor [ca. 1295–96], and then he was transferred to be clerk of the Ministry of Revenue. He held in succession positions as assistant in the Bureau of Military Affairs and the Secretariat. He became a ranked official at the rank of Gentleman of Fostering Uprightness as a proofreader in the Secretariat and a secretary in the Ministry of Justice, then judge in the Bureau of Military Affairs, then director of the Lingbei branch secretariat. From first to last, he never left government service and always had praiseworthy accomplishments.[4]

In Zhending, when he assisted the prefect in deciding cases, amid a great drought, it suddenly rained [an auspicious sign]. None of those he interrogated while serving in Hedong complained of injustice. In the Censorate, when he accompanied the censor to distant places, he maintained his composure even when causing officials to be mortified by what they had done, thus assuring that they would never again dare neglect their responsibilities.

In the Ministry of Revenue, he assisted the vice-director of the Ministry of Rites, Gao Fang [1264–1328], in dealing with the [Buddhist] White Cloud Society case [ca. 1306–1309]. In western Zhejiang, the White Could Society was strong, and the rich followed each other in contributing substantial wealth to put pressure on those in high positions. The society gradually made use of Buddhist teachings and set up official bureaus to organize the populace and entice them to grab and steal, collecting followers in the tens of thousands to over-whelm the prefecture and county. Mr. Su was able to distinguish those who corruptly profited by not following the law. He sent away those misled by them. The land and houses liable to confiscation reached into many tens of thousands. Several hundred boys and girls of good family who had been caught were returned to their families. During the two years he was examining the case, he returned to the capital five times to report on it in detail.

While at the Bureau of Military Affairs, Mr. Su assigned posts to all the poor sons and grandsons of soldiers and clerks who had been wait-ing ten or more years to inherit their positions. The Son of Heaven sends high officials to inspect the border regions, and in the northern regions Mr. Su assisted them. [As a consequence] he received gifts of bows and arrows, clothing, and saddles. While he was in the Secretar-iat, it so happened that the Department of State Affairs was set up. As its power was evident, many of the clerks in the Secretariat accepted transfers to it, all except for Mr. Su, who stayed as fixed as an anchor in his department. When the Department of State Affairs was abolished [in 1311], and those who had worked there were evaluated for reassign-ment, Mr. Su scrupulously followed the rules in dismissing those who had done illegal things.

[After Mr. Su became a ranked official] as proofreader, he recov-ered the overpayments of money or goods worth thousands made by the Ministries of Works and Revenue. Several dozen times when the ranks assigned by the personnel office missed the mark, he corrected them. While at the Ministry of Justice, [he had many achievements]. He was able to reject the higher officials' plan to ignore previous viola-tions. He was able to object when the ministers of the time wanted to kill those who stole money from the inner treasury even though the evidence was not conclusive. He was able to expose the main thieving clerk who had enticed good people to join. He was able to edit the legal stipulations to make them more convenient to use. While in the

Bureau of Military Affairs, he was able to recognize that a younger brother by a concubine mother was slandering his elder brother and have him dismissed.

Taking it all into account, Mr. Su was someone who never neglected his responsibilities in any situation. But his political achievements in Karakorum were the most extraordinary. It was through military might that our dynasty first ruled all within the seas, and so officers with military accomplishments were honored. But the schedules for the transport of money and grain, the budgeting for construction, the examination of rewards and punishments, and the right terms for things are all activities that can only be done by those wielding writing brushes. Recognizing this, after he began his service as a clerk, Mr. Su was in no hurry to become a ranked official through other means.

Dukes and ministers, generals and chancellors, in the end everyone falls into one category or the other [civil or military]. When matters are decided, the military generals have fixed ranks. But, on the civil side of government, from the beginning the clerks were in charge. As a result, all the literati in the realm who had talent, wisdom, and good behavior and wanted to be of use to the world had to follow this route to become officials. It was not that they wanted to establish themselves in this way but rather that they were urgently needed. And yet in the world there are people who specialize in finding flaws in those able to handle situations, who are familiar with documents and able to perform calculations. Such critics probably have not fully considered the situation. Otherwise, how could they look down on men like Mr. Su because they began their careers as clerks?

When Mr. Su was child, he did not like to play and rarely spoke or laughed. He took care in choosing friends. When he served as a clerk, he looked at documents in terms of whether or not they could be applied and did not wait to be asked to give his opinion. When he came home from work, he would close his door and not entertain guests or pay visits.

With his wife and children, Mr. Su was as serious as with teachers and friends, and was solemn whether at home or away. He loved to read and especially revered *The Greater Learning* and *The Memorials of Lu Xuangong* [Lu Zhi, 754–803], which he never put aside. He was serious in teaching his son, and, when he had some surplus funds, he would buy books to give him. His son was also a good student and in time became a well-known scholar, fulfilling Mr. Su's ambitions for him.

Mr. Su's ancestors were from Luancheng in Zhaozhou [Hebei] but after two moves settled in Zhending [Hebei]. His great-grandfather was Yuanlao, his grandfather was Cheng, and his father, Rongzu. [Rongzu,] because of Mr. Su's high rank, received the posthumous rank of Grand Master for Forthright Service, Acting Prefect of Zhongshan, Commandant of Flying Cavalry, Baron of Zhending County. His mother was from the Wu family and received the posthumous title of Lady of Zhending County. Information on these ancestors is in the stele for the ancestral graveyard.[5] Mr. Su married Madam Liu, who was given the title of Lady of Zhending County. She was the granddaughter of Yi the Black Army Myriarch and the daughter of Hundred Household Patrol Leader Cheng. He had one son, Tianjue, who through testing high at the Academy was given the rank of Gentleman of Attendance and made assistant prefect of Jizhou in Dadu Circuit. He carried out his father's funeral according to Confucian ritual and was able to avoid Buddhist services. Mr. Su had three daughters. The first married Gong Tianzhen, commissioner of agriculture; the second married Zhang Meng; the third married He Andao, with the rank of Gentleman for Rendering Service, serving as office manager of the Henan branch secretariat, and was given the title of Respectful Lady. He has a grandson named Yuan.

Mr. Su lived to sixty. Although he served for a long time, he was always assisting others, never in charge himself. Valued by his contemporaries, his sudden death saddened men of character.

The rhymed elegy reads:

Solemn Mr. Su held fast to virtue, never deviating.
Deep, silent, he restrained himself, not drawing attention to his
    talent.

When first associating with his peers, his love of the good was
 already apparent.

How to study or farm? One gains by not seeking.

Getting not by seeking, one's *qi* is straight and shines forth.

Speaking forthrightly, in no hurry, how would he do anything
 wrong?

Following the upright path made him seem arrogant, a disadvan-
 tage in dealing with people.

He maintained his serious self-confidence from the start to the
 end.

Five times an assistant to a high official—his position lowly but
 his goals were achieved.

Four times given appointments by the court, his accomplishments shining forth.

The grand city of Karakorum is under our accomplished emper-
 or's rule.

Taking charge of the north was easy for Mr. Su—what is a thousand or ten thousand *li*?

The compatriots [Mongols] live there, in the valleys where
 horses prosper like clouds.

Whether coming or going, how all-encompassing his feelings!

[While serving as a clerk] the documents of the Censorate, he
 single-mindedly composed them.

Even those who harmed him he treated ethically.

[For his service in the Bureau of Military Affairs] the Son of
 Heaven complimented him; the great chariots went to pro-
 claim it.

[The ruler] said, "From me, this bow and horse for you."

He returned [as an office director] to the region, acting with
 method and kindness.

As a person he was perceptive, and as a clerk his language was
 highly literary.

Generally calm, yet easy to disturb, he responded to the
 occasion.

Tending as attentively as a mother bird, his post came first.

The people of the border area cherished him, but he did not stay long.

He went in all haste to his next assignment but became ill and died.

He neither showed eagerness for glorious posts, nor did he change when on a cold bench.

What should be done he did; where distinctions should be drawn, he drew them.

At home, he was able to think things through, closing his door and dwelling in the deep.

He was very strict in administration and his movements accorded with Confucian ritual.

Confucian conduct, a teacher for clerks, both can be found here.

He had books filling his hall to pass on to his son.

His son was able to study them and also to put them into practice.

How is his son's achievement as an official his alone? He also fulfills Mr. Su's personal goals.

It is the source [that is, Mr. Su] that makes a river deep and the stream [that is, his son] that makes it long.

To be continued and passed down, now in this dark chamber.

Source: Quan Yuan wen 全元文, edited by Beijing shifan daxue guji yanjiusuo (Nanjing: Jiangsu guji chubanshe, 2004), 27:882.379–83.

Notes

1. *Quan Yuan wen*, edited by Beijing shifan daxue guji yanjiusuo (Nanjing: Jiangsu guji chubanshe, 2004), 27:884.400–402; 21:650.153–55; 38:1195.335–38; 30:965.115–16.

2. This is, of course, an exaggeration. At 2 *li* to a kilometer, it was more like 2,600 *li*—still a formidable distance.

3. This would be approximately enough to feed people for a year.

4. Su Zhidao's *shendaobei* (spirit path stele) says he was a clerk for twenty years before becoming a ranked official. *Quan Yuan wen* 38:1195.337.

5. Yu Ji also wrote this. See *Quan Yuan wen* 27:884.400–403.

Further Reading

Dardess, John W. *Conquerors and Confucians: Aspects of Political Change in Late Yuan China*. New York: Columbia University Press, 1973.

de Rachewiltz, Igor, Hok-lam Chan, Hsiao Ch'i-ch'ing, and Peter W. Geier, eds. *In the Service of the Khan: Eminent Personalities of the Early Mongol-Yüan Period*. Wiesbaden: Harrassowitz, 1993.

Langlois, John D. "Yu Chi and His Mongol Sovereign: The Scholar as Apologist." *Journal of Asian Studies* 38.1 (1978): 99–116.

Mote, Frederick W. "Chinese Society under Mongol Rule, 1215–1368." In *Cambridge History of China*, vol. 6: *Alien Regimes and Border States, 907–1368*, edited by Herbert Franke and Denis Twitchett, 616–64. Cambridge, UK: Cambridge University Press, 1994.

Overmyer, Daniel L. "The White Cloud Sect in Sung and Yüan China." *Harvard Journal of Asiatic Studies* 42.2 (1982): 615–42.

15

A Mongol Rising to the Defense of the Realm

Epitaph for Grand Guardian Sayin Čidaqu 賽因赤荅忽 (1317–1365), by Zhang Zhu 張翥 (1287–1368)

TOMOYASU IIYAMA

As one of the few epitaphs for a non-Han person from a non-office-holding family, this biography offers glimpses of the multiethnic society of north China during the late Yuan period.

UNDER THE RULE OF THE MONGOL EMPIRE, MASSIVE INFLUXES of migrants from Central Asia, the Mongolian Steppe, and Manchuria came into China proper. Among them, non-Han elite garrison troops called Tammači (mounted scouts) constituted one of the cornerstones of Mongol rule in China. The subject of this epitaph, Sayin Čidaqu,[1] whose undisturbed tomb was excavated in 1990 on the outskirts of Luoyang (Henan), was from a hereditary Tammači military household. As one of the few epitaphs for a non-Han person from a non-office-holding family during the late Yuan, this funerary biography written in Classical Chinese gives us rare insights into the lives of non-Han migrants and their descendants in north China from the emergence of the Mongol Empire down to the turbulent Yuan-Ming transition.

By the end of the twelfth century, the tribe that Sayin Čidaqu belonged to, the Baya'ut (or Bayaɣud), was one of the nomadic groups found in the Mongolian steppes. *The Secret History of the Mongols*, a thirteenth-century Middle Mongolian literary work, narrates that, in exchange for one thigh of a three-year-old deer, a man of the Ma'aliq Baya'ut (a subgroup of Baya'ut) in desperate straits gave a son of his to Dobun Mergen, the eleventh descendant of the mythic Blue-Gray Wolf and Fallow Doe, the celestial apical ancestors of the Mongolian people. Thereafter, *The Secret History of the Mongols* continues, the descendants of the Baya'ut child became the hereditary household servants of Temüjin's (Činggis Qan, or Genghis Khan) direct ancestors.[2] And, in fact, Temüjin had a hereditary Baya'ut retainer named Sorqan. After the founding of the Mongol Empire, when its ruling elite became marriage partners of the imperial household, the Baya'ut produced military commanders, civil officials, and imperial concubines throughout the empire, including, for example, Kökejin Qatun, the Baya'ut princess who traveled with Marco Polo by sea from China all the way to Iran to marry Arɣun (r. 1284–1291), the fourth Ilkhan, the monarch of the Ilkhanate.[3]

Compendium of Chronicles, a Persian world chronicle completed by Rashīd al-Dīn (1249–1318) in 1314, records that one of the sons of the above-mentioned Sorqan of Baya'ut, named Kökečü, fathered Julči (or Julji) Baɣurči, who served as a major military commander in the Ilkhanate. Although it seems unlikely due to the clear dissimilarity of political status between the descent lines in China and Iran, some scholars believe that the Kökečü that appears in *Jāmiʿ al-Tawārīkh* is the same person as the great-grandfather of Sayin Čidaqu in this epitaph and thus that Sayin Čidaqu traced his ancestry back to the hereditary Baya'ut retainer of Činggis Qan (Genghis Khan).

Sayin Čidaqu would have lived an unremarkable life as a Tammači soldier, but the outbreak of the Red Turban Rebellion utterly changed his life. In the fifth month of 1351, Liu Futong (1321–1363) rose in rebellion together with his companions in Yingzhou (in Anhui). Liu initially supported Han Shantong (d. 1351), the leader of the White Lotus Society, a Maitreyan Buddhist sect, who proclaimed himself the messianic

"Radiant King" and the legitimate descendant of Emperor Huizong (r. 1100–1126) of the Northern Song. After Han was executed, Liu himself mobilized the White Lotus believers, and, calling themselves Red Turbans, they rapidly spread his dominance over the neighboring regions. Later, supporting Han Lin'er (d. 1366), the son of Han Shantong, the Red Turbans eventually occupied Bianliang (Kaifeng, Henan) and reestablished the "Song" dynasty in 1358.

Faced with the Red Turbans invading his homeland, Čaɣantemür (d. 1362) of the Nayiman tribe (called King Zhongxiang in the epitaph), who was also from a Tammači military family that had resided in Shenqiu County (Henan) for four generations, organized hundreds of local young men into a volunteer army. Sayin Čidaqu followed Čaɣantemür from his emergence and distinguished himself by repeatedly defeating Red Turban detachments. The two men became close kin. Sayin Čidaqu married Fo'er, the sister of Čaɣantemür, who later adopted the couple's first son, Köketemür. The Yuan army led by Čaɣantemür, now one of the most eminent Yuan generals, managed to recapture Bianliang in 1359, and the Red Turbans fell into infighting. The leader to emerge from these struggles, Zhu Yuanzhang (1328–1398), would eventually found the Ming dynasty.

The author of Sayin Čidaqu's epitaph, Zhang Zhu (1287–1368), was an eminent poet. He was Han, not Mongol, a rare sign that Sayin Čidaqu's family had substantial contact with Chinese literati. Writing in Chinese, Zhang provides a straightforward narrative of his subject's life, enumerating the names and posthumous titles of Sayin Čidaqu's forefathers, summarizing his major military achievements, and recounting the official careers of his sons. Reading of all his victories in battle, one would think that Mongol forces had gained the upper hand and were close to destroying all opposition. But that was not the case. During the early 1360s, the Yuan army fell into disorder, and the rebels, now calling themselves the formal army of the Ming dynasty, captured the imperial capital, Dadu (modern Beijing), in 1368. The sons of Sayin Čidaqu, Köketemür (d. 1375) and Toyintemür (d. 1388), assumed control over the Yuan army following the assassination of Čaɣantemür and fought for successive khans after the Mongols abandoned China proper and retreated into the steppe. The fates of Köketemür and Toyintemür are recorded in Ming sources.

Sayin Čidaqu's epitaph helps throw light on a multiethnic northern Chinese society comprising peoples with conflicting interests and diverse cultural backgrounds. Both anti-Yuan rebels and pro-Yuan militants, such as Čaɣantemür and Sayin Čidaqu, emerged in the same region, Ruzhou and Yingzhou. Whereas Red Turbans were mainly Han, the majority of the pro-Yuan militias were organized by non-Han leaders from Tammači military households. Wielding bows and swords, weapons banned for Han, the non-Han garrison soldiers and their families consisted of people identifying themselves as Mongol, Nayiman, Baya'ut, Tangut, Kyrgyz, Uyghur, and other migrant groups from North and Central Asia. They formed a specific social group, weaving marriage ties with each other for generations.

Epitaph for the Late Mr. Sayin Čidaqu, Grand Guardian, Recipient of Edicts in the Hanlin Academy, Grand Master of Imperial Entertainments with Silver Seal and Blue Ribbon, Drafter, Compiler of the Reign History of the Great Yuan

Authored by Zhang Zhu, Hanlin Academician, Recipient of Edicts, Grand Master for Glorious Happiness, Drafter, Compiler of the Reign History; calligraphy by Chen Zuren, Grand Master for Palace Attendance, Chancellor of the Directorate of Education; title on the epitaph cover written in seal script by Zhang Qi, Grand Academician in the Academy of Scholarly Worthies, Grand Master for Splendid Happiness, Commandery Duke of Teng

Mr. Sayin Čidaqu was of the Baya'ut tribe of the Mongols. His ancestors served in Emperor Shizu's [i.e., Qubilai Qaɣan, r. 1260–1294] campaign to pacify the lands south of the Yellow River. They were stationed in Gushi County, Guangzhou [Henan], and eventually settled down there. Kökečü, his great-grandfather, was posthumously bestowed the titles and offices of Grand Master of Palace Attendance, assistant administrator of the Shaanxi Branch Secretariat, and Military Protector, and was enfeoffed as Commandery Duke of Yunzhong. Šiju [or Šiču], his grandfather, was posthumously bestowed the titles and offices of Grand Master for Promoting Goodness, assistant director of the Left

Sichuan Branch Secretariat, and Senior Military Protector, and was enfeoffed as Commandery Duke of Yunzhong. Bayaɣudai, his father, was posthumously bestowed the titles and offices of Grand Master for Glorious Happiness, manager of governmental affairs of the Huguang Branch Secretariat, and Pillar of State, and was enfeoffed as Duke of Ji. Lady Kyrgyz, his great-grandmother, and Bayaɣujin, his grandmother, were both enfeoffed as Commandery Mistress of Yunzhong. Ölǰeilün, his mother, was enfeoffed as Mistress of Ji.

Mr. Sayin Čidaqu loved learning, exercised administrative clerical skills, and had profound ambitions. He was skilled at shooting on horseback and was exceptionally strong. In the *xingmao* year of the Zhizheng reign period [1351], bandits rose in insurrection, and many cities and towns in Ruzhou and Yingzhou [in Henan and Anhui, respectively] fell to them. Garrison commanders, routed, fled from their assigned posts, and the devastated cities were occupied by the brigands. Mr. Sayin Čidaqu used his own funds to buy weapons and recruit robust men to form a righteous army [that is, one to defend the Yuan government]. Having established a stronghold at Aiting [Anhui], he seized every strategic mountain pass to contain the bandits, who did not dare to attack after seeing his preparations. He soon joined King Zhongxiang's [i.e., Čaɣantemür's] troops to pacify Luoshan County [Henan] and was appointed disciplinarian of his battalion of the Pacification Commission in Yingzhou and Xizhou Prefectures [in Anhui and Henan], with the prestige title Commandant for Manifest Loyalty.

In the *yiwei* year [1355], the grand army subdued Junzhou, Xuzhou, and Ruzhou [all in Henan]. Mr. Sayin Čidaqu was promoted to vice brigade commander of the Pacification Commission, with the prestige title General for Military Strategy. In the *bingshen* year [1356], he captured Mengjin, Gong, and Wen Counties [all in Henan]. He then conquered Xingyang [Henan], Sishui [Shandong], and Heyin [Henan], and fought in Sui [Henan] and Bo [Anhui], killing and capturing countless enemies. For his exploits, Mr. Sayin Čidaqu advanced to Hedong vice pacification commissioner, with the prestige title

General for Militant Virtue. Subsequently, he followed [King Zhongxiang's army] to take Shanzhou [Henan] and subdue prefectural and county seats including those of Pinglu and Xia Counties [Shanxi] and Lushi County; Guozhou County; Lingbao County [all in Henan]; and Tongguan County [in Shaanxi]. This led to his promotion to the post of Hedong assistant surveillance commissioner, with the prestige title Grand Master for Governance. Next, he was transferred to Hedong associate pacification commissioner, with the prestige title Lesser Grand Master of the Palace, then advanced to Hedong vice surveillance commissioner. At the time, the lands west of Tongguan and Shanzhou were strategically significant to check the brigands, but they were isolated. Bandits therefore used them as the base of their operations. King Zhongxiang, keen to vanquish them and recover the area, dispatched his subordinate generals to march there from multiple directions simultaneously. Mr. Sayin Čidaqu was in charge of one of the fronts and recovered Huazhou, Huayin County; Fengxiang, Pingyang County; and Longzhou [all in Shaanxi], and defeated the bandits that had roamed the southern mountains [presumably the Qinling Mountains]. [For his merits, he] was advanced to Hedong pacification commissioner, with the prestige title Grand Master for Palace Attendance.

In the *wuxu* year [1358], a bandit chieftain known as the "King Who Sweeps the Earth" abruptly stormed into and rampaged through Shanxi and Hebei. Mr. Sayin Čidaqu fought and defeated him at Cold Water Valley, and the remnants of the bandit army were routed. As a result, he was promoted to be assistant commissioner of the Henan Branch Military Affairs Commission. [By then] Bianliang [Kaifeng, Henan] had fallen to the deceitful "Young Radiant King," Han Lin'er, who established his court and stationed his army there. Han Lin'er originally intended to seize the Central Plain but was defeated by King Zhongxiang, and Henan was pacified. Mr. Sayin Čidaqu was subsequently promoted to Assistant Director of the Left at the Henan Branch Secretariat, with the prestige title Grand Master for Assisting toward Goodness for his merit [during the campaign against Han

Lin'er]. This was soon followed by an appointment as Assistant Director of the Right [of the same branch secretariat], with the prestige title Grand Master for Assisting Virtue. [Then he was] transferred to vice-commander of military affairs and advanced to manager of governmental affairs at the Henan Branch Secretariat, with the prestige title Grand Master for Glorious Happiness. Shortly after that, he was made Hanlin Academician and recipient of edicts, and immediately after this received the post of grand guardian, concurrently holding the post of recipient of edicts, with the prestige title Grand Master of Imperial Entertainments with Silver Seal and Blue Ribbon.

In the first month, the twenty-ninth day, of the *yisi* year [1365], Mr. Sayin Čidaqu passed away at home from illness at the age of forty-nine. He had married Fo'er of the Nayiman, who was so austere and articulate that all the female family members acted on her principles. She passed away at the age of [empty space] in Luoyang five years before her husband's demise and was posthumously enfeoffed as Mistress of Ji. Her body is now buried with Mr. Sayin Čidaqu's.

Mr. Sayin Čidaqu had three sons. The eldest is Köketemür, who is naturally agile and sharp, with extraordinary talents. As a child, Köketemür was prone to illness. King Zhongxian, as his mother Lady Nayiman's brother, regarded Köketemür as his own son and eventually adopted him. From his youth, Köketemür followed the king and built his career in the army. The king relied on him for everything, which he would complete as expected. When the king passed away,[4] by an imperial edict, Köketemür was ordered to take supreme command over his adoptive father's army. He then pacified Shandong and subdued Yunshuo [i.e., northern Shanxi]. When the imperial crown prince led an army on a southern tour, Köketemür served as an imperial retainer. Once the imperial capital region was cleansed, with his name and exploits highly acclaimed, Köketemür advanced to Assistant Director of the Left of the Secretariat and Grand Mentor.[5]

Mr. Sayin Čidaqu's second son is Toyintemür. Gentle and unselfish, Toyintemür was recognized by the emperor and the crown prince, and as a symbol of exceptional imperial grace he was granted the post of assistant administrator of the Henan Branch Secretariat, with the prestige title of Grand Master for Palace Attendance. The third son, Nailu, is still young. A daughter, Guanyingnu, has not yet married.

The tomb of Mr. Sayin Čidaqu is located on the plain at the foot of the northern Mang Mountains. He was buried there on [empty space] day in the eleventh month [of 1365]. Alas! During a time filled with sufferings and hardships, talented men aspire to rise high. Men of humble origins in the countryside who used to drift around villages and hamlets joined the army and rose to positions as esteemed administrators and great generals. With regard to their initial lack of experience in official service, even Han Xin [d. 196 BCE], Peng Yue [d. 196 BCE], Zhou Bo [d. 169 BCE], and Guan Ying [d. 176 BCE. were also mere ordinary men [at the beginning].[6] Once they served in office, with the suddenness of wind arising or lightning striking, and the simplicity of hands clapping and gentle smiling, they set far-reaching goals. When Heaven wants to assign a task to a man, it certainly holds him back for a time, intending to eventually use him to benefit the world. How could the achievement of a person like Grand Guardian Sayin Čidaqu be a mere coincidence? With that, I append a rhymed elegy as follows:

The magnificent sovereign dynasty wields executive authority
    over everything under Heaven,
Who dare not to offer up tribute and present themselves for
    imperial audience?
Those freakish and delusive demons then spread out their fren-
    zied violence,
They raged ferociously like covetous fat boars and insatiable
    owls.
At that point, Mr. Sayin Čidaqu raised a righteous army with his
    manifest martial prowess,
Marching with the decorated battle flag, his bravery was
    irresistible.

From Shanxi and Shaanxi in the west to Song and Liang
[Henan] in the south,
Mr. Sayin Čidaqu went around cleaving the enemy's elbows and
thighs and gripping their throats.
Ascending in ranks through abundant exploits, he made his
glory brilliant,
Here his family tombs under the vaulted sky will be prized for
countless years to come.
Those who will succeed to his legacy, make yourselves familiar
with this inscription.

Sources: Luo Huojin 罗火金, "Yuandai saiyinchidahu muzhi kao" 元代
赛因赤答忽墓志考, *Wenxue shijie* 2004.4:20-21; Luoyangshi tielu-
beizhan bianzuzhan lianhe kaogu fajuedui 洛阳市鐵路北站編組站聯合
考古發掘隊, "Yuan Sanyinchidahumu de fajue" 元赛因赤答忽墓的發
掘, *Wenwu*, 1996.2:22–33.

Notes

1. The name means, in Mongolian, "one who can do things well."
2. See *The Secret History of the Mongols*, translated and annotated by Igor de
   Rachewiltz (Leiden: Brill, 2006), vol. 1, 3.
3. See Peter Jackson, "Marco Polo and His 'Travels,'" *Bulletin of the School of Orien-
   tal and African Studies* 61.1 (1998): 82–101.
4. While laying siege to Yidu (Shandong), Čaɣantemür was stabbed to death by his
   subordinate generals Wang Shicheng and Tian Feng (d. 1362), who used to be
   Red Turban leaders.
5. The "southern tour" and "cleansing of the capital" are metaphors depicting the
   1364 coup d'état against the imperial crown prince Ayurširidara (1340–1378),
   with whom Köketemür sided, and the consequent reprisal against Bolodtemür
   (d. 1365), the eminent warlord who led the coup. Facing the advancing rebels,
   Ayurširidara fled to Taiyuan (Shanxi), the power base of Köketemür, who then
   retook Dadu (Beijing) as protector of realm in 1365. This epitaph was authored
   sometime between Köketemür's capture of Dadu in the eighth month of 1365
   and the interment of Sayin Čidaqu's body in the eleventh month of the same
   year.
6. Han, Peng, Zhou, and Guan were all famous generals of the Han dynasty.

Further Reading

Allen, Thomas T. *Culture and Conquest in Mongol Eurasia.* Cambridge, UK: Cambridge University Press, 2001.

Amitai, Reuven. *Mongols, Turks, and Others: Eurasian Nomads and the Sedentary World.* Leiden: Brill, 2004.

Biran, Michal. "Periods of Non-Han Rule." In *A Companion to Chinese History*, edited by Michael Szonyi, 129–42. Malden, MA: Wiley Blackwell, 2017.

Iiyama, Tomoyasu. "A Tangut Family's Community Compact and Rituals: Aspects of the Society of North China, ca.1350 to the Present." *Asia Major* 27.1 (2014): 99–138.

A Merchant Aspiring to Gentlemanly Virtue

Funerary Biography of the Gentleman Residing at Home Cheng
Weiqing 程惟清 (1531-1588), by Wang Shizhen 王世贞 (1526-1590)

TRANSLATED BY YONGTAO DU

Commercialization of the economy led to the rise of a new wealthy
class and the blurring of social boundaries in late Ming China. In this
epitaph, a prominent scholar-official celebrates the life of a merchant
from Huizhou, the best-known home region of merchants in late
imperial China.

FROM THE HAN DYNASTY ON, ORTHODOX CONFUCIAN IDEOLOGY
elevated literati to the top of the social order, as the noble and cultured
gentlemen meant to rule, and assigned merchants to the bottom as profit-
seeking social parasites. Thus, for centuries literati and merchants, as the
high and the low in Chinese society, were kept apart. However, in the
last hundred years of the Ming dynasty it became increasingly common
for the two to mix socially, and literati in this period wrote hundreds of
biographies for merchants. The funerary biography of the merchant Cheng
Weiqing (1531–1588), translated here, is one example. It was written by
Wang Shizhen (1526–1590), a high-level official and a leading figure in
the literary and scholarly realm of the late sixteenth century.

Many factors contributed to this dramatic change in the relationship between the two social classes. Probably the most powerful one was the substantial commercialization of the economy. Trade and commerce had long since been a common factor in Chinese economic life, but the wave of commercialization that picked up momentum in the sixteenth century went both deeper and wider. For example, not only luxury goods, but also low-priced bulk commodities such as grain, cotton, and cloth were bought and sold over long distances. One can make sense of this situation by looking at the agricultural changes in the Yangzi delta. During the Song dynasty, the previous high point in the development of China's market economy, the Yangzi delta was an important area of grain production, as reflected in the famous Song proverb "When Suzhou and Huzhou harvest, the all-under-Heaven is fed." But by the late Ming, because of the increase in cash crops in this area, grain had to be imported from the middle Yangzi region. Accordingly, the Yangzi delta exported cotton and cloth to almost all regions of the Ming empire.

Commercialization of the economy led to the rise of a new wealthy class in late Ming China, as it did in Western Europe during roughly the same time period. The newly rich, not surprisingly, sought to share the glamour and social esteem of the old elites. The rise of the nouveau riche played out differently in China than in Europe, however. In late Ming China, this process took a form that some scholars call the "confluence of literati and merchants."[1] The merchants often had at least a rudimentary level of education; some even pursued a scholarly career before embarking on mercantile pursuits. They sponsored art and learning, and mingled with and befriended literati.

In late imperial China, there was no true aristocracy with inheritable titles. Success in the civil service examinations was virtually open to all. In these circumstances, many families hedged their bets by letting one son pursue scholarly training and prepare for the examinations, while others entered the world of business. In this way, mercantile wealth could be used to support the increasingly elusive goal of examination success. As a result, merchants and literati not infrequently came from the same family background. Wang Daokun (fl. sixteenth century), one of the most vocal defenders of the dignity of merchants, was himself a son and grandson of merchants. After he earned the highest degree in the examinations, he had a successful career as a civil official. In such cases, late Ming commercial wealth resulted in the blurring of social boundaries. Still, the merchants' financial power and their assertive manners also caused widespread unease among the old literati elites over such issues as the scholar's dignity, the decline of simple rural virtues, and the vulgarization of aesthetic tastes.

When it came to social and moral values, merchants did not pose any threat to the established order. Values such as filial piety, kinship solidarity, and ritual appropriateness that had been advocated by Confucian scholars for centuries were fully embraced by the merchants. The highest praise for a merchant was that he looked or behaved like a Confucian scholar, resulting in stock phrases such as "Confucianized merchant" or "both a Confucian scholar and a merchant" commonly found in late Ming sources. A frequently used honorary title for merchants in their biographies, as here in the case of Cheng, was "gentleman residing at home" (*chushi*), a term that originally referred to a scholar not currently holding an office. The career of a Confucian scholar was always more desirable than that of a merchant so that moments when one had to embark on the latter role, as seen from available biographical sources, were often accompanied by disappointment and regret. Thus, it was highly appropriate for a merchant to demonstrate his admiration of Confucian virtues.

The first and foremost way merchants could make positive use of their commercial wealth was by assisting kinsmen in need and contributing to lineage construction. The lineage institution—kin groups organized around the principle of patrilineal descent—was one of the most important social institutions in late imperial China. Since the Song dynasty, lineage building had been energetically promoted by Neo-Confucian literati and constituted an integral part of their agenda for social reform. The moral foundation, regular practices, as well as social significance of the lineage were all explained in Confucian terms: descendants of the same ancestor should be reminded of their common root through collective rituals of ancestral worship; the duty of filial piety and ritual appropriateness requires people to clarify, recognize, and maintain proper ritual relations with their kinfolk; good social and moral order of "all-under-Heaven" starts with proper relationships among kin, and so on. The literati spearheaded lineagewide charitable works and continued to play the leading role in charitable and other activities of the lineage in the late Ming, but merchants loomed increasingly large in this domain, as they did in other areas traditionally reserved for the literati.

Many of these celebrated characteristics of late Ming merchants are reflected in the life story of Cheng Weiqing. His home county, Xiuning, and neighboring She County were both in Huizhou (Anhui), which is arguably the best-known home region of merchants in late imperial China. Its mountainous topography and limited arable land made it necessary for men to leave to seek income from commerce; its highly developed lineage institutions and deeply rooted lineage culture provided both financial aid and personnel support for the merchants' adventures and enterprises. The Huizhou merchants achieved great mercantile successes and accumulated huge amounts of wealth. In late Ming literature, they were the stereotypical nouveau riche who embarrassed the cultural establishment and challenged the social order. However, the mercantile wealth that they sent home greatly enhanced lineage construction and promoted Confucian learning, making Huizhou one of the most socially conservative places in the country. In some ways, Cheng Weiqing and his fellow Huizhou merchants epitomized both the potential and the limitations of China's "commercial revolution."

Funerary Biography of the Gentlemen Residing at Home
Cheng Weiqing

In She County [Anhui], it is the custom to rank clans, and the Cheng clan and the Wang clan are at the very top. The Chengs are all descendants of Cheng Lingxi, the Honorable Mr. Zhongzhuang [of the Tang dynasty].[2] Lingxi dwelled in Huangdun of She County. By the Song dynasty, Mr. Xuanyi moved to Likou of [neighboring] Xiuning County. About a dozen or so generations later, there was Weijie. Weijie begot Jingyin, Jingyin begot Zhonglie, and Zhonglie is the father of our gentleman residing at home.

Mr. Cheng's taboo name is Jie; his courtesy name is Weiqing. Rivers converge near the village where he lived, so he adopted the courtesy name Liantan [Clear Pond, lit. "a pond as clean as white silk"]. His father had four sons, and Mr. Cheng is the third. His two older brothers both made their fortunes as merchants. Mr. Cheng was clever as a child and had studied *The Classic of Changes* with learned elders of the clan. When he was about to complete his study, his father pressed him to become a merchant, saying, "It is not that I do not appreciate learning, but our family has many mouths to feed; why don't you assist your brothers in business and make some income to ease my burden? When your younger brother grows up, he may follow the path of becoming a scholar." So Mr. Cheng entered the salt business with his brothers in Huaiyang [the Yangzhou region of modern-day Jiangsu].[3] Soon he himself invested in lending businesses in places like Juqu and Zhongshan [both in the modern-day region of Nanjing, Jiangsu]. For about ten years, he was busy traveling around, north and south. In time, the business did well, with a return on his investment of several fold.

Mr. Cheng was good at sizing up situations. He was able to make adjustments according to local custom and to adapt to change over time. He never forced his will just to be frugal, nor did he own anything extravagant. All he had he shared with his brothers, and they turned everything over to their father. Mr. Cheng provided sweet and crisp seasonal foods to his parents and was never tiring in his service to them. When his parents and brothers died, his sorrow was devastating. On each occasion, he threw himself upon the body or the coffin, always demonstrating his grief with utmost sincerity. He raised and nurtured his brothers' orphans. From finding them good teachers to helping them marry, he put them ahead of his own sons.

Mr. Cheng was forgiving, kind, and loved to extend charity. He always had a broad mind. There was hardly any among his extended relatives who had not benefited from his generosity. When disputes among clansmen were brought to him, he would resolve them immediately. The clan used to have an ancestral shrine, but it did not include Mr. Gongyi, the branch ancestor of his own branch, so he built a special shrine dedicated to Mr. Gongyi. In addition, he thoroughly renovated the tomb of another ancestor, Mr. Yide, who was a Tribute Scholar in the Song dynasty. Never miserly, he paid for these projects out of his own pocket. His clansmen were grateful that he was so high-minded and asked to establish a stele in his honor. Mr. Cheng did not give them permission, saying, "I did not take these actions in order to gain a reputation." He once named the main room of his house Cultivating and Ordering. He explained that, as a commoner, one dares only to extend one's duty to "cultivating the self and ordering the household."[4] By then, his three sons were all being educated as scholars and had good reputations. He looked at them and said, "I like to see you working hard toward the goal I could not achieve; you youngsters strive for it."

There was a time when famine persisted for several years. Mr. Cheng opened his storehouse and issued a large quantity of grain to provide relief to the poor. Several times servants cooked fresh meat for him, but he waved them away, saying, "I cannot stand it that the cost of one meal for me is equal to the value of several lives of the poor."

From his youth, Mr. Cheng had been strong and had never been sick. In middle age, he repeatedly mourned the death of close relatives and cared for the survivors. This gradually wore him down and made him ill. In the last moments of his life, seeing that the clothing prepared for his burial was overly fine, he put on a serious face and said, "You three sons are too extravagant. Haven't you heard about the admonitions of [Confucius's disciple] Master Zeng? Your great-grandfather did not get such luxuries from your grandfather, and your grandfather did not get them from me and my brothers, so how can I feel comfortable getting them?" A friend responded, "Didn't *The Book of Rites* say that [the performance of appropriate] rituals must take into consideration the [available] means and the [suitable] time? This is the duty of a gentleman." At that, Mr. Cheng merely gave a slight nod. In tears, the three sons asked what last words he had for them, and he said, "Inscribe in your mind and heart the teachings of filial piety, friendliness, diligence, and frugality. That's all." After saying that, he expired. The time was the twelfth month of the *xuzi* year of the Wanli reign period [1588], fifty-eight years since his birth in the *xinmao* year of the Jiaqing reign period [1531].

His wife, surnamed Xiang, has womanly virtues. He had three sons, all registered students in the Imperial University: Yuanzheng was married to Madam Huang and [after Huang died] to Madam Wu; Yuanheng was married to Madam Dai; and Yuanren is engaged to Madam Wu. He had three grandsons and one granddaughter. His record of conduct was composed by Wu Zhiyu, instructor of the Southern Capital Region Confucian School. Wu Zhiyu is a trustworthy and cultured person, and a friend of mine. [The eldest son,] Yuanzheng, who came to ask for the funerary biography, is a refined and courteous gentleman. So I agreed to write this funerary biography with an elegy for Mr. Cheng.

The elegy reads:

Why was he called a "gentleman residing at home"?
Because he behaved like a gentleman.
He was a gentleman hiding in the occupation of a merchant.
Is there a precedent for this gentleman-cum-merchant?
The Grand Historian [Sima Qian, 140s–80s BCE] said,
"A merchant could have the righteousness of a gentleman residing at home and yet still enjoy abundance and prosperity."
Oh, well, who says mercantile wealth is always a detriment?

Source: Wang Shizhen, *Yanzhou shanren sibugao xugao* 弇州山人四部稿續稿, Siku quanshu edition, 122.4a–5a.

Notes

1. On the mixing of merchants and literati, see Yu Yingshi, "Business Culture and Chinese Traditions—toward a Study of the Evolvement of Merchant Culture in Chinese History," in *Dynamic Hongkong: Business and Culture,* edited by Wang Gungwu (Hong Kong: University of Hong Kong Center of Asian Studies, 1997); and Kai-Wing Chow, *Publishing, Culture, and Power in Late Imperial China: The Making of Early Modern Culture* (Stanford: Stanford University Press, 2004). For a critical review of the merchant-literati convergence thesis, see Antonia Finnane, *Speaking of Yangzhou: A Chinese City, 1550–1850* (Cambridge, MA: Harvard University Asia Center, 2004), 264.

2. Cheng Lingxi was a legendary figure in the local history of the region, who once organized and led a local militia to defend the community during the chaos that preceded the founding of the Tang dynasty. Later on, Cheng Lingxi became a local god worshiped by people in several counties of Huizhou Prefecture, including She and Xiuning.

3. Salt merchants, who operated with licenses from the government, could build huge fortunes, and among them the salt merchants of Yangzhou were especially famous for their wealth.

4. In distinction to scholars, whose duties included "running the government and bringing peace to the entire realm," according to *Great Learning,* one of the Four Books central to education in late imperial China.

Further Reading

Du, Yongtao. *The Order of Places: Translocal Practices of the Huizhou Merchants in Late Imperial China.* Leiden: Brill, 2015.

Finnane, Antonia. *Speaking of Yangzhou: A Chinese City, 1550–1850.* Cambridge, MA: Harvard University Press, 2004.

Guo, Qitao. *Ritual Opera and Mercantile Lineage: The Confucian Transformation of Popular Culture in Late Imperial Huizhou.* Stanford: Stanford University Press, 2005.

Lufrano, Richard J. *Honorable Merchants: Commerce and Self-Cultivation in Late Imperial China.* Honolulu: University of Hawai'i Press, 1997.

A Ming General Turned Warlord

Funerary Inscription for Military Officer Mao
(Mao Wenlong 毛文龍, 1579–1629), by Mao Qiling
毛奇齡 (1623–1716)

TRANSLATED BY XING HANG

This funerary inscription provides an intimate and personal snapshot of the early stages of the dynastic transition from Ming to Qing rule. The career of a military officer in the porous region of Northeast Asia reveals the simultaneous flexibility and rigidity of the Ming political and military system during its final decades.

THE MILITARY SYSTEM OF THE MING DYNASTY INITIALLY RELIED on a hereditary population of soldier-farmers. Specialized military households would supply soldiers in rotation and support their needs by means of state-assigned agricultural lands. A network of garrisons would oversee and train them to maintain a general level of military readiness. By the early seventeenth century, however, the system had broken down as military affairs came under the increasingly strict oversight of civil officials. In this climate, society held soldiers in contempt. Even high-ranking military commanders were forced to kneel and endure abuse at the hands of haughty civil authorities. Stigmatized and demoralized, many soldiers of the hereditary households chose to abscond from their specialized settlements or contrive ways to take their property off of the official registers.

Even as the traditional military structure collapsed, the Ming experienced a military revolution that involved the importation and adaptation of European muskets, cannons, and fortresses, and the development of new battle formations and siege tactics. The new modes of warfare drastically increased the cost, deadliness, and organizational demands of warfare. The court, lacking the motivation and means to maintain a permanent standing army, opted instead for the expediency of authorizing field commanders to recruit and outfit units with their own resources on an ad hoc basis. This measure allowed the Ming to achieve significant successes in eradicating piracy on the southeastern coast and repelling the Japanese invasion of Korea in 1592. However, many of the units would later transform into fully fledged private armies, and their commanders would become semi-autonomous warlords.

The career trajectory of Mao Wenlong (1579–1629), the subject of the inscription below, reflects the intensified pace of militarization and privatization during the final years of Ming rule. The early decades of the seventeenth century witnessed a severe breakdown in the flourishing commercial economy, characterized by monetary deflation, famines, and food shortages that hampered effective governance by the court. As a result, peasant rebellions rocked the country. At the same time, the Jurchens, a group of semi-agriculturalist hunter-gatherers on the Northeast Asian frontier of Manchuria, united under the ambitious chieftain Nurhaci (1559–1626, r. 1616–1626). They soon grew into a formidable power, subjugating Mongol tribes and seizing most of Liaodong, a forward base for the Ming and the densest concentration of Han in Manchuria. The Pass of the Mountains and the Sea, where the Great Wall meets the Bohai Sea, was the last major defensive barrier that separated this northeastern frontier from north China and the capital at Beijing. The Jurchens, known as the Manchus after 1635, would go on to seize the city in 1644 and establish it as the seat of their new Qing state, China's last imperial dynasty.

The Ming court, pressed by domestic and external military threats and straitened financial circumstances, resorted to the time-tested expediency of deputizing commanders to raise their own forces. This practice, in turn, provided unprecedented opportunities for mobility outside of the civil service examinations, the traditional avenue of advancement in late imperial China. As his funerary inscription reveals, Mao Wenlong, orphaned at a young age, detested studying the Confucian classics in preparation for the examinations and killing time gambling. His real passion lay in military strategy and adventures into the frontier. With the support of the Liaodong grand coordinator, Mao was able to recruit his own troops and forge a base on Pi Island in the Yellow Sea off the coast of Korea. Between 1621 and 1629, his private army, the Dongjiang Garrison, controlled the waters around Manchuria as a virtually independent power.

For a while, Mao's hegemony managed to check and even turn back the Jurchen advance. He even managed to secure defections from Nurhaci's ranks, including a highly prominent commander named Liu Aita (or Liu Xingzuo, d. 1630), who would remain loyal to him until the very end. The success of Mao's garrison owed much to its ideal geographic location. The porous maritime boundary between Manchuria and Korea provided a strategic lifeline for his forces to obtain necessary supplies and provisions. The Joseon dynasty (1392–1910) had always maintained a close tributary relationship with the Ming and had a similar form of government based on shared Neo-Confucian ideals. Those ties had grown even closer when Chinese forces aided the Koreans in repelling Japan's invasion of the peninsula in 1592. The rise to power of a staunchly pro-Ming faction in the Joseon court in 1623 caused it to adopt a hostile policy toward the Jurchens. The Koreans thus worked actively with Mao Wenlong and provided generous assistance in food and provisions. Another source of Mao's income came from the lucrative profits raked in through his participation in the robust East Asian trading network that connected the Chinese coast with Japan and Southeast Asia. A similar set of factors had facilitated the rise of warlordism in other restless frontiers of the troubled empire. The most prominent of them was the pirate-turned-merchant mogul and Ming commander Zheng Zhilong (b. 1661) in coastal Fujian.

The emergence of men like Mao and Zheng reveals the simultaneous flexibility and rigidity of the Ming system. The court proved capable of employing the services and even commanding the loyalty of semi-autonomous actors in order to achieve pressing aims, such as fighting piracy or repelling the Manchus, that it had been unable to handle with only its own resources. However, such an arrangement fueled intense conflict with the established Ming practice of civilian control over military affairs. Once someone like Mao Wenlong grew powerful enough, the fear of internal subversion equaled or even exceeded concerns over external threats.

This inherent contradiction would spell the doom of the Dongjiang Garrison and its commander after Mao came into direct confrontation with Yuan Chonghuan (1584–1630), appointed by the court to command all the Ming regular forces in Liaodong in 1626. That year, Yuan won a decisive victory over Nurhaci at Ningyuan, the Jurchen leader's first and only major defeat. Nurhaci would perish of wounds inflicted in this battle several months later. It was this victory, according to the inscription, that caused Yuan to grow arrogant and overconfident in his ability to retake Liaodong through his own efforts. He came to view Mao Wenlong with intense jealousy as a competitor who stood in the way of his path to glory. However, the inscription claims that Mao played a crucial role in deterring the Jurchens from concentrating their entire manpower on Yuan's forces. Instead of working together with him, Yuan, with the full support of officials at the court, ordered the size of the Dongjiang Garrison to be drastically cut to 28,000 men from a peak of several hundred thousand soldiers. He further placed tight restrictions on the flow of supplies and provisions to the islands under Mao's control. Finally, in 1629, he paid a personal visit to Mao and surrounded his garrison with troops. Yuan then had Mao executed on the spot. Without a strong and unifying leader like Mao, the garrison soon dissolved. Many of his former subordinates, such as Kong Youde (ca. 1602–1652) and Shang Kexi (1604–1676), surrendered to the Jurchens. They would later play an instrumental role in the early Qing occupation and consolidation of China.

Ironically, Yuan Chonghuan would soon encounter a similar fate. In 1629, Jurchen forces under Nurhaci's son and successor, Hong Taiji (1592–1643, r. 1626–1643), launched a surprise offensive on Beijing. Although Yuan's troops repelled the Jurchens, he was severely criticized for his handling of the campaign, with some court officials and eunuchs even accusing him of collusion with the enemy. A year later, the Chongzhen emperor (1611–1644, r. 1627–1644), who had newly ascended the throne, ordered Yuan to undergo a slow and painful execution by slicing. Yuan's demise was especially ironic because he, like Mao Wenlong, fell victim to the wide gulf of distrust that had developed between civil and military officials over the course of the Ming.

The Ming, too, would perish at the hands of peasant rebels in 1644. By then, Hong Taiji had given his Jurchen people the new ethnic label of Manchu and proclaimed himself the emperor of a Chinese-style Qing dynasty. Although he passed away in 1643, the solid institutions and bureaucracy that he established laid the foundations for the Manchus to take advantage of the disorder in China to occupy the former Ming realm. In many ways, the inscription below provides an intimate and personal snapshot of the early stages of this dynastic transition from Ming to Qing rule.

The funerary inscription of Mao Wenlong is typical of those produced over the imperial period in China. Such inscriptions were largely composed of words of praise that aim to portray the individual according to an idealized Confucian archetype, which, in the case of Mao, was that of the loyal and wronged minister. A prominent member of the literati elite who enjoyed considerable standing in his community but often did not know the subject personally would be invited to write the epitaph. The author of Mao Wenlong's funerary inscription, Mao Qiling (1623–1716; also the author of Selection 20), was a poet, writer, and artist. He hailed from Wenlong's hometown of Hangzhou and shared his surname. He initially joined the Ming loyalist resistance against the Manchus, but, after it was largely crushed during the 1660s, he served the Qing as a Hanlin Academician and participated in the initial drafting of *The History of the Ming Dynasty*. What stands out about his eulogy for Mao Wenlong is his sensitivity to the political situation, especially since he had to pay homage to an enemy of the current dynasty. Mao Qiling was thus careful to avoid negative references to the general's Jurchen adversaries, referring to them using the anachronism "Great Qing," a dynastic title that did not come into being until 1636, well after the events described had occurred.

Funerary Inscription for Military Officer Mao

The son of the general Mao Wenlong, Chenglu, could not escape the negative impact of his father's wrongful death. During that time, the trees had withered and everything was in a hurried and unsettled state. Therefore, Chenglu was not able to make proper arrangements to lay his father to rest. The Great Qing had grown powerful, and the commanders and officials formerly under Wenlong played meritorious roles in founding and establishing the state. Kong Youde, the Prince Who Stabilizes the South, was assigned to garrison Guangxi. While passing through Hangzhou, he searched for the general's son, but his efforts came to naught. The general's old residence, three rooms in all, had already changed ownership. Prince Kong left, sobbing. Some of Mao Wenlong's other subordinates and officials who have since received honors and titles from the imperial court also passed through Zhejiang on their way to Guangdong and Guangxi, in the far south. An old lieutenant discovered the whereabouts of the general's son and later visited him, bestowing lavish gifts upon him. The officer then solemnly wept as he paid his respects to the general. He blamed himself for not having given Wenlong a proper burial, with the result that his remains continued to float around in the sea. After discussions with Prince Kong Who Stabilizes the South, the two men decided to bury the general's cap and gown at Lingfeng Village [near Hangzhou], where a tablet was erected. Since General Mao and I both trace our roots to the Ji clan,[1] I was entrusted with the writing of his epitaph.

Previously, I had heard conflicting views regarding the general's behavior during the former [Ming] dynasty. Time and again, he went against the current [Qing] dynasty in his attitude and actions. His misdeeds are certainly not worth recording. Besides, *The Great Qing Veritable Records* have not yet been promulgated, so his legacy is not officially set in stone. How dare I advance my own interpretations prematurely? Yet, for ages people have kept both historical records and clan biographies even though they disagreed with each other. Moreover, officials and commoners all have achievements worthy of being etched in stone to record and commemorate their lives. If records of the general's deeds perished, and no one memorialized the court on his behalf, where is justice and moral principle? Therefore, I record this inscription based on the record of conduct (*xingzhuang*) that circulated during his time. I would rather let my narrative err on the side of not being useful in order to record, albeit briefly, his innocence, which should benefit his wrongly accused clan.

According to the record of conduct, the general's surname is Mao, with a taboo name of Wenlong and a courtesy name of Zhennan. He was a native of Hangzhou. Having lost his father as a boy, he followed his mother to live in the home of his maternal uncle, Shen Guangzuo. Shen had passed the civil service examination of 1595 and received a Presented Scholar (*jinshi*) degree. He served as the provincial administration commissioner of Shandong. From a young age, General Mao went to school, but he disliked reading books in preparation for a career as a civil official and thought of dropping out. When, on one occasion, a guest commented on Sunzi's *Art of War*, he asked for a copy of the book and proceeded to scrutinize it carefully. All of a sudden, his mind opened. He soon surprised Shen Guangzuo with his knowledge of military affairs. While Shen Guangzuo was serving in Shandong, Mao Wenlong gambled and accumulated debts, so he had to hide in his uncle's office. When, out of boredom, he would listen to the urgent news coming from the frontier, he felt a sense of helplessness. Once, he secretly journeyed to the Pass of the Mountains and the Sea [Shanhaiguan, Hebei] and Ningyuan [Liaoning], and surveyed the layout of the mountains and the rivers.[2] He patted his leg and sighed, but in the end he could do nothing. Wang Huazhen [d. 1632], the grand coordinator of Liaodong [Liaoning], was a native of Shandong and a good friend of Shen Guangzuo. Before leaving to assume his post, he called on Shen to ask for advice. Shen said:

> For my whole life, I have never studied military matters. How dare I speak lightly about them? But my sister's son, Mao Wenlong, is a rare genius, who is fervent and capable of strategic thinking. He has been following current affairs in Liaodong with great concern for some time. See if you could give him

some troops to lead. He will certainly serve the country with success and earn fame and rank for himself. However, if you put him under the command of your other officers, then Mao Wenlong certainly will not be able to show his full talents.

Wang Huazhen agreed and posted a formal summons on General Mao's door [to recruit officers]. On a date planned in advance, he selected ten men and hosted them at a banquet. He assigned each of them to the post of military commissioner, with General Mao receiving the highest rank. As Mao Wenlong prepared to set out amid the sound of drums and flutes, Wang Huazhen gave him flowers, personally changed his clothes, and helped him onto his horse. Deeply moved, General Mao wept and kowtowed. Breaking apart the leather belt of his new outfit, he swore: "If I refuse to give my life for the sake of this country, may I end up just like this belt!"

By this time, Liaodong had completely fallen [to the Jurchens]. The troops of the Great Qing were seizing a hundred villages a day. [The successful offensive brought Jurchen forces to the gates of Beijing. At this moment of desperation, several officials raised the idea of occupying and fortifying island outposts off the coast of Korea to use as bases for reconnaissance operations and for striking the enemy's rear, thereby halting their advance or even causing them to turn back. Wang Huazhen accepted the proposal.]

Accordingly, General Mao was dispatched to Dengzhou and Laizhou [both in Shandong], and he secretly ensconced himself on the islands. He was given the title of Mobile Corps Commander Who Trains Troops and was allowed to decide military maneuvers on his own accord. He surveyed the coastline and established a naval camp. He recruited strong and brave men to serve as sailors and to assist and reinforce the Liaodong naval forces. At night, the troops entered the island of Lianyun [near Dalian, Liaoning], under the jurisdiction of Gaizhou [Liaoning]. Gaizhou, Haizhou, and Jinzhou [part of present-day Dalian] are all strategically important crossroads of Liaodong. Because Yang Yuwei, the Great Qing's brigade commander of Gaizhou, and Shan Jinzhong, patroller of Fuzhou, were both Liaodong natives, General Mao secretly communicated with them. With their connivance, he could seize and occupy Lianyun. He then proceeded to launch an attack on Boar Island [in the Bohai Sea, northwest of Dalian]. At the time, heavy gales prevented his men from advancing. A private vessel floated past Boar Island occupied by Li Jingxian, who had come to seek refuge there. A native of Deer Island [to the southeast of Dalian in the Yellow Sea], he knew much about the state of the defenses there. General Mao hastily led his troops to attack Deer Island and killed the official in charge, Hu Kebin. Nearby Jidian, Shicheng, and all the other islands were seized one after the other. General Mao captured the soldiers on the islands and their flat-bottomed junks, Liao ships, and wave-stabilizing junks. He soon attracted and settled tens of thousands of migrants in his maritime bastion. Then his troops searched and destroyed the Qing generals and soldiers on the upper and lower reaches of Zhenjiang [Dandong, Liaoning, on the border with modern North Korea].

At the time, the Great Qing forces were powerful and flourishing. They rolled over everything in their path. The supreme commander of Jiliao [Tianjin and Liaodong], Xue Guoyong [1573–1621], commented that "the Ming won no victories, whereas the Great Qing suffered no defeats." Only after General Mao took charge did the reputation of the Ming forces slightly improve. Yet, because his base was remote and his troops few, he ultimately could not maintain his resistance. The Great Qing forces, thirsting for revenge for their earlier defeat, sought to recapture Zhenjiang. Realizing that he was stretched thin, General Mao appealed for reinforcements, but none were authorized. He then requested soldiers from Korea but waited in vain for a reply. The assistant regional commanders under him had to defend the islands, and he did not dare to budge an inch from them. The supervising secretaries of the Office of Scrutiny for War, Cai Sichong [1559–1642] and Zhang Heming [1551–1635], called for reinforcements on the grounds that General Mao's army was isolated. But the court refused.

General Mao realized that he was in a disadvantageous position. Since he was unable to advance farther, there was no benefit to the continued defense of Zhenjiang. Therefore, he opened up the island of

Pi, known as Dongjiang at the time. He recruited strong and brave warriors and welcomed displaced refugees, the total reaching hundreds of thousands. Dongjiang bordered Korea to the east. To the south were hundreds of islands, the largest of them being Boar Island, Mustang Island, the Larger and Smaller Long Mountains, and others. They connected to Dengzhou [Shandong], with all the strategic points defended by troops. It was only 40 *li* [20 km] northwest to the mainland and just over 300 *li* [160 km] to Shenyang. General Mao sent his cavalry in all directions to await the arrival of the Great Qing forces. Regardless of size, if his men could attack, they would. If they could not, then they would board their ships and head back to Pi Island. Few of the Great Qing troops were familiar with the currents, and their weapons and ships were not comparable. In no time, the ranks of the Qing soldiers would fall into disorder on the sea. General Mao would take these opportunities to attack them. As soon as they saw an inkling of his nearby stockades, the Qing troops would be warned not to go west. If they went west, they would be taken prisoner. Therefore, the Great Qing forces placed tremendous importance on containing General Mao's activities. Once they had done so, they recaptured Zhenjiang, and General Mao did not dare confront them. Xiong Tingbi [1569–1625, the Liaodong regional inspector] was overjoyed when he heard the news and said that the fall of the garrison proved him right. Although contained militarily, General Mao continued plotting ways to launch an offensive and break through the enemy lines.

For their part, the officials in charge of defending the Pass of the Mountains and the Sea and Ningyuan disliked the pressure caused by the containment. They thought that the forces of the Great Qing should be easy to handle and had no particular strengths. Seeing that the Great Qing armies were not advancing farther, they started to comment negatively about the way General Mao handled the situation in Dongjiang, saying that, if General Mao continued to act arrogantly and his powers remained unchecked, he would become a threat in the future. Also, there was a famine at the time, and, since the state refused to provide funds from its coffers, the soldiers on the island experienced an acute shortage of funds. Dongjiang was then separated from Guanning [the garrison in charge of Ningyuan and the Pass of the Mountains and the Sea] to form its own command. Those who wished to slander the Dongjiang command clamored for cutting funds to the garrison and downsizing its troops. After a while, they also started calling for the removal of the commander himself, General Mao. They hated him to the point that they would not stop until they got him removed. They did not comprehend that the Guanning and Dongjiang Garrisons were able to survive for eight years precisely because of him.

Initially, when all the islands had no troops, the Great Qing army saw no sufficient reason to worry about the four Ming transport commands. Then, when General Mao undertook a reconnaissance mission with heavy forces toward the east, the Great Qing army realized that Lüshun [part of present-day Dalian] constituted the gateway to the southern transport command. Jinzhou stood in the middle, commanding the four garrisons and also putting pressure on Lüshun. Accordingly, the Great Qing troops were sent to sack Jinzhou [Liaoning] and cut off the pathway to Lüshun. After all, this stranger, Mao Wenlong, who sleeps soundly on the side of our territory was a threat and had to be uprooted and removed. Once, during a night when the water around Pi Island had frozen over, the Great Qing troops made secret plans to sneak across and attack. But word of the scheme soon reached General Mao. He proceeded, in advance, to chop up the ice. Although the ice would later freeze together again, it would become far more fragile, which nobody would expect. At dusk, rain mixed with snow accumulated in large amounts on the ground. The Great Qing troops saw their chance and started crossing. Halfway through, the soldiers on Pi Island beat their drums and bells and shouted at the top of their voices. Horses and humans within the Qing ranks stepped on each other, and over half of them sank into the sea. From then on, the Qing soldiers told each other to refrain from crossing over to the island.

At the time when Emperor Zhuanglie [the Chongzhen emperor] ascended the throne, there was a shortage of military provisions. There was talk of reducing the forces on the islands. Previously, during the final years of the Tianqi reign [1621–1627], the Hanlin Academician Jiang Yueguang [1584–1649] and Wang Mengyin, a supervising secretary of the Office of Scrutiny for War, were dispatched to the islands to inspect the troops. They purposely underreported the total number of the garrison by over one hundred thousand. The general had to make up the deficit of provisions and supplies for these men through opening markets and engaging in maritime trade. But his troops still numbered over a hundred thousand. Now, the investigating censor Wang Tingshi, acting on instructions from officials in the Grand Secretariat, ordered a drastic reduction of troop numbers down to 28,000 men. The soldiers met the news with shock and disbelief. The people on the islands gathered together and wailed loudly. Gradually, some came forward to propose a mutiny. Only after General Mao beheaded two of his officers did a semblance of calm return. Incrementally, he demobilized the surrendered soldiers, and destitute refugees left, across the seas, one after another. The islands were in an uproar.

By that time, Mao Wenlong had already received the rank of regional commander and carried the seal of a general. He had been given a sword and enjoyed the privilege of executing on the spot. Yet, even these honors proved insufficient to deter the crisis. His memorials were not accepted. Additionally, Yuan Chonghuan, the commissioner-in-chief of the armed forces, intended to confiscate the supplies and provisions for Mao Wenlong's 28,000 men to compensate for the extra number of recipients in prior years. Yuan Chonghuan also issued regulations mandating that henceforth the food and weapons of the Dongjiang soldiers would all be transported from the gate of the Pass of the Mountains and the Sea. At Juehua Island [off the southeastern coast of Liaoning], they would be loaded onto ships and delivered to Dongjiang via Lüshun. Grain shipped from Tianjin would have to arrive at Juehua Island via Jinghai [Weihai, Shandong]. Shipments that did not bear the registration of the commissioner-in-chief's office were forbidden from exiting the gate.

Mao Wenlong at one point memorialized the court:

In transporting provisions and supplies, there are complicated and straightforward paths. It is convenient and easy to go from Dengzhou to Lüshun. The route from the gate of the pass to

Lüshun is convoluted and difficult. Everybody knows this. The intention of the commissioner-in-chief is nothing more than to place me entirely under his control. But he does not understand the unsustainable and impracticable nature of certain courses of action. I only need to speak of the winds. Because there is a southwesterly that blows for half a day from Dengzhou to Lüshun, shipments can arrive early. Yet there are still occasions when our soldiers feel that they take too long to arrive. Why is that? People eat during the morning and get hungry in the evening; they cannot wait. If the supplies and provisions arrive from the gate of the pass, however, they must first catch the westerly for two days to get from the Niutou River [in Shandong] to the Changshan Islands [off present-day Yantai, Shandong]. Then, a southwesterly for half a day is needed to reach Juehua Island. Subsequently, the shipment must catch a northwesterly for one day and one night to arrive at the Northern River Checkpoint. Another westerly for half a day would blow toward the Southern River Checkpoint. From there, a northwesterly for a day would allow the shipment to arrive at Talian Island [off Dalian]. After one more southerly lasting for half a day, Lüshun can finally be reached.

Ships sail on water. They cannot jump from one shore to another. Furthermore, there are no ways to force wind to blow east in the morning and west at dusk. As a result, there are very few shipments every year, and for men who normally grow impatient for their meals to wait for their food is equivalent to killing them. The transport route from Tianjin to Lüshun is also fundamentally convoluted. In each of the previous years, only six or seven out of ten shipments arrived, with the rest either wrecked or sunk. Since I understand the situation, I have no choice but to frankly report the matter. The transport routes are already making things highly difficult. Any further restrictions will harm the fate of the garrison. If shipments must go through Juehua Island, they then must register at Ningyuan. The farther the route, the greater the wastage and loss. By the time they reach the garrison, the provisions will have been reduced to nothing.

Before the general sent this memorial, Qian Xilong, an official of the Grand Secretariat, had already come to loathe the general. Every time he visited Yuan Chonghuan's residence, he secretly ill-mouthed Mao Wenlong. Qian Xilong asked, "Who can get rid of the man on Dongjiang?" Yuan Chonghuan replied, "I can do it." At the time, Yuan was the intendant for the Ningyuan and Jinzhou Circuit. He subsequently received a promotion to commissioner-in-chief. In recalling Mao's words, Yuan deeply resented his lack of propriety. Yuan remarked on one occasion, "Huh! How can Mao behave like this?"

Ming custom looked down on military men. If someone received military training and intended to become a soldier, even his relatives despised him. Although military men could rise to the rank of commander and take charge of five prefectures, they must bow before a county magistrate and shower him with gifts. The magistrate would act arrogantly when receiving military men. When it was time for the magistrate to pay back the visit, he often just sent his calling card carried by a petty official and would not pay a personal visit. When visiting the Board of Military Affairs, regardless of the rank of civil officials in the hall, all military men beneath the rank of commander had to take off their cloaks and kneel. When taking leave, they had to maneuver their knees in the manner of a snake, while saying, "If you have anything to request from me, I will certainly fulfill it." Whenever a situation arose, they could not lead troops on their own without being an official at or above the rank of the five prefectures. Even if they led forces, civil officials had to supervise them. Because only one surveillance commissioner was assigned to a unit, the military men had to present themselves daily at his office to acquire permission for their actions. If he said, "Don't move!" then, even if there were a million soldiers on the field, they dared not move. Therefore, despite there being plenty of soldiers, from the imperial bodyguard to the frontier troops as well as the guards, none of them could function independently.

General Mao alone stood out for his pride and arrogance. Wherever he went, he refused to yield. He did not mind defying even his own supervisors. All of the officials at the court were in shock. They wondered what had allowed this practice of strict civilian supervision over the military that had worked for three hundred years to break down suddenly in one day. At this time, Zhou Xigui and Wang Zizhi, two guests at Yuan Chonghuan's residence, planned to return to their hometown. They volunteered to travel to Dongjiang to survey its terrain and layout. They hoped that, by presenting themselves before Mao Wenlong as protégés of the commissioner-in-chief, they could expect rich bribes. When they arrived, Mao Wenlong served sweet wine for them to savor but did not provide any meat. The gifts they received merely consisted of some goblets and silk. Filled with extreme anger and hatred, they reported to Yuan Chonghuan that Mao Wenlong held the commissioner-in-chief in contempt. They spoke about Mao Wenlong in secret for an entire day and night before leaving. During that time, Yuan Chonghuan saw himself as a commander of great genius and capability who could win victories. Meanwhile, the Great Qing forces rested and did not launch any particular offensive, so they let Yuan Chonghuan have his way to a certain extent. Yuan grew overconfident and claimed he could manage matters in the east on his own. The Dongjiang Garrison, the final obstacle to his complete success, had to be uprooted. This is just like when one has a deep-rooted ulcer: one not only treats it with acupuncture, but also should follow up by using a decoction of herbal medicine. Those who do not understand the nature of the disease may recklessly doubt the usefulness of the latter. They would only use acupuncture but not the decoction. As a result, the ulcer comes back, and the patient becomes incurable.

Liu Aita [d. 1630] was a man of Liaodong who was captured by the Great Qing army at the age of twelve. He grew up to be brave and ferocious. His younger brothers, Xingzhi [d. 1631] and Xingxian [fl. 1631], were also in the army. Emperor Taizu of the Great Qing [the posthumous title of Nurhaci] highly esteemed him and bestowed upon him the name of Aita. Aita had the additional meaning in Chinese of "loving him." At the time, Aita served as the commander in charge of Jinzhou's defense. General Mao plotted to communicate with him. Wang Bing, the commander of Fuzhou [now part of Dalian], discovered Aita's intention to rebel. The attitude of the emperor changed, and Aita almost lost his life. At this moment, a group of people came to his rescue, accusing Wang Bing of slandering Aita out of personal hatred, and called instead for Wang Bing's execution. As a result, Aita was released without further questioning. Aita then sent his younger brothers to join the Dongjiang Garrison. He clothed a corpse with his garments and burned the corpse's face [to fake his own death]. He then sneaked away to Gaizhou during the night. He picked up his four hundred soldiers and four hundred horses and led them to Lüshun. From there, General Mao welcomed them to the islands. Soon afterward, with Aita acting as a guide, Mao Wenlong's forces landed on the shore of Gaizhou and slaughtered two thousand men. Accordingly, Aita received the title of Bright and Brave General. Yuan Chonghuan was greatly incensed when he learned that Aita had not gone to his headquarters but instead surrendered directly to the Dongjiang Garrison. Yuan repeatedly sent people to invite Aita, but he did not go. Yuan then asked General Mao to hand over Aita, but Mao did not send Aita to Yuan either. Yuan's houseguest Zhou Xigui personally visited Aita on the islands and even tried to entice him with offers of a rank of nobility, but still the offer was declined.

At the time, Emperor Taizu of the Great Qing visited a hot spring. When Aita got word of it, he advised the general to set up a trap. They were about to proceed with the plan, but then the emperor died, so they did not dare attack. After Emperor Taizu died, Yuan Chonghuan dispatched a Tibetan monk to offer condolences. Meanwhile, General Mao sent a memorial to the [Ming] imperial court in the name of Aita, mentioning that he together with Aita would plot the recovery of Liaodong and penetrate the Pass of the Five Mountains. Filled with tremendous hatred and jealousy, Yuan memorialized the court in the fifth month of the second year of the Chongzhen reign period [1629]. He requested permission to visit the Dongjiang Garrison in person and discuss the offensive. An edict commanded him to join Mao Wenlong and Aita. Coincidentally, Yuan had left his sword and seal of authority at his Ningqian Circuit office [responsible for the defense of the Pass of the Mountains and the Sea]. Therefore, he again made a request to take along his sword and seal. His memorial read: "The house guest of your minister, Zhou Xigui, said that by grace of Your Majesty's splendor, the Dongjiang Garrison would surely undergo a rejuvenation of its strength and confidence. May all its decision-making authority at the Ningqian Circuit be delegated to Zhao Shuaijiao [1569–1629], with Zu Dashou [d. 1656] assisting him." He then requested 100,000 piculs [six million kilograms] of provisions and had them carried along to give to the Dongjiang soldiers. He selected two hundred particularly brave and ferocious officers and soldiers. They boarded ships and sailed to the Twin Islands [located southwest of Dalian on the Bohai Sea] from Lüshun.

The Lüshun brigade commander, Mao Yongyi, welcomed them with his troops. Yuan Chonghuan stepped onto the island and paid respects at the Shrine of the Dragon King. He summoned Mao Yongyi and his company and proclaimed, "When our dynasty was established and pacified, the Prince of Zhongshan, Xu Da [1332–1385], combined infantry and naval forces. As a result, he could capture Caishi [Anhui] and battle on Lake Boyang [Jiangxi]. With these deeds, it is said that one could traverse the desert and still not flinch. Today, I would also like to let all the Dongjiang officers and men serve the Ningqian Circuit [thus combining the land and sea forces]. How about that?"

Some among the crowd agreed, but others disagreed. Yuan Chonghuan threatened the naysayers with death but then released them. He told them: "In the past, no rationale existed for rejecting the words of the commander-in-chief. All of you have long forgotten the rules! So I am here to teach you." Only then did the crowd agree. Then, the general arrived and bowed to Yuan Chonghuan, who returned the greeting. Yuan personally reported to General Mao's tent and borrowed a tent for himself. He found a space on the island to pitch it. He served up wine and invited General Mao over for drinks, using the opportunity to speak about official business. Yuan said, "This matter depends on the two of us. We must be of one heart and act together. Today I come with the intention to survey the overall conditions of Dongjiang. Because of the gap of mistrust between us, I did not hesitate to humble myself and seek you, general, in order to achieve great feats with you." General Mao, weeping, replied, "I have been out on the seas for eight years. Although I am in want of little, if we continue to be deprived of horses and weapons, I am afraid that empty bellies and bare hands cannot accomplish anything. What can we do?" Yuan said, "The provisions will arrive afterwards, so you do not need to worry about hunger." At this time, Yuan demonstrated great propriety and respect, and the tone of his words was agreeable. They spoke privately into the night. It was not until after 9:00 p.m. that they exited the tent.

Thereupon, General Mao set up a banquet for the Dongjiang officers and soldiers as well as the surrendered men and those who came to greet him. Everybody received a token of appreciation. When they started drinking, a soldier serving wine stood up with a knife. Yuan shouted angrily and ordered him to withdraw. As they enjoyed their wine, Yuan brought up four proposals: (1) moving the garrison, (2) establishing rules for the camp, (3) setting up circuits and departments, and (4) separating Lüshun into eastern and western commands. Lüshun East would come under the authority of the regional commander, whereas Lüshun West would fall under the jurisdiction of the commissioner-in-chief. General Mao refused to agree to any of them. Then, Yuan Chonghuan provided 100,000 piculs [six million kilograms] of provisions and feasted the Dongjiang officers. At dusk, he called on Wang Zhu, a vice-general of the Ningqian Circuit, and spoke with him until midnight.

During the next morning's archery competition, Yuan Chonghuan told General Mao, "I will return to Ningqian. The security of the country's outer seas heavily relies on you, General. Please accept my respectful bow." As they took their leave, Vice-General Wang Zhu and Assistant Regional Commander Xie Shangzheng secretly ordered the commissioner-in-chief's forces to form four rings, thereby completely surrounding Mao Wenlong. He and his accompanying Dongjiang officers were blocked within the innermost ring. His soldiers were kept outside the rings and not allowed to go near their superiors. Yuan Chonghuan then inquired after the surnames of Mao Wenlong's accompanying officers. "Mao," they replied. Yuan said, "How can all you officers have only one surname? This is illegal." He then called for them to come before him and said,

You are all the cream of the crop who have served this country for a long time. Even if you do not have the surname of Mao, how can the country forget to reward your efforts? Now, you are out on the sea and have to undertake many times the labor and hardship as those on land. And your food and salaries have been reduced by the Ningqian Circuit. It pains me. I will memorialize and petition for an increase in your rations. At the moment, I have nothing to reward you with. Please accept my respectful bow.

The crowd of accompanying officers bowed back.

Yuan Chonghuan now took advantage of this opportunity to spell out the general's crimes. He continued to speak of nothing else but the four matters discussed earlier. Then he shouted sternly, "Your parochial arrogance, on par with the Marquis of Yelang, has gone on long enough already.[3] After I kill you, if I cannot recover the land of Liao to repay you, then I, too, will use a sword to kill myself on another day." He then turned to Mao Wenlong's accompanying officers and said, "This edict is confidential and does not apply to any of you. Do not fear." He then asked for the imperially bestowed sword to behead Mao Wenlong. General Mao said not a word as he met his death.

Mao's soldiers began to bicker and rise up, but when they viewed the majestic stateliness of the commander-in-chief and further suspected that a secret imperial edict had been issued, they dared not advance. Yuan Chonghuan wept and conducted a funeral ceremony. He broke apart a horse shed to serve as a coffin. Then, he dressed the body and placed it inside. Yuan delegated the affairs of Dongjiang to Liu Xingzuo, who, weeping, refused. Yuan then divided the garrison into four joint commands, with Liu Xingzuo as one commander and the general's son, Mao Chenglu, as another. The other two were Xu Fuzou, the signal bearer, and Vice-General Chen Jisheng. Liu Xingzuo was in fact Aita's original name. This took place on the fifth day of the sixth month [1629]. Then, the officers of Dongjiang got together and wept. They wanted to chase down and kill Yuan Chonghuan, but Mao Chenglu steadfastly stopped them. That evening, a huge star was seen falling into the sea, accompanied by a flash of light and a thunderous sound. The spectacle lasted for a long time. Witnessing this, everyone sighed, "The general has died. It is the will of Heaven." Everybody soon scattered. Kong Youde, Shang Kexi, and Geng Zhongming [d. 1649] all surrendered to the current dynasty. They later stayed at the emperor's side and were enfeoffed as nonimperial princes. They were known as the Three Princes. Only Aita exclaimed, "I will not follow you [and betray the general]." He then fled to some other islands with his brothers. No supreme commander was appointed to replace Mao Wenlong, and no military encampment was established after him. With all of the islands left neglected in the middle of the sea, the Dongjiang Garrison had effectively perished.

General Mao cut a handsome figure with a flowing beard. His face had pockmarks and was blackened and crinkled. He walked like a tiger, standing at five *chi* nine *cun* tall [1.97 meters]. His household was impoverished and did not make a livelihood as ordinary men did. While on the islands, he traded daily goods from Korea, Siam, and Japan to support his forces. The 100,000 ounces of silver income each month entirely went to provide for the military and to accommodate visitors. On the day of his death, he had no surplus money left in his room.

Before Aita fled, he paid his respects to General Mao, saying, "I will not let Yuan Chonghuan survive on his own and therefore let you down, General." Later, when the emperor did, in fact, order Yuan Chonghuan torn apart from limb to limb, Aita said, "My will has been fulfilled!" At the time, Sun Chengzong [1563–1638], an official of the Grand Secretariat, succeeded Yuan in taking charge of defending the Pass of the Mountains and the Sea. Sun was happy to have the service of Aita and would pat his back and say to him, "You are a righteous official who can certainly achieve success and fame in serving the country." Sun took off his own sash and gave it to Aita. Aita set up a military colony at Yongping [on the border between present-day Liaoning and Hebei]. Afterward, Circuit Intendant Zheng Guochang [d. 1630] moved Aita to Jianchang [in Liaoning]. Aita encountered the Great Qing forces at Maotou'er [Liaoning]. He ordered all of his generals to lie in ambush in three places. He then personally selected eight hundred men to directly confront the enemy at night. He secretly replaced the Ming banners with those of the Great Qing. Moreover, he knew the Manchu language and code words. Since it was pitch black and nobody could see each other, Aita crushed one force and took several hundred heads. When dawn finally cracked through the skies, the great cavalry of the Qing arrived and joined the battle, causing the trap to fail. Aita was hit by a stray arrow and perished. Liu Xingxian surrendered, and his brother Xingzhi returned to the islands. The commanders on the islands suspected that, because Liu Xingxian had defected, his brother's arrival would certainly jeopardize their position. Infuriated, Liu Xingzhi attacked and killed twenty commanders before he was, in turn, eliminated by the island soldiers. Mao Chengdou, the son of the general, changed his name to Jue. The name of Mao Wenlong's grandson was Youhan.

The elegy reads:

The general died a wrongful death,
When, in fact, the motivations behind his actions are as clear as
    the sun at dawn.
Much of the general's aims and aspirations remain unrealized.
Recording onto the stone tablet to first shine light on his
    accomplishments
And to pass down his legacy,
How is anything out of the ordinary in doing this?
As of now, one can no longer find the general's cap and gown in
    this grave,
But I still get to write his epitaph.

Source: Jia Naiqian 賈乃謙, ed. and annot., *Dongjiang shujietangbao jiechao (wai erzhong)* 東江疏揭塘報節抄（外二種）(Hangzhou: Zhejiang guji chubanshe, 2013), 213–20.

Notes

1. Ji was the surname of the ruling house of the Zhou dynasty (1046–256 BCE). One branch of the clan was expelled from the capital and enfeoffed along the eastern frontier, where they assumed the surname of Mao to distinguish their line.

2. The Pass of the Mountains and the Sea is a gateway flanked by the easternmost section of the Great Wall, which terminates at the Bohai Sea. Historically, this strategic defensive barrier separated Manchuria from the north China plain. Ningyuan refers to a garrison in present-day Xingcheng, Liaoning, which defended the northern approach to the pass.

3. This Chinese proverb is derived from Sima Qian's *Historical Records* (Shiji), the first comprehensive history of China. It refers to a small vassal state of the ancient state of Dian in southwestern China during the Western Han dynasty whose ruler severely underestimated the power and sophistication of the Han and behaved in a condescending manner toward its envoys when they requested passage through his realm to reach India. The proverb that emerged from this incident has since been used to refer broadly to extremely arrogant and conceited behavior, whether on the part of states or individuals, based on willful ignorance and refusal to assess the reality of their surroundings.

Further Reading

Andrade, Tonio. *The Gunpowder Age: China, Military Innovation, and the Rise of the West in World History.* Princeton, NJ: Princeton University Press, 2016.

Struve, Lynn. *The Southern Ming: 1644–1662.* New Haven, CT: Yale University Press, 1984.

Swope, Kenneth M. *The Military Collapse of China's Ming Dynasty, 1618–44.* London: Routledge, 2014.

Wakeman, Frederic Jr. *The Great Enterprise: The Manchu Reconstruction of Imperial Order in Seventeenth-Century China.* Berkeley: University of California Press, 1985.

Zheng, Yangwen. *China on the Sea: How the Maritime World Shaped Modern China.* Leiden: Brill, 2011.

A Brother Remembers His Sister

Epitaph for My Sister Madam Fang (Qian Huan 錢還, 1600–1668), by Qian Chengzhi 錢澄之 (1612–1698)

TRANSLATED BY MARTIN W. HUANG

By narrating seemingly insignificant anecdotes, a literatus offers intimate insights into his sister's personality. This biography reveals the author's attachment to his sister, the importance of her natal family to a married woman, and the ways an indulgent mother could help her daughter after she left home.

IN A PATRILINEAL SOCIETY SUCH AS THAT OF PREMODERN China, a man's relationship with his married sister was complicated by the rupture that often occurred when she married and moved away to live in her husband's home. Once a member of his family, now she belonged to another man's family. Yet, at the same time, she remained his close kin. Having "lost" her when she moved away and married another man, he would lose her once more if she passed away before he did, a factor that might have contributed to the unusually strong show of emotion in some of the epitaphs for women authored by their brothers. These epitaphs draw our attention to the close relationship between a married woman and her natal family, an aspect of a woman's life that otherwise receives little exposure. Qian Chengzhi's (1612–1693) epitaph for his sister allows us to glimpse both his attachment to his sister and the importance of her natal family to a married woman.

Qian was a well-known Ming loyalist poet, scholar, and historian. He wrote memorial essays for several of his family members including a lengthy record of conduct for his first wife, who chose to commit suicide rather than face the possibility of being violated by bandits during the chaotic days of the Ming-Qing dynastic transition.[1] Her brief biography is included in the Lienü (Exemplary women) section of *The History of the Ming Dynasty* compiled under the sponsorship of the Qing imperial government. Translated here is the epitaph he wrote for his elder sister.

"Epitaph for My Sister Madam Fang" is a telling case of how an epitaph could yield intimate insights into the private life of a deceased woman if its author happened to be someone very close to her, complicating the common assumption that epitaphs were often scripted and formulaic. A commissioned epitaph writer, who often did not know his subject personally, had to rely on the record of conduct provided by a relative or associate of the deceased. Compared to the epitaph, it tended to be much less rigid in format and more personal in nature. Further adding to its flexibility was its assumed "unfinishedness" because it was meant to be a source of first-hand materials a future biographer or epitaph writer would rely on. When an epitaph writer knew the deceased well, however, he was more likely to write the epitaph as if it were a record of conduct since he now relied on his own personal memory rather than that of another person. Here the boundaries between an epitaph and a record of conduct become blurred. This is especially true in the case of a literatus writing about his female relatives, where he was more likely to focus on seemingly insignificant details in their private lives since women were not supposed to have a public life. At the same time, writing about one's sister offered our author unique freedom and flexibility, which he might not have in writing about his other female relatives: he did not have to worry about appearing too indulgent in the eyes of the more orthodox, as he might when he wrote about his own spouse. By the same token, he would not feel pressured to present his female subject as so great a moral exemplar as he would when he, out of filial reverence, wrote about his mother.

What is so remarkable about Qian Chengzhi's epitaph for his sister is the utter unremarkableness of its female subject as he presents her. Freed of the pressure to present his subject as a moral exemplar, Qian apparently perceived no need to apologize for writing an epitaph on the very ordinary life of his sister. Thus, it reads like a personal memoir at a time when the personal memoir was just beginning to emerge as a distinct genre. Conveying her endearing personality with all her flaws from the perspective of a brother, the epitaph points to a new trend in the writing of memorial essays in seventeenth-century China—blurring the distinctions of such different genres of elegiac prose as the epitaph, record of conduct, and biography.

The epitaph is relatively long, underscoring how much Qian as a brother felt he had to say about his unremarkable sister, who does not seem to have too many extraordinary acts of Confucian virtue to boast of. Qian mourned her simply because she was an elder sister whom he felt he had been very close to. Their mother gave birth to six children, among whom his elder sister was the only daughter, a possible reason why the mother doted on her so much. Unfortunately, her husband, though enjoying a reputation as an intelligent child when he was young, failed to pass the provincial examinations after as many as ten attempts. He died a frustrated examinee at the age of forty-seven. Although Qian Chengzhi never explicitly blames his brother-in-law or his family for the miseries his sister suffered, the reader still feels that her husband's career failures contributed to her suffering. Then, when the country was thrown into chaos during the violent dynastic changeover, his family's fortunes went downhill rapidly as bandits began to ravage their area. After their residence was burned down, the situation became even more perilous for his sister with the death of their mother.

According to Qian, when their mother was still alive, if his sister disliked any of her maids, their mother would simply choose a good one among her own maids and send the maid over to serve his sister. As a result, the number of maids serving his sister was several times larger than that of those serving all the brothers. After their mother died, within a few years, all the maids of his sister were gone: they either died or ran away because, as Qian tells us, his sister was a mistress "lacking generosity," implying that she might have treated them harshly. Because of her relatively easy life when her doting mother was still alive, she seems to have been ill-equipped to deal with hardships later in her life after her natal family could no longer help her.

Qian's portrait of his sister differs in interesting ways from his portrait of his mother.[2] Their mother was strict in raising her children and efficient in managing the household. Qian Chengzhi's main intention in mentioning his mother's doting on his sister in this epitaph was to show how precious his sister was to the former. However, the mention of doting complicates the mother's image, since it contributed to the sister's later misery as she needed to learn how to manage a household on her own. Writing about his mother, Qian Chengzhi describes in detail how effectively she supervised all the servants and the maids, even though she was actually kind to them, a sharp contrast to the clumsiness on the part of his sister. In this respect, Qian Chengzhi was far more candid in presenting his sister, whereas, in writing about his mother, presumably out of filial deference, he celebrated her as an exemplary mother. Such a contrast draws our attention to the different strategies a literatus author often adopted when he remembered and wrote about his different female relatives.

Qian did not mean to speak ill of his sister; he was just describing her as she was. For the most part, Qian presents her in loving terms, betraying his deep attachment to her. In Qian's vague memory, his much older sister was almost like a mother figure to him, although she moved away before he was old enough to remember her that well (he was only four when she married at the age of sixteen). As he says in the concluding rhymed elegy, he authored this epitaph so that future generations would know her.

Compared with the record of conduct he wrote for his own wife, who was celebrated as a female martyr to chastity, Qian's epitaph for his sister, interestingly enough, is much more intimate. This was partly because Qian tried to keep a deliberate distance from his late wife as a biographical subject in order to convince his readers that he was writing as an objective historian about the life of a remarkable chastity martyr. In contrast, availing himself of the format of the epitaph, he chose to write a personal memoir about his late sister, a woman characterized by her seemingly unremarkable life.

Epitaph for My Sister Madam Fang

My mother, Madam Long, gave birth to six of us. I have four elder
brothers and one elder sister. My sister was the third among my siblings, making the next three younger than her. My sister married
Mr. Fang at the age of sixteen. That year, my brother-in-law, Fang Boying,
had just passed the prefectural examinations. Earlier, when Boying was
younger, my father really took a liking to him. I had another elder
sister [born to a different mother], Wan. However, that sister died not
long after my father had her engaged to him. My father was very sad
and composed a poem to mourn her. Later, when my sister was born,
my father was happy, saying, "This girl must be the reincarnation of
my previous daughter," and thus he named her Huan [the one who has
returned] and then had her engaged to my brother-in-law. This was
why my brother-in-law was five years older than my sister. My mother
doted on my sister and almost exhausted our family fortunes to prepare for her dowry. After she was married into the Fang family, mother
continued to give her whatever she wanted. Her family was 20 *li* [about
6 miles] away from us. A servant was assigned to make daily deliveries
to her family, which my father did not begrudge at all.

Boying had the reputation [of a smart young man], but he failed to
pass the provincial examinations ten times. After our mother passed
away, we no longer sent things over to the Fang family, which became
quite poor. Their house was destroyed during the chaos of the war.
Boying moved a hundred miles away. He suffered many frustrations in
life and died at the age of forty-seven from an illness. At that time, our
father had already passed away, and I moved my family to live in
Baimen [Nanjing, Jiangsu]. It was my brothers You'an and Ruoshi who
helped take care of the burial matters and brought his body back to the
hometown. Ruoshi had his daughter engaged to my sister's fifth son,
on whom my sister was especially dependent. Later, I sought refuge in
the Sanwu area [Jiangsu] after becoming a victim of the factional
fighting in Baimen [in the politics of the Southern Ming, 1644–1663],
and then I lived in the areas of Min [Fujian] and Yue [Guangdong].
After seventeen years, I eventually returned to my hometown.

On my return, I went to visit my sister. Although she was barely over fifty and her hair had not turned completely gray, she looked so old and worn out that she was simply a copy of our mother in her old age, only much more haggard. There is a saying "Having many children makes a mother's life hard." Both my sister and my mother had a hard life due to having many children, and yet my sister's life was much unhappier than that of my mother. This was why she aged much faster. I composed a poem before I left her. The poem was quite depressing, and my sister felt sad whenever she had others read it to her.

My sister was twelve years my senior. When I was little, I was sick all the time. She often carried me in her arms when I cried and seldom put me down. I do not remember that well the time when she got married. I can only recall the day when she returned to visit us for the first time after the wedding: Elegant and respectful, all dressed up and with the tingling sound of her bracelets, she got out of the carriage and entered through the courtyard. Seeing her, my mother was so happy that she was in tears.

My sister had a quick temper, and yet she served her mother-in-law with great patience. Her mother-in-law, Madam Ruan, was strict with her daughters-in-laws, who were often not allowed to leave after paying respects in the morning. My sister did not show any sign of resentment even though she had to wait on her all day. After she had her own daughters-in-law, she often led them to pay respects to her mother-in-law. The latter would have all her granddaughters-in-law sit while she treated my sister as she used to. Some would fault the mother-in-law for this, but my sister instead tried to defend her by denying that this had ever happened and never complaining. She treated the concubines of her husband as if they were her own sisters so the family enjoyed great harmony.

It was the custom in the village that a woman did not withdraw in the presence of her younger brother-in-law. Boying had a brother, Zhongfu, who was two years younger than he, and yet my sister always withdrew when he was present. Someone pointed out that he was her younger brother-in-law, but she replied, "Even though he is my younger brother-in-law, he is older than I, and I should withdraw in his presence." This shows how carefully she followed the ritual proprieties.

Earlier, when my mother was still alive, my sister's family would be given whatever she wanted from us, and this became routine. She already had quite a few maids, but if she happened to dislike any of them, my mother would select a good one to send to her. As a result, the number of her maids was several times that of the maids serving us brothers. Within a few years after our mother's death, because of her lack of generosity, her maids and servants either died or ran away. In her old age, she had to do all the chores herself and suffered great hardship. Once she sighed to me in tears: "Good Heavens! How did I come to this? I had not realized that everything in daily life, no matter how small, cost money."

My sister was content with a simple life. She was a good household manager, and she arranged the marriages of several of her sons while leading a frugal life herself. Without any land, her sons had to make a living elsewhere by serving as tutors or clerks, but her daughters-in-law did not serve her as well as she did her own mother-in-law. Frequently, You'an would hear about this and would want to talk to them about how a daughter-in-law was supposed to behave. Knowing his intention, my sister would meet You'an before he could reach their home and tell him that recently her daughters-in-law had become quite respectful. Consequently, he had to return without saying a word. She spoiled all her daughters-in-law; their failure to serve their mother well was all due to my sister's excessive generosity.

My sister had a daughter. She became a hunchback after a carbuncle grew on her back. Almost every member of the family could not wait for her to die except for my sister, who really loved her. A few years later, she indeed died. My sister cried for her for several years, asking, "Why is Heaven so cruel to have taken her away from me?"

My sister had a tendency toward melancholy, easily shedding tears. This was especially so after she grew old. She would cry whenever my mother was mentioned; she would cry whenever Boying was mentioned; every time we brothers visited, she would cry; and she would do the same when we were about to say good-bye. Alas! Everyone says that my sister was easily given to melancholy, but one should not fault her as she could not help feeling depressed over what had happened to her. My wife, Madam Fang, was an orphan, and she treated my sister as her mother. When alive, her mother, Madam Wang, got along well with my sister as in-laws. Madam Wang asked my sister to find her daughter a good son-in-law. That was how my wife married me. My wife's mother, Madam Wang, was a chaste widow. My wife followed me when I was fleeing from the factional fighting [of the Southern Ming regime]. She became a martyr of chastity [by committing suicide to protect her chastity] in the Wujiang [Jiangsu] area. After hearing the news, my sister cried a lot and then said: "She did not let her mother down. This is a sad but also admirable act." This shows how much importance she attached to the great principles of loyalty and chastity.

After I returned to my hometown [from the South], I sojourned in Baimen for two years. Thinking that among my siblings only my sister and my second brother were still around, I wrote two poems, titled "The Wheat Garden" and "The Pepper Hill" to express my brotherly feelings. The next year when I returned, my second brother had passed away. Later, to avoid possible persecution as a result of being slandered by others, I moved to the Min region and married Madam Xu. After another three years, when I took my wife with me and returned home, I went to see my sister immediately. She looked very old. Knowing that she would reach seventy the following year, I told her: "Our mother did not live to seventy, nor did any of our brothers. Fortunately, sister, you will be seventy next year. We will definitely invite you to my home to celebrate your seventieth birthday with all the members of the younger generations." My sister agreed. Who could have known that that winter my son would be killed by bandits! On hearing the news, my sister was overwhelmed by shock and distress. Her sickness got worse, and she passed away before she could reach seventy! The time when my sister was growing up was a peaceful period undisturbed by disorder. For generations, men in our family had been scholars. At home, one would consider a man almost an alien if he did not study for the examinations. Ever since the upheavals [accompanying the fall of the Ming dynasty], many in the family had to change our professions. My sister would still judge things by the old standards: she was always upset that her sons were unable to fulfill their father's hopes. Once, pointing at me, she told her sons: "In the past, I saw your uncles studying. When it was becoming dark, our mother would measure the lamp oil [before giving it to her sons]. When the lamp oil was burned out at midnight, some of them would knock at her door for more. She would give more lamp oil to those who had studied hard and would treat them to porridge. However, those who had been sitting there playing would get neither oil nor porridge. Now I am old, and I still weave during the night. It has been quite a while since I have heard people reading aloud in the family."

Then she recalled how I could not count money when I was young. I had a problem counting whenever the number reached ten. I spent all my time reading, and people considered me stupid. [She would wonder] why people nowadays are so obsessed with calculating and counting [money]. She would become depressed after saying this. Alas! This is truly sad!

My sister was born in the *gengzi* year of the Wanli reign period [1600] and died in the *wushen* year of the current reign period [1668], at the age of sixty-nine. She had six children and several grandchildren. She was buried on the hill behind her residence. I, her younger brother, authored this epitaph. The rhymed elegy reads:

Large was the house when sister got married.
With her pendants tingling, she stepped onto the wedding
    carriage.
Suitable for maintaining the harmony of her husband's family,
    our mother was pleased.
Life began to become hard with our mother passing away.
Drifting and suffering from poverty, she lost her husband.
Along with her children, she brought her husband's coffin home,
    a virtuous woman she was.
With the old house burnt down, they had no good dwelling to
    live in.
With all the servants and maids deserting, sister had to tend to
    everything herself.

Not complaining about hardship, she became easily distressed.

Crying often, she looked much older than her age.

Not far away from her residence was the site of burial.

Alas! What about her soul when her spirit must have felt
attached here?

Why is it that she could not tear herself away but her children?

With all the loving memory who could remember her faults?

This humble epitaph was authored by her younger brother.

So that, one hundred generations later, people remember we
were siblings.

Source: Qian Chengzhi, *Tianjian wenji* 田間文集 (Hefei: Huangshan
shushe, 1998), 445–48.

Notes

1. For a discussion of this record of conduct, see Martin Huang, *Intimate Memory: Gender and Mourning in Late Imperial China* (Albany: State University of New York Press, 2018), 63–71.
2. See his "Xianmu Pang anren xinglüe," in *Tianjian wenji*, 554–56.

Further Reading

Bossler, Beverley. "A Daughter Is a Daughter All Her Life: Affinal Relations and Women's Networks in Song and Late Imperial China." *Late Imperial China* 21.1 (2000): 77–106.

Carlitz, Katherine. "Mourning, Personality and Display: Ming Literati Commemorate Their Mothers, Sisters and Daughters." *Nan Nü: Men, Women and Gender in China* 15.1 (2013): 30–68.

Huang, Martin W. *Intimate Memory: Gender and Mourning in Late Imperial China.* Albany: State New York University Press, 2018.

Lu, Weijing. "Personal Writings on Female Relatives in the Qing Collected Works." In *Overt and Covert Treasures: Essays on the Sources for Chinese Women's History*, edited by Clara Wing-chung Ho, 403–26. Hong Kong: Chinese University Press, 2012.

19

A Chinese Bannerman Expert in Waterworks

Epitaph for Director General of River Conservancy
Jin Wenxiang 靳文襄 (Jin Fu 靳輔, 1633–1692),
by Wang Shizhen 王士禎 (1634–1711)

TRANSLATED BY R. KENT GUY

This epitaph for a Chinese bannerman serving the Manchus highlights his career as an accomplished river manager who envisioned the
lower Yellow River and the Grand Canal as a single hydraulic system.

THE YELLOW RIVER POSED A GRAVE CHALLENGE TO ALL CHINESE
dynasties. Bearing an enormous load of silt as it flows south and east, the
river builds up its own bed, which can be higher than the surrounding
farmlands. When this occurs, the river needs to be restrained with levees
and guided with water gates. If this is not done, the river can change its
course, causing serious floods. Every several hundred years, the river radi-
cally changed directions, flowing to the sea either to the south or to the
north of the Shandong Peninsula. In the beginning of the Qing dynasty,
the Yellow River had been flowing out through its southern mouth for
over four hundred years and had built up substantial silt and mud.

Controlling the Yellow River was complicated by the fact that its lower
courses, in northern Jiangsu, were linked with the Grand Canal. The

latter was a crucial waterway, which transported much of the grain, known as "tribute grain," that fed the capital. Early Qing managers of this river system, known as "directors of river conservancy," were not terribly successful, with the result that there was flooding in nineteen of the first thirty years of the dynasty. Since the ability to maintain hydraulic infrastructure was one mark of a dynasty's success in governing, central governments paid close attention to what went on in northern Jiangsu.

The funerary biography translated below presents the life of Jin Fu (1633–1692), who served as director general of river conservancy from 1676 to 1688 and from 1691 to 1692. It was written by Wang Shizhen (1634–1711), a distinguished poet and high official of the Qing. Jin Fu was a Chinese bannerman, a member of a family that held a hereditary position within the army of Chinese subjects formed by the Manchus before their conquest of Beijing. He was born eleven years before the conquest and moved with the Manchus from Shenyang in Manchuria to Beijing in 1644 or shortly thereafter. He occupied a series of positions in the capital before being sent to govern Anhui province in 1671 at age thirty-eight. He served five years in Anhui and was then promoted to the post of director general of river conservancy in 1676.

Jin Fu and Wang Shizhen both served as bridges between Manchus and Chinese in the very early years of the dynasty. Bannermen translated for the Qing rulers and in the early years often served as the face of the new rulers for Chinese populations in the provinces. Wang Shizhen too served as the Manchus' face: as a local official in Yangzhou between 1660 and 1665, he had helped to reconstruct social life in a town devastated by the Qing conquest armies. He went on from there to posts within the central Qing state. Wang Shizhen and Jin Fu may have met, but, if they did, their meeting was not recorded. The occasion for the epitaph was a request from Jin Fu's eldest son that Wang memorialize his father. Wang had access to Jin family papers as he prepared the biography, and he also was able to listen to the stories that the family told of itself. The account he prepared was the only one of the seven extant biographies for Jin Fu that was written by one of his contemporaries.

A tantalizing detail about the Jins in Wang's epitaph is the claim that, when the Ming conquered Shandong in the late fourteenth century, Jin

Fu's ancestors joined the Ming army, membership in which was hereditary, and were assigned to guard Liaoyang (Liaoning), near the Manchu homeland. As the Manchu order grew in the early seventeenth century, the Jins joined it, forsaking the Ming. If true, it would appear that, in the seventeenth century, the Jins traded posts as hereditary military servants of the Ming for positions as hereditary military servants of the Qing. Why the Jins joined the Manchus is unclear. There is no way to corroborate the Jins' service to the Ming or surrender to the Qing, and none of the other biographical accounts extant included this detail. However, Wang Shizhen's epitaph likely reflects the Jins' image of themselves as occupying a service niche in the middle reaches of the late imperial state, a niche that existed regardless of who actually held the throne.

Jin Fu had four sons and two daughters with his two wives, Yang and Bai. The sons were named Zhiyu, Zhiyong, Zhilu, and Zhiqi. This confident servant of the Qing named his four sons after the rulers of the ancient Chinese states of Yu, Yong, Lu, and Qi. With these names, he was hoping for sure positions for his sons not at the top, but safely nestled in the state order. His hopes were in fact realized, as all four sons occupied government positions at the time of his death. As Jin became more senior, Wang's epitaph relates, he established an ancestral temple and carefully compared liturgies for family rituals by Sima Guang (1019–1086) and Zhu Xi (1130–1200) to determine the appropriate ceremonies for special occasions. Research has shown that many seventeenth-century Chinese families, particularly ones with complex histories of dual loyalties like the Jins, were pressed to reflect on the question of what made them Chinese. The most common answer was that the essence of Chineseness lay not in political loyalties, but in fealty to a set of inherited rituals. But which were the correct rituals? Sorting through extant accounts of ancient Chinese rituals was a major concern of scholars in the late seventeenth century and also of families trying to understand their place in the Sino-Manchu sociopolitical order. Behind the Jins' apparent confidence may have been a shade of doubt about what they were doing serving a state run by foreigners.

Suggestive though these details are, they represent only passing notations in Wang's epitaph, which is in the main concerned with describing

Jin's work along the lower Yellow and Huai Rivers. Here, too, the special access Wang had to the family and its papers was important, as it enabled him to quote from Jin's unpublished memorials. Probably after his death, 108 of Jin's memorials were published by his son Jin Zhiyu. Many of the passages Wang quoted can be found in this collection, but several passages seem to be from documents not included. Wang's account is not exactly chronological; rather it emphasizes the highlights of Jin's work, showing the close empirical observation and analytical thinking that lay behind Jin Fu's river work. Several scholars who have studied Jin's work find his perspective at least protoscientific, approximating modern hydrology. Jin Fu was unique among early Qing river managers in envisioning the lower Yellow River and the Grand Canal as a single hydraulic system, in which changes to any single feature affected the system as a whole. The systematic structure he created largely prevented flooding for over one hundred years, until corruption and silting in the river brought massive floods (and a change in the mouth of the river) in the nineteenth century.

If Wang's biography takes us into the Jin family circle, as it were, there are also places it does not take us. These include Jin Fu's relation with his private secretary Chen Huang (d. 1689), his longstanding disagreement with the emperor and the Jiangnan elite over the cause of flooding in central Jiangsu, and the facts of his cashiering in 1688. Summaries here will have to suffice, as each of these issues was complex. Chen Huang, who died in prison after Jin was cashiered, was the acknowledged author of many of Jin's memorials, enjoyed an extraordinarily close relationship with his employer, and even penned a catechism in which Jin Fu asked questions about issues in hydrology and Chen answered them. Jin's disagreement with the emperor and the Jiangnan elite was based on their different understandings of lower Yangzi hydrology; Jin was stubborn almost to the point of intransigence in defending his point of view. Jin and the court also disagreed over the merits of creating military agricultural colonies on reclaimed lands in Jiangnan: the Jiangnan elite saw this as stealing their land, and the Kangxi emperor was inclined to agree. Although twentieth-century scholars, like Wang Shizhen, admired Jin Fu's achievement, many in his day found him arrogant and unbending.

Recalcitrance was never a good idea in relations with a Chinese emperor; and, in Jin's case, it provided an opening for an investigating censor to impeach Jin.

During the time Jin spent out of office, he prepared *On Managing Rivers*, which Wang recommends and quotes, although the work was not printed until some years later. Jin Fu's time out of office lasted only three years. When the emperor saw and admired Jin's masterwork, the Central Canal, in northern Jiangsu, he reappointed Jin to office, where he served until his death. The life of Jin Fu embodied how Chinese men strived to make a mark in a realm ruled by foreigners.

Epitaph for the Grand Master for Splendid Happiness, Director General of River Conservancy, Military Superintendent, Minister of War, Right Vice Censor in Chief, Mr. Jin Wenxiang

On the nineteenth day of the eleventh month, the thirty-first year of the Kangxi reign period [1661–1722], Mr. Jin, who was director general of river conservancy [with concurrent appointments as] military superintendent and minister of war, exhausted himself in the service of the monarch and died in office. When he was notified, the emperor was stunned and saddened, and ordered that the burial be with full ritual; he also bestowed on Jin the posthumous name Wenxiang [Cultured and Completed]. Thereupon, the orphaned son Zhiyu, who was a vice-director in the Ministry of War, among other posts, undertook to have the remains buried at a grave site granted him in Mancheng County [Baoding, Hebei]. The monarch's words were inscribed on the tombstone, which rested on a base of river dragons and divine turtles carved out of stone so that the lavish display of dynastic grace would be illumined in perpetuity. The family also wanted an inscribed tablet next to the grave prepared by the inelegant Wang Shizhen. I could not refuse.

When a country is at the height of its glory and wants to build something large and long lasting, it must have an official of profound ability, an extraordinary man whose name will be known through posterity and whose deeds will illuminate Heaven's accomplishments. His energy will accomplish great deeds; his wisdom will resolve great doubts. His talent will achieve great merit, and his loyalty will unite with the monarch's mind and quiet frivolous notions. With his accomplishments and reputation firmly established, he leads senior and junior in common efforts; there are none under Heaven or in the future who do not believe in him. Such an accomplished person should be the subject of the "recording good deeds" (*chunshi*) tradition so his reputation will pass on unceasingly. Such a man was Mr. Jin.

According to his record of conduct, Mr. Jin's taboo name was Fu, and his courtesy name was Ziyuan. His ancestors were from Licheng [Jinan, Shandong]. During the time of the Hongwu emperor of the Ming [r. 1368–1398], their first ancestor, Qing, joined the military as a company commander together with a hundred households and defended the Liao region, thus becoming Liaoyang [Liaoning] natives. After Qing died in battle, his descendants were granted hereditary leadership of a regiment [a thousand households]. After several generations, Shouchen was born; Shouchen begat Guoqing, and Guoqing begat Yingxuan. Yingxuan was Right Assistant Commissioner of the [Qing] Office of Transmission and was Mr. Jin's father. Because of Mr. Jin's noble accomplishment, these three generations of ancestors [Shouchen, Guoqing, and Yingxuan] were posthumously bestowed by the emperor the titles of Grand Master of Splendid Happiness, Director General of River Conservancy, Military Superintendent, Minister of War, Right Vice Censor in Chief.

Mr. Jin's inborn nature was trusting and kindly. When he was nine, his mother died, and he carried out the full mourning rituals expected of an adult. At age nineteen, he entered the Hanlin Academy as a compiler. He thoroughly learned the dynasty's regulations and precedents and was promoted to the director of the Bureau of Operations in the Ministry of War, then served as Right Vice Commissioner in the Office of Transmission. He was then promoted to Academician of the Wuying Throne Hall, concurrently serving as vice-minister of the Ministry of Rites.

In the tenth year of the Kangxi reign period [1671], Mr. Jin was appointed governor of Anhui, an exceptional promotion, with concurrent rank as Right Vice Censor in Chief. When *The Veritable Records of the Shunzhi Emperor* [r. 1644–1661] was issued, his rank and salary were raised one step. Anhui had been devastated by a drought, and many of its people had fled. After Mr. Jin acted vigorously to relieve their suffering, several thousand households returned. The land around Fengyang [Anhui] had long been neglected, and Mr. Jin presented three memorials on reclamation for the instruction of the throne, titled "Summoning People to Recover the Land," "Providing the Essentials to Encourage Cultivating [Reclaimed] Land," and "Six-Year Tax Breaks [for Reclaimed Land]."

Another memorial he submitted said:

The way of governing lies in first securing the people's sufficiency. It does not lie in asking for relief or remitting land tax, but in using the people's strength and teaching them how to earn a profit. How do the broad wheat lands of Fengyang compare to those of Suzhou and Songjiang [in Jiangsu]? The Su-Song region is an area of 300 *li,* and its tax yields are the highest in the empire. The Fengyang area is 500 *li,* and it does not produce onetenth of the tax revenue of Su-Song. Granted that the land includes both rich and barren lands, still, why should the difference between Fengyang and Su-Song be this great? The Su-Song people have built irrigation works, and theirs is a land of streams and small rivers; during droughts there is relief, and during floods there is drainage. Even though rains are variable, there is no cause for concern. North of the Yangzi River, the old irrigation works have been completely lost. If there is drought, the land turns to stone. Now, if we want there to be no wasteland and no years of dearth, nothing would be better than vigorously building irrigation works.

Irrigating fields carries on the spirit of the ancient well-field system.[1] However, marking each acre of the well field with an irrigation channel of the proper width and depth can be onerous. Irrigation systems begin with one channel, and repairing and managing them is quite easy. The method is as follows: Ten *mu* [approximately 1½ acres] is taken as a plot; for every twenty plots, there is one irrigation ditch. Among the twenty plots, a little over three *mu* are set aside as borders. Surrounding the twenty plots is a deep irrigation channel. The land allowed for the irrigation ditch is 1 *zhang* and 8 *chi* [4 meters]; the ditch itself is 1 *zhang* and 2 *chi* [3½ meters]. The depth of the channel is 7 *chi* and 5 *cun* [2½ meters]. The dirt dug out of the channel should be piled on either side, creating a wall 5 *chi* [1½ meters] higher than the field. The base of the channel is 7 *chi* and 5 *cun* lower than the surrounding field. This makes the channel appear 12 *chi* and 5 *cun* [5 meters] deep. When there is a flood, waterwheels in the fields will push the water into the channel; and, when there is drought, the waterwheels in the channel can carry water to the fields.

Building irrigation channels has four advantages. First, it alleviates worry about flood and drought. Second, when the channels are clear, water can flow through them, and those who live downstream need not worry about flooding. Third, tax revenues increase. Fourth, because land boundaries are clearly marked, there can be no abuse involving hidden lands and [baseless] compensations.

The memorial was submitted and was just about to be referred to the board for discussion of its implementation when crises occurred in Dian [Yunnan] and Min [Fujian]. Wan [Anhui] lies at a strategic meeting point in Chu, where three provinces come together.[2] In the south, She County is close to the Fujian border. Mr. Jin organized troops, gathered a militia, firmed up fortifications, and sent spies out great distances, thus greatly increasing military preparedness. The bandit Song Biao created havoc from a base in the mountains of She; his reputation frightened those far and near. With a clever stratagem, [Song] was apprehended at Lake Chao [in Anhui], and peace was restored.

The Ministry of War proposed that the costs of the courier system be reduced in order to cover military expenses, and the matter was referred to provincial governors for proposals. Mr. Jin memorialized: "To save expenses, one must first reduce the work undertaken. At present, governors general, governors, and provincial and regional military commanders send a special messenger for each item of business, a huge waste every year. I propose that only dispatches about the military situation be conveyed by special messenger; the rest may be sent in batches. Let us set three matters of business as a standard, with one messenger sent to convey three items." His proposal was submitted to the emperor, approved, and made the law. In the course of a year, a million *liang* was saved in courier expenses. Mr. Jin was given rank as minister of war.

In the sixteenth year of the Kangxi reign period [1677], the levees broke between the Yangzi and the Huai Rivers, and the emperor, knowing Mr. Jin's talents, ordered him to move to the Wanjiang region [both sides of the Yangzi River within Anhui]. Retaining his rank, he was appointed director general of river conservancy. At that time, the river levees and the Grand Canal had greatly deteriorated. From Xiao County downriver, the waters of the Yellow River flowed through many small streams and never reached the sea. The breaks in the north were in the levees as the river flowed through Suqian, Shuyang, Haizhou, and Andong Counties. The breaks in the south were as the river flowed [to the west] into Lake Hongze and [to the east] to the seven downriver counties. The canal at Qingkou was completely blocked with silt. Mr. Jin traveled for a thousand *li* up and down the rivers, treading through the mud, and observed, sighing, "The deterioration of the river works is extreme! It cannot be repaired by inches or feet. The whole situation must be mastered so that it can be repaired from beginning to end. Only then can the situation be resolved."

Thereupon, he submitted eight memorials on the appropriate management of river works. They said, in general: "There are some matters in which it is best to follow precedent and some in which current circumstances must be weighed; there are some matters in which things to be done first must be separated from things to be done later and some matters in which everything must be done at once. The guiding principle must be to properly rely on the force [of the current]." Court discussion was critical of Mr. Jin's plan because of the need to pay for provisions for the armies [engaged in suppressing the Rebellion of the

Three Feudatories].³ Thereupon, it was ordered to only repair those deemed to be most crucial.

Mr. Jin again memorialized:

Below Qingjiangpu, if we neither build levees nor dredge, the Huai and the Yellow Rivers will have no route to the sea. Above Qingkou, if we do not dredge, the Huai will not flow easily. If the breaks in the levees along Gaoyan are not repaired, then the current of the Huai River will be divided and will not scour the mud; water will be forced into the Yellow River, and the downriver Qingshui Lake will be a crisis point. Moreover, if we don't rebuild the levees on the south bank of the Yellow River, then Gaoyan will be threatened. If the levees on the north bank are not repaired, then the rivers east of the mountains [i.e., in Shandong] will back up. In the matters of building levees, forcing the water downriver, and repairing breaks, there can only be the question of what to do first; there can be no question of which is more urgent. If at present we don't make a plan to accomplish the work once and for all, then the levees built year after year will be broken year after year. These past disasters are lessons as clear as daylight. They are not merely a waste of the people's resources but will be endless, and the river system will steadily deteriorate.

The memorial was submitted, but the discussion at court was the same as before.

The emperor, judging that river affairs were very important, sent the records of the court discussion to Mr. Jin and asked him to memorialize again. Mr. Jin once more set forth the importance of waterworks, and the emperor approved of his requests. Mr. Jin later memorialized again, recommending that water gates be installed on both banks of the Yellow River to prevent the most violent floods from harming the levees, which the emperor again approved. This was because the emperor knew well that Mr. Jin was loyal and intrepid and could be entrusted with a major project. Therefore, he rejected the criticisms and employed him. Mr. Jin was grateful for the emperor's recognition. Trusting in Heaven, fearing neither callouses nor injuries, he expressed no resentment and was not affected by expressions of sympathy or hatred.

Not many years later, the Huai and Yellow Rivers were restored to their original courses, and the Grand Canal was again navigable. The work at Qingshui Lake was the most dangerous in the Yangzi-Huai region. The Huai absorbed the excess water of the Yellow River, and this was channeled into Gaoyu and Baoying Lakes. Channeling the water at this point was for the benefit of those in downriver counties and departments. The rivers there frequently backed up and flooded, causing years of unceasing labor. When Mr. Jin built on the edge of these lakes, he avoided the dangerous points and selected shallow areas; the levees he built had firm foundations.

Earlier, the Ministry of Works had estimated that the work along the lakes could not be completed for less than 600,000 *liang*. But, up to this point, the work cost only 100,000 *liang*, thus saving tens of thousands of *liang*. Mr. Jin also recommended the elimination of unnecessary positions in the river conservancy administration, assigned responsibilities, and was stern with rewards and punishments. He switched to having soldiers do the work, supervised by military officials. All of the tasks of gathering wood, transporting supplies, sweeping and cutting down trees, building up low places, and reinforcing thin spots were assigned to local communities. Their work was observed and evaluated daily and monthly, and the abuses of passing responsibility to others and embezzlement were eliminated. All of Mr. Jin's actions served to discipline those who indifferently followed the old tradition and aimed at long-lasting impact. The above examples all fit into this pattern.

In the winter of the seventeenth year of the Kangxi reign period [1688], Mr. Jin reported by memorial that all the breaks in the river and lake levees had been closed. The emperor was delighted and responded with a letter of commendation, heaping praise and encouragement on him. Before this, grain tribute barges had to pass between the southern and northern mouths of the Grand Canal. The Grand Canal and the Yellow River flowed together, and the river was often filled so that every year it had to be dredged, causing much misery for both residents and officials. The northern mouth of the canal was formerly in Xuzhou to the east of Liucheng [Jiangsu]. Later, it was moved to the Zao River in Suqian County [Jiangsu]. Moreover, for 300 *li*, when the Yellow River flooded, silt was a problem. Mr. Jin dredged the Zao River for a distance of 20 *li*, hence controlling the water flow of the canal.

He also wrote:

> It is the nature of water to flow downward. One *li* [of watercourse] ought to descend by one *cun* [3 inches]. If the Xin River is 2 *chi* ¾ meter] higher than the Yellow River, then the Yellow River will not flow into the canal. However, if we move the water gate at the southern mouth of the canal into the Huai itself, we will capture all the water of the Huai. The water of the Huai is clear, and that of the Yellow River is muddy, so the sand from the Yellow River is not deposited. Even if the current of the Yellow River were stronger than of the Huai, the water forced into the Huai would steadily build up; once the Huai River is full, the silt will be washed away completely.

When the two mouths of the canal were repaired, problems going back centuries were eliminated. Mr. Jin also wrote: "The nature of water is yielding, but, when the wind blows, it can be hard so that planks and stones are not able to resist it." Therefore, on the edge of Lake Hongze, he built sloped banks to decrease the force of the water and protect the levees. Thinking that this worked, he then ordered river officials to plant willow trees along the levees. The trees could be used in the future as materials that buttress up the levees. As a result, the levees are stronger, and there is no need to purchase building material from far away. With that, the river protection system was complete.

In the twenty-third year of the Kangxi reign period [1684], the emperor observed the river from his carriage on his southern tour.

His heavenly countenance showing pleasure, the emperor wrote a poem, "Observing the Levees," which he presented to Mr. Jin along with a *jiaha* boat,[4] an imperial barge, and the curtains used by the emperor, all of them truly extraordinary gifts. Once the Yellow and the Huai Rivers had been restored to their original courses, Mr. Jin then memorialized, asking to dredge the Central Canal for a distance of 300 *li* [100 miles] in order to direct the waters from Shandong. Initially, when the Yi, the Si, the Wen, and the Jia Rivers from Shandong flooded, the waters reached Suqian, Taoyuan, Qinghe, Andong, Shuyang, and Haizhou, flooding uncounted acres of the people's land [in Anhui and Jiangsu]. They also merged with the Yellow River. The angrier the Yellow River becomes, the more it influences the Huai. The three streams flow together as they pass Qingkou. The broader the flow is upriver, the slower the downriver flow. The slower the flow, the more silt builds up, causing further flooding of the upriver regions.

In the 200 *li* [60 miles] after the tribute boats leave the Yellow River, the winds and currents create unseen dangers. Therefore, the exertions of the hired hands [i.e., tribute boat pullers] were inestimable. Once the work on the Central Canal was completed, the force of the Yellow River was contained, and the danger to the seven prefectures was relieved. Tribute boats sailed smoothly, like crossing a bed. Analysts regard the project of building the Central Canal as benefiting the state for a hundred generations, equivalent to Song Li's [1358–1422] digging of the Huitong Canal or Chen Xuan's [1365–1433] boring out the Qingjiang River.[5] During Mr. Jin's ten years of managing the waterways, he had decisively separated the flows, building channels according to the topography. Each attained its place, and the rivers were well managed.

In the twenty-sixth year of the Kangxi reign period [1687], the emperor raised the issue of how to manage the downriver flows of the Huai and the Yangzi. Mr. Jin emphasized that, "in order to regulate the downriver region, one must first completely regulate the upriver," a position many opposed. Accusations exploded like swarming bees, and Mr. Jin was dismissed from office. In the spring of the twenty-eighth year [1689], the emperor made another trip south to the riverbank, and

Mr. Jin greeted him at Huai'an [Jiangsu]. The emperor asked whether the reconstruction work after flooding had been completed and restored Mr. Jin to his original rank, praising him as "wholeheartedly devoting himself to his office."

While Mr. Jin lived at home for three years, the emperor, remembering his unforgettable accomplishments, sent him three times to investigate the river and summoned him once for an audience. In the thirty-first year [1692], the emperor specially ordered him to leave his home and return to his original position as director general of river conservancy. Mr. Jin tried to decline on the basis of advancing age and ill health, but he was not permitted to do so.

At this time, because a drought in Fengxiang and Xi'an in Shaanxi had caused famine, there was an imperial order to retain 200,000 *shi* [2,666,000 pounds] of grain in the south and ship it up the Yi River for storage at Puzhou [Shanxi] to relieve those suffering from famine in Shaanxi. The emperor ordered Mr. Jin to manage the project. Unable to refuse, despite his ill health he took to the road. In consideration of Mr. Jin's age and illness, the emperor again assigned him a *jiaha* boat and a royal barge to honor and distinguish him. Once Mr. Jin arrived, he set about planning the westbound transport, carefully thinking through the details. From Qinghe through Rongze [Henan] and up through the Sanmen Gorges and Dizhu Mountains, all proceeded smoothly and safely. Throughout the entire time, not one laborer was drafted and all was accomplished.

When the western transport was almost done, Mr. Jin memorialized the emperor describing his health problems. The emperor specially ordered Mr. Jin's eldest son, Jin Zhiyu, to travel to see his father and ordered Mr. Jin to return to the Huai region to recover. At this time, Mr. Jin's illness worsened, but he still managed to submit a memorial of several tens of thousands of words, setting forth the reconstruction work necessary along the river and the procedures and appropriate actions in river work. He urged that rivers be opened up and that levees be built around land that would have been wasted so that taxes could be collected on lands that were no longer inundated with mud. The emperor sent Grand Secretary Zhang Yushu, Minister

Tu Na, and Minister Xiong Cilü to assess the situation and help him with the work. A short time later, Mr. Jin again requested retirement because of illness, but the emperor still would not permit it and once again sent his son Jin Zhiyu to see him. Jin Zhiyu had not yet arrived when Jin Fu again requested retirement, which the emperor finally permitted. On this very day, Mr. Jin expired at his official residence. The date was the nineteenth day of the eleventh month of the thirty-first year of the Kangxi reign [1692].

The emperor sighed fondly on reading Mr. Jin's posthumous memorial. He ordered his remains returned to the capital and carried through the official city before being returned to his home. This ritual was unprecedented. The emperor ordered that all the great officials and guardsmen come out to offer wine and tea [as the coffin passed]. He ordered the Ministry of Rites to recommend how to handle the funeral and the Grand Secretariat to recommend a posthumous name. He was granted the name "Wenxiang." His funeral rites were without parallel. Alas! In his interactions with his ruler, Mr. Jin's virtuous name was well established, he was treated with full ritual from beginning to end, and what he was granted by the emperor can be described as generous.

On the request of the emperor, Mr. Jin wrote *On Managing Rivers*, in twelve chapters. The several chapters of memorials that he wrote while in office have been published. [In his writings,] he discussed the reasons why river maintenance projects have succeeded and failed over the ages. He argued:

> Among those scholars who have recently written of river affairs, there are none who have not given a lot of space to Jia Rang's [fl. 7 BCE] "Three Proposals." I don't believe it should be thus. One of Jia Rang's proposals envisioned moving the people of Jizhou [Hebei],[6] but the river has changed its course since Song times and no longer follows the Han bed. The second [middle] proposal emphasized water gates. During droughts, they could be opened so that the water would flow downriver to the east; with the great gates opened, the water would flow into several smaller streams. Jia Rang did not realize that the channel [edges] of the

river was lower than the mud in its bed, so where would the river go when it was released years later? Moreover, when *The Tribute of Yu* wrote "in the nine provinces there are banks," what it calls banks we today would call levees. Now the river is level, but the surrounding topography has high and low points; thus, unless levees are constructed to channel the water, how will the water, as it flows to the low points, not flood? Jia Rang's third proposal, reinforcing the old levees and expanding those thin and weak, is just the opposite of *The Tribute of Yu*. How could Jia Rang's wisdom be superior to that of the sacred Yu? These were just the current scholars' opinions.

Therefore, Mr. Jin's way of managing rivers completely corrected Jia Rang's writings, emphasizing the building of levees to control the water. The good that he accomplished is all detailed in *On Managing Rivers*; later readers can examine it in detail and understand his ideas. What he has drawn together will constitute a mirror for a thousand years of river defense.

Mr. Jin's heavenly endowed nature was both filial and friendly, and he waited on his father with sincerity and met all his needs. His father's elder brother Vice-Commissioner Yanxuan died without an heir. Jin Fu buried him with full ritual. His father's cousin Chengxuan died leaving an orphan son; Mr. Jin educated him, arranged for his marriage, and planned a livelihood for him. He loved his younger brothers Bi, the section director, and Xiang, the prefect of Nan'an [Fujian]. He treated them as he would himself and their sons like his own children. Within his household, he was stern, as is prescribed by the dynastic ritual code; he wrote a clan genealogy and a set of precepts for his family and made his descendants honor them. As his rank rose, he established an ancestral temple. For all auspicious occasions, funerals, and sacrificial ceremonies, he searched for appropriate ceremonies by comparing the liturgies of Sima Guang and Zhu Xi, and recorded his choices in the family history.

Never careless with his words or gestures, once he uttered a word, it could be depended on. There is much more that could be written of his conduct and his management of his family. [However,] the most important fact was that his merit as an official rested on his work on river management, he added to state revenue, and he extended his goodness to the people. In all respects, "he worked much and ate little" and was utterly dedicated in service to the state. He was truly what the ancients called a "pillar of the state."[7]

Mr. Jin was born during the seventh year of the Tiancong reign period [1633] and died during the thirty-first year of the Kangxi reign period [1692], having attained the age of sixty. His first wife, surnamed Yang, was granted the rank of first grade consort; his successor wife, surnamed Bai, was also granted the rank of first grade consort. He had four sons, Zhiyu, vice director of the Bureau of Operations of the Ministry of War, with concurrent rank of assistant commandant; Zhiyong, prefect of Hunyuanzhou; Zhilu, an eighth rank official; and Zhiqi, a local educational official. He had two daughters, one married into the Gao family and one married into the Zhu family. He had eight grandchildren, Shuji, Shuqiao, Shuzi, Shuwan, Shuyu, Shude, Shugong, Guangning, and one great-grandchild. The rhymed elegy reads:

> The Yellow River flows a thousand *li* from Kunlun,
> Descending through the Jishi Mountains and past Longmen
>   [Henan].
> Guiding the channel, the works of Yu remain,
> The nine rivers deriving their orderly flow from them.
> In the Han "Songs of Gourd City," the banks of the river were
>   thick with bamboo,
> When an image of a white horse and a jade disk were submerged
>   to honor the effort.[8]
> The Great River ran by day to the southeast,
> Agitated by ferocious waves and fearsome fish.
> The emperor sent a trusted official to take up residence,
> To ride in Yu's cart and tread in the mud, forgetting dynastic
>   reward.
> Now that the River God's spirit prevails, and the waters are tamed,

The Yellow and the Huai no longer threaten chaos.

From Yangzhou and Xuzhou for a thousand *li* grains flourish,

And myriads of tribute barges flow steadily along.

The emperor repeatedly bestowed rich rewards,

Mr. Jin took ten years to accomplish everything but never
flaunted his merits.

Now he is with Sagittarius and Scorpio, and the people are
grieving,

There was weeping in the lanes as the [funeral] catafalque
passed, banners fluttering.

The emperor presented sacred funeral markers for the grave,

Richly endowed with gifts of gold and grain.

Heavenly rewards and auspicious events attended his burial,

Heavenly carriages and horses did not darken the sun.

The mountains and waters are safe and bountiful,

And will benefit descendants for myriads of years.

Source: Wang Shizhen, *Wang Shizhen quanji* 王士禛全集 (Jinan:
Qilu shushe, 2007), 3:1865–72.

Notes

1. The well-field system was a classical utopian scheme of land division, in which the field was divided into nine equal plots in a checkerboard pattern resembling the character for well, *jing*. Jin proposed to similarly divide land in Anhui, using irrigation ditches as borders.
2. Chu was a preimperial Chinese state; the term functions here generally to identify the south central region of China. Anhui borders Jiangxi and Zhejiang on the south; the border is about 199 kilometers from Fujian.
3. The Rebellion of the Three Feudatories broke out in 1673 and was suppressed in 1680.
4. A *jiaha* was a type of riverboat.
5. Both these were early Ming efforts to secure the Grand Canal.
6. This is a general expression for much of the eastern end of the north China plain.
7. These are two four-character phrases drawn from the Classics to describe a dedicated official's commitment to his work.

8. The poems, purportedly by Emperor Wu of the Han (r. 140–86 BCE) were written during a visit he made visit to Guazi Kou (Henan) to observe the Yellow River. To encourage the work, the emperor ordered that a white horse and a jade disk be submerged in the river.

Further Reading

Spence, Jonathan. *Emperor of China.* New York: Random House, 1974.

———. "The Kang-hsi Reign." In *The Cambridge History of China,* vol. 9: *The Ch'ing Dynasty to 1800,* edited by Willard J. Peterson, pt. 1, 120–82. Cambridge, UK: Cambridge University Press, 2002.

Kessler, Lawrence D. *Kang-hsi and the Consolidation of Ch'ing Rule.* Chicago: University of Chicago Press, 1976.

Guy, R. Kent. "Governing Provinces." In *The Cambridge History of China,* vol. 9: *The Ch'ing Dynasty to 1800,* edited by Willard J. Peterson, pt. 2, 1–76. Cambridge, UK: Cambridge University Press, 2016.

A Woman Determined to Die

Epitaph for the Joint Burial of Scholar Wu (Wu Xi 吳錫,
1666-1687) and His Martyred Wife, Madam Dai 戴氏 (1666-1687),
by Mao Qiling 毛奇齡 (1623-1716)

TRANSLATED BY JOLAN YI

This joint biography for a young couple by a leading scholar in the
early Qing focuses on the husband's anguish over failing the civil service examinations and his wife's single-minded pursuit of death once
her husband passed away. The epitaph illustrates the influence of the
"cult of widow chastity" and the "cult of *qing*" in late imperial China.

IN MING AND QING TIMES, YOUNG WOMEN WHO REFUSED TO
marry after their husbands died were celebrated for upholding the womanly virtues of loyalty and chastity. Many chaste widows were publicly
honored, especially if they devoted themselves to their husbands' family
for decades. Some bereaved women went even further, not just refusing
to remarry but killing themselves to reunite with their deceased husbands. There were also cases of young women who had been betrothed
to marry who refused to marry anyone else after their fiancés died; they
were known as "faithful maidens." This "cult of widow chastity" was promoted by the government through the awards it conferred on chaste
widows and by literati and officials who wrote admiring accounts of these
women as moral heroes. Research has shown that the more intense the

competition in the civil service examinations, the more biographies of chaste women were written. Men who were finding it difficult to raise the status of their family through government service, it would seem, found other avenues to promote their families by bringing attention to the merit of their women.

The joint epitaph translated below is for Wu Xi (1666–1687), a government student who died at twenty-two, and his equally young wife, Madam Dai (1666–1687), who took her own life not long afterwards. The author, Mao Qiling (1623–1716), was one of the leading scholars and philologists of early Qing China, famous for vehemently opposing the orthodox commentaries on the classics by Neo-Confucians in the Song dynasty such as Zhu Xi (1130–1200). An erudite scholar, Mao compiled works on the Confucian classics as well as phonetics, music, history, geography, and philosophy. A native of Xiaoshan County in Zhejiang, he refused to serve the Qing government after the fall of the Ming dynasty in 1644. In 1679, however, he took part in and passed a special honorary examination held by the Kangxi emperor (r. 1661–1722) to attract scholars who had yet to announce their allegiance to the new dynasty. Mao was then appointed to the official branch charged with compiling the *Ming History*. After retiring from office in 1685, he went to live in Hangzhou, where he taught several disciples. "Epitaph for the Joint Burial of Scholar Wu and His Martyred Wife, Madam Dai" was written during his retirement.

Mao Qiling at first supported the ideal of the faithful maiden, claiming that, once a woman promised to marry a man, she was to be seen as his wife. But later, around 1702, he changed his position, arguing that a faithful maiden had yet to fully carry out her wedding and therefore could not be considered a true wife. In 1711, he even expressed his regret for writing this epitaph for Wu and Dai, even though they had been married, most likely out of fear that praise for the act of suicide might push those in grief in the direction of taking their own lives. Already in this epitaph he expresses misgivings about bringing positive attention to suicide.

Wu and Dai, whose deaths were only forty-two days apart, were buried in the same chamber in the same tomb.

Joint burial appeared as early as the Warring States period. During medieval times, husbands and wives (and sometimes parents and children) were often buried together or promised a posthumous reunion with kin at some future time, practices that remained common in Ming and Qing times. The dead would be buried either in one chamber or in a multichambered tomb, which often was the case when the deaths occurred years apart. In this epitaph, we can also detect the influence of what has been called the "cult of *qing*" (emotion, affection, love), as writers took to celebrating passion or ardor.

From Tang to Qing times, there was a historical shift in how authors discussed the husband-wife relationship. In Tang epitaphs, husband and wife were often described as harmonious, which is less common in funerary inscriptions in the Song. Song epitaphs tended to emphasize the harmonious relationship between a wife and her husband's family members or a wife's life as a widow. In the mid-Ming, there was a fairly standard language of mourning for women. Literati in the late Ming did not shy away from a realistic portrait of how their subjects got along with their wives. By the late seventeenth century, however, the "cult of *qing*" began to have less impact on writing about marital relations.

In this joint burial epitaph for a couple, Mao Qiling depicts both Wu and Dai as passionate people. He portrays Wu Xi's anguish over trying to pass the civil service examination and Madam Dai's single-minded pursuit of death once her husband passed away.

Epitaph for the Joint Burial of Scholar Wu and His Martyred Wife, Madam Dai

The Wus and the Dais were prominent families [of Hangzhou, Zhejiang], and they intermarried with each other. The Wus had a son who, at four years old, could read *The Comprehensive Mirror to Aid in Government* [by Sima Guang, 1019–1086] and recite it after transcribing it a few times. When he was five, he could discuss the histories of the dynasties and the reasons for their rise and fall. He could also make judgments on the good and bad in people and events. By the age of seven, he was proficient in classics such as *The Book of Songs, The Classic of Documents, The Classic of Changes, The Spring and Autumn Annals, The Strategies of the Warring States*, as well as *The Historical Records, The*

History of the Han Dynasties, and other famous works of early thinkers. At eight, he started to study writing civil service examination essays. The next year, his family took him to take the examinations. He received the exam sheet in the *chen* hour [7:00 to 9:00 a.m.] and handed in his answer sheet in the *si* hour [9:00 to 11:00 a.m.]. The education intendant took pity on his youth and said: "Are you able to take on the duties of a 'cultivated talent'?" He attempted to pass the exams again the next year. His literary talent had improved, and so he was granted a place in the Qiantang County [Zhejiang] school. By this time, Wu Xi was quite well known. People saw him as a gifted boy and said: "It can only be that his talent has been bestowed by Heaven!" Therefore, he was given the name of Xi [bestowed], and his courtesy name was Tianyu [granted by Heaven]. In the neighborhood lived a daughter of the Dai family who was ten years old. When her father passed away, she wept and was so overwhelmed with grief that she almost lost her eyesight. People in the community called her a filial daughter and said: "Shouldn't the filial daughter be matched with the gifted boy?" Thus, the Wu family betrothed her. At sixteen they were married, and at seventeen Wu Xi fell ill.

Previously, when Wu Xi was fifteen years old, he took the provincial examination and failed. He was resentful and wrote a poem to express himself, imitating Li He's [790–816] "Farewell to Shen Yazhi," written upon failing the imperial examinations. In the autumn of 1684, at the age of eighteen, he took the provincial examinations with his younger brother Yao. Wu Xi was self-confident, and his brother was young as well. They went together and both thought they would pass the examination, but they both failed. Wu Xi became more resentful. Reciting Meng Jiao's [751–814] poem "Failing the Examinations Again," when he came to the line "I got up many times during the night [due to short dreams]," he declared, "what is the point of getting up!" He lay down during the day and wrote hundreds of characters in the air. Sometimes he forcefully drank strong wine and felt uneasy and emotional. After a while, he abandoned practicing exam essays and bolted his door. He took out old rhapsodies that he had read from the Han and Wei dynasties, and sat upright and worked over them. In addition to such emotional strain, his mountain studio was very remote. Living deep in the woods from dawn to dusk, with the vapors of the dense vegetation saturating him and emaciating him, he grew ill. After three years, he became gravely ill and died.

When her husband was ill, Madam Dai devotedly served him medicine, neglecting to take care of herself. She sold her jewelry to pay for Buddhist rituals and Daoist rites, hoping that they would bring him some slight relief. When she realized that Wu Xi could not be cured, she asked to die before him. Wu Xi responded: "I am not dead yet, and you want to die before me. Do you want to speed up my death?" She wept and ceased her attempt to commit suicide. When Wu Xi was near death, he called his younger brother Yao and said: "I know that your sister-in-law will certainly commit suicide after I die. When I die, enjoin the family to watch over her. If you cannot prevent it, then just follow her will."

Sure enough, when Wu Xi died, Madam Dai could not stop weeping. She knocked her head on the coffin, injuring her head and covering her face in blood. The family kept close watch over her. She tried to kill herself seven times, hanging herself with a towel and stabbing herself with a knife. Finally, she swallowed pieces of gold but did not die.

Her mother comforted her and said: "You are well known for your filial piety. Now, with your mother still alive, how can you kill yourself?" She replied: "Before I was married, I would have died for my father. Now I will die for my deceased husband. This is my destiny. I am not filial and cannot take care of you anymore." She secretly smashed a glass vase and swallowed the pieces, which tore up her intestines. She coughed up volumes of her precious blood and died, forty-two days after her husband. That day marked the sixth week of mourning.

[Moved by her outstanding conduct,] fifty-eight townsmen, including Zhao Pei and others along with forty-five county school students from Renhe and Qiantang Counties in Hangzhou [Zhejiang], including Wang Dacheng and others, gathered and went to the county seat. There, they publicly requested that Madam Dai be recognized as a martyred wife.

The magistrates turned in the petition to the governor general, the governor, and the educational intendant. These officials forwarded the documents to the Provincial Administrative Commission, the Surveillance Commission, and the prefectural and county offices, supplying the facts of her case in order to recommend that she be commemorated with the construction of a memorial arch.

The Wu and Dai families were originally from Xin'an [Anhui]. They had been selling salt in Hangzhou for generations, so the merchants from Xin'an living in Hangzhou along with one hundred members of the gentry, led by Yang Dasheng, also submitted a petition to the Salt Control Censorate, requesting that they join in the commemoration recommendation. They first hung a placard above the door of the Wu residence and donated money to buy articles for the ceremony, and they personally composed funerary prayers for her in the mourning hall. Clansmen and fellow townsmen [from Xin'an] raised funds to build a shrine for Madam Dai at West Lake on the south side of Ge Hong Hill, a location selected through divination. They decided to bury Madam Dai and Wu Xi together next to the shrine on the fourth day of the fourth month of the following year [1689] and asked me to write this epitaph.

I have heard that in the past the wifely way was "to be faithful to one's husband unto death" and "to be in harmony with one's husband, unchanging throughout one's life." Thus, it was said that one should be faithful and that one should not remarry, but I have never heard that one must follow her deceased husband to the grave. If a woman was forced against her will [that is, raped], or she was harassed and insulted, then she would pledge her life to show her loyalty. To make a pledge is fine, but this does not mean that she must commit suicide. Even in the case of suicide, she should first give an indication that she intends to kill herself, whether by stabbing her nose, cutting her face, breaking her arm, or cutting her hair, instead of actually killing herself. When a woman has not been forced and yet pledges to die, and then, having pledged to die, sees death as necessary and carries it out in the end, is that not a case of her going too far? Between the times of Emperor Yao of high antiquity and the Song dynasty, all the loyal officials, filial sons, dutiful brothers, and faithful friends always behaved in extraordinary ways, with great displays of emotion to demonstrate their wills. They never hesitated to do what they should; never scrupled when they had to withdraw. In this they completely matched what Madam Dai has done. In ancient times, Bo Yi obeyed his father [and then died because he was not willing to serve in the Zhou court]; Yi Yin brought the king to worship the king's ancestor [and then dismissed the king when he was not good enough]. Prince [Yaoli assassinated Prince Qinji and then] sacrificed himself [by committing suicide]; Taibo and Yuzhong both gave the throne to their younger brothers; Zuo Botao, [who left food and clothes for] Yang Jiao'ai, died for friendship. These are all examples of heroic behavior.

Ever since conformist views arose, people began to overthink. They examine themselves before they take any action; they go back and forth, looking nervously in all directions as they fear deviation from the norms. For example, subsequently, they concluded that Boqi's self-exile was merely submission to his parents; Yurang was seen as simply chivalrous [for killing himself after his assassination mission failed]; Huo Guang was viewed as unlearned; Tian Hui [who gave away his official position] and Deng Yuo [who gave up his own son to save his nephew] were seen as abnormal; Zhi Junzhang and Xun Jubo were seen as casually sacrificing their lives for their friends. Thus, although people were loyal, filial, and upright, there were obstacles to seeing them this way. Therefore, when the Song dynasty ended disastrously as the rulers perished and the state collapsed, none of the Neo-Confucian scholars gave their lives for their country. Fortunately, their ideas did not reach as far as the women's chambers.

When I was young, I went to the local official school, where the teachers spoke of filial piety. The stories included Guo Ju burying his own son [out of devotion to his mother], Ding Lan carving his mother's portrait in wood [to serve as his real mother], and so on. I felt terrified when I first heard of this and then sighed over it, and my heart beat quickly. I thought, how can I not try to live up to such inspiring examples? When I came back home, I told my family what I had heard at school. Some became very emotional and some wept before I finished the story.

My elder brother, who had long taught in the local school, was disgusted with what I told them. He said: "Young boy, you have learned it wrong. That is not proper conduct, and it is not worth mentioning. Burying one's own son would cut off the family succession; repudiating one's wife does harm to husbandly grace; carving a wood portrait of one's mother damages the community; lying on ice to catch fish to feed one's parent goes against one's nature. Any one of these deeds goes against filial piety; how much more so to gather them into a collection! Have you never read the Ming dynasty legal code? One would be punished for self-harm or suicide, for cutting off one's own flesh to feed one's parents, or for residing in a hut at a parent's tomb. For you to esteem these as extraordinary virtuous deeds is too much!"

When I heard this, I was at a loss. Hopeless, I gave up on improving myself. It has been more than fifty years since then, and, because of that single remark, I have been unable to be a filial son or a dutiful brother. Now, having seen what Madam Dai has accomplished, I should reform myself.

Wu Xi died on the thirteenth day of the second month, the twenty-seventh year of the Kangxi reign period [1687], and his martyred wife died on the twenty-fourth day of the third month in the same year. Both of them lived to the age of twenty-two.

Mr. Fuzhong, Wu Xi's father, once said to someone: "This martyred wife married my son at sixteen and died at twenty-two. I was happy to have my son for sixteen years, but his joy with his wife lasted only six years. My son died in the second month, and his martyred wife died in the third. Before the third month, I grieved at the loss of my son. From the third month, I grieved at the loss of my daughter-in-law. I grieved over my son's death for only one month, but I will grieve for his martyred wife for the rest of my life." He also said: "Each time the martyred wife attempted to kill herself, we saved her. The more we saved her, the more pain she felt. In the end, she was in such extreme pain that she could not be saved." Alas! Thus, I have written a joint epitaph for this couple. The rhymed elegy reads:

At the beginning people said the filial daughter was a good
    match for the gifted boy.
We did not expect a scholar's wife would finish her life as a martyr.

They were born in the same year, and they died in the same year
as well.
Now they are buried in one grave together. As it is said, "She has
been faithful to her husband."
The burial mound lies between the base of Mount Ge and the
eastern side of West Lake.
It is planted with catalpa trees and empress trees.
Mandarin ducks dwell there,
Female and male pairing with each other.
They stay together day and night,
They may soar to the west or to the east,
They may be separated or joined together,
They may diverge or converge.
The only ones who cannot be separated lie within the grave.

Source: Mao Qiling 毛奇齡, *Xihe wenji* 西河文集, Guoxue jiben congshu
國學基本叢書 edition (Taipei: Taiwan shangwu yinshuguan, 1968),
muzhiming 8.

Further Reading

Carlitz, Katherine. "Shrines, Governing-Class Identity, and the Cult of Widow Fidelity in Mid-Ming Jiangnan." *Journal of Asian Studies* 56.3 (1997): 612–40.

Lu, Weijing. "Faithful Maiden Biographies: A Forum for Ritual Debate, Moral Cri-
tique, and Personal Reflection." In *Beyond Exemplar Tales: Women's Biography in
Chinese History*, edited by Joan Judge and Ying Hu, 88–103. Berkeley: University of
California Press, 2010.

Mann, Susan. "Widows in the Kinship, Class, and Community Structures of Qing
Dynasty China." *Journal of Asian Studies* 46.1 (1987): 37–56.

Ropp, Paul S., Paola Zamperini, and Harriet T. Zurndorfer, eds. *Passionate Women:
Female Suicide in Late Imperial China*. Leiden: Brill, 2001.

T'ien, Ju-kang. *Male Anxiety and Female Chastity: A Comparative Study of Chinese
Ethical Values in Ming-Ch'ing Times*. Leiden: Brill, 1988.

A Wife's Sacrifices

Living Funerary Inscription for My Wife, Madam Sun 孫氏
(1769–1833), by Fang Dongshu 方東樹 (1772–1851)

TRANSLATED BY WEIJING LU

Written for a wife while she was still living, this premortem epitaph
brings to life a strong, resilient, and capable woman who managed her
household effectively despite a severe disability. Calling his wife a
good friend, the biographer is not shy in confessing his affection for
her as well as his strong sense of indebtedness.

THE HUSBAND AND WIFE RELATIONSHIP IS ONE OF THE FIVE
cardinal relationships in Confucian teaching, regarded as foundational
to an orderly human society. The Confucian canon stressed the difference between husband and wife, although it also acknowledged their ritual parity, signified in their essential roles in performing ancestral rites.
It held mutual respect and a wife's obedience toward her husband as
principles for marital interaction. However, beyond Confucian moral
rules, Chinese culture recognized the great importance of affection
between husband and wife. Iconic symbols of marital affection, such as
the pairing of mandarin ducks, have lasted to modern times. In the late
imperial period (1368–1911), cultural celebration of emotion and love
(the cult of *qing*) and admiration for the literary and artistic talents of
women helped forge a new kind of marital ideal based on affection and

intellectual compatibility. An eighteenth-century example is the memoir *Six Records of a Floating Life* (Fusheng liu ji) by Shen Fu (1763–1832), which details Shen's blissful marital life with his wife Yun in the midst of tensions with his parents and brother.

During the Qing period, educated men and women employed several genres to express their affection toward each other and profess their gratitude for their spouses' companionship. Poetry, which both men and women wrote, was popular for conveying sentimental feelings. Biography and epitaph, written mostly by men, in contrast, focused on praising their late wives' virtuous conduct and their indebtedness to their wives' contributions to household preservation and even their career success. The convention of writing an epitaph for a deceased wife was established in earlier times (see Selection 13), but it grew "secularized" in the late imperial period, in the sense that women from less prestigious families became the subjects for this genre, and their portrayals became more mundane.[1]

Fang Dongshu (1772–1851), a native of Tongcheng, Anhui, was a leading member of the Tongcheng literary school.[2] A student of the eminent scholar Yao Nai (1731–1815), he later became an influential teacher himself. Fang's intellectual interests extended from the Confucian classics to other schools of thought and Buddhism. A firm follower of Song Learning, he advocated ideological and philosophical approaches to the study of the Classics rather than the philological one that was favored by the eighteenth-century Han Learning intellectual movement called "evidential scholarship."[3] Fang wrote profusely, leaving behind numerous works, the most famous of which was "A Discussion of Han Learning," which he wrote to discredit the Han Learning School.

Despite his stature in nineteenth-century intellectual history, Fang Dongshu's public career left much to be desired. After obtaining the lowest degree at age twenty-two, he failed in his ten attempts at the provincial examinations, held every three years. He finally gave up when he was in his mid-fifties. Pressed by poverty, he traveled constantly looking for employment opportunities as a teacher or on the staff of local officials. While employed in Guangdong by Governor General Ruan Yuan (1764–1849), he took charge of the compilation of the comprehensive gazetteers of Jiangning and Guangdong. In his late years, he served as head of a number of academies. Although deprived of a chance to serve as an official, Fang took interest in social and political issues. In the late 1830s, while on the staff of Governor General Deng Tingzhen (1776–1846) in Guangdong, he was said to have urged the assassination of British Superintendent of Trade Charles Elliot to eliminate the problem of the opium epidemic.

Fang spent much more of his life time away than he did at home. His constant absence from home and the hardships and disappointments he encountered give a distinctive tone to the funerary inscription he wrote for his wife, Madam Sun. This "living funerary inscription" was written in 1831, when he was sixty and Sun sixty-three. At the time, he was serving as the head of Susong Academy in Anhui and had just finished writing a family biography. His wife would live for another two years. A few months after her death, on her sixty-fifth birthday, he composed a long postscript. In that text he revealed how, in the months leading up to her death, he was constantly on edge, afraid his wife would die, and, when news of her death reached him, he was so devastated that he was not sure if he could continue to live without her.

Fang's funerary biography for his wife is unusual in that Fang wrote it while Sun was still alive. Fang explained his decision in the epitaph and again in the postscript: "I wrote a living epitaph for my wife because I wanted her to read it. It was to console her." The epitaph would be read by others, but it was intended primarily for her eyes.

Fang's premortem epitaph brings to life an extraordinary woman, one whose severe disability highlighted in a powerful way the strength, capability, resilience, and endurance of women as household managers. Sun was completely disabled at age forty-four, following years of suffering from a less severe stage of paralysis. Yet she managed to overcome nearly impossible obstacles and to perform her managerial duty superbly year after year. An important part of the background to this extraordinary show of willpower was Fang's constant travels. This case, therefore, also illustrates the centrality of the wife's role in preserving the household at a time when the itinerant life became a common experience for educated men of little means. The normalization of prolonged conjugal separation must have had a profound effect on spousal relationships.

Fang's affection for his wife comes through clearly in this piece. To be sure, Fang had no intention of presenting their relationship as one between equals. He constructed Madam Sun's virtue mainly in terms of the framework of wifely devotion to their household and to him personally. Still, his own personal attachment is evident, as seen in the postscript: "Every life ends with death, which can be expected to happen within a hundred years. One can never forget those with whom one endured poverty. Since I have few brothers and other relatives, the only one to care whether I leave or stay was my wife, who took pity on me for my hardships and understood my character. From now on, I have no one with whom to commiserate."

Fang's description of his wife's life and conduct was imbued with a heavy sense of indebtedness. He did not take her labor and sacrifice for granted. His praise of her virtue and accomplishments was also an admission of his own inadequacy as a husband: it was his misfortune that brought her hardship. Many of the qualities Fang saw in his wife were usually associated with men. Fang remarked on his wife's composure: her face did not reveal her feelings, and she did not complain. He portrayed her as more broadminded and generous than he was himself. What emerges from this account was more than a dutiful wife or a virtuous woman, but rather an individual of outstanding character.

Fang called Sun a "good friend" when describing the joy of coming home to be in her company and discussing people and political events with her. Being able to connect at an intellectual level added additional satisfaction to their relationship. As a high-minded moralist, Fang probably would have frowned on a romantic relationship between husband and wife, but the epitaph he wrote offers us rich material to think about marital relationships in new ways.

Living Funerary Inscription for My Wife, Madam Sun

My wife, Madam Sun, was born on the thirteenth day of the ninth month in the *yichou* year [1769] of the reign of the Qianlong emperor. She married me at age twenty-five, thirty-nine years ago. Taking pity on her for all kinds of hardships she has endured and for the fact that she is dying from old age and illness, I therefore write this epitaph in advance to console her by describing her suffering and her conduct so that she can read it while alive. I do this because she understands the value of writing and because she is happy that I can write. I hope that this text will keep memories of her deeds alive forever.

My wife married me in the winter of the *guichou* year [1793]. Two years later, she lost her mother. She was so emaciated [from excessive grieving] that she nearly died. Her younger brother was not yet married, and her father was sojourning far away. Therefore, she went to manage her natal family, returning one year later. At the time, my family was in straitened circumstances. My late father was trapped [by a stalled career] at home, and my grandmother was old and ailing. There was nothing available to provide for our daily needs. Pressed by this need to earn a living, I left home to teach the classics to earn money to support my family. Because the income from my teaching job was meager and not enough to cover all our needs, my wife often resorted to pawning things to get by. In the *yiwei* year [1799] of the Jiaqing reign period, I was working in Jiangyou [Anhui]. That year, smallpox struck in my hometown. Within one month, my younger brother and sister and two of our daughters all died. My wife held her son and cried for her daughters. She caressed their dead bodies but could not find clothes to dress them for encoffining. My wife once tried to describe to me what had happened but could not finish her words.

Because our home was located in a low, narrow, and wet place, she was stricken with an ailment that made her weak and lame. In the beginning, she could manage to hold a cane to stand up. But a doctor prescribed the wrong medicine, causing her to be completely disabled, and both her hands and legs suffered from spasms. That occurred in the *guiyou* year [1813]. Three years later, when I was on Vice Censor in Chief Hu's staff in Jiangsu, my father passed away. My mother was old and ailing and could not manage the funeral. As the daughter-in-law of the oldest son, my wife took charge of the family. She fulfilled her responsibility and spared no effort to manage this major undertaking, doing nothing that violated ritual. The following year, I was working in

Jiangning [Nanjing, Jiangsu] and was trapped by poverty in Yangzhou [Jiangsu], when my grandmother also died. Compared with the time of my father's death, this time my wife had fewer resources for the funeral. These two major deaths occurred within two years. An unfilial son, far away, I avoided my responsibility and placed all of it on my wife. This is why I felt so sad and ashamed of myself that I could not utter a word.

The following year, I took a job in eastern Guangdong and my wife managed the marriage of our eldest son. For nineteen years, beginning in the *guiyou* year [1813], she had someone carry her to sit on a couch every morning and carry her back to lie down in her bed late at night. This was her routine. For the rest of the time, she crouched on a couch, and matters were brought to her continuously, ranging from rice and salt for daily needs to government demands for taxes and services, supplies for burial and sacrifices, and the visits of friends and relatives. With her one mouth and one heart, she managed everything. Alas, even a strong and healthy man would not be able to deal with all this, yet this woman in poor health handled it all. This was not easy.

My wife read books and excelled in the Mao Commentary on *The Classic of Poetry*. She taught our sons to read before they began formal schooling with a teacher. Her disposition was firm, straightforward, and solemn; she was reserved and did not reveal happiness or anger on her face. Even in an urgent situation, she did not lose her composure. She did not look worried or speak sadly despite our poverty. She did not moan or call on her parents or Heaven even when she was in great physical pain. She was sincere and not pretentious when speaking with people. When weeping over a death, she truly grieved; when she saw other people suffering, she was kind and merciful. Her conduct was constant, and she understood the great principles. When it came to things that had to be done, she did them even when she was short of money.

I was born with a weak constitution and from childhood on often got sick. At the time my wife married me, I was so delicate and weak that I did not have a normal physique. Moreover, I often coughed blood. My wife was afraid that I would die. For this reason, she always thought of me as sickly, whether I was home or traveling. She would not think of her own illness but would be worried about mine. She was like that for the past several decades, which have passed in a blink. During my infrequent returns from travel, she looked after me extremely solicitously, making sure I had enough to eat and wear. If I wanted to do something, she would dutifully make it happen as soon as she learned about it. Not once did she argue, complain, or refuse to do something. She would quietly figure out what I needed and would get it promptly arranged without waiting to hear from me. I often thought this: a man would be called a filial son if he served his parents the way my wife served me. Therefore, although my wife did not have extraordinary ability or great virtue, judged by criteria for wifely conduct, nothing was lacking in her conduct. She can be called a female gentleman.

I made ten attempts at the provincial examinations and failed them all. My wife said to me, "Before I was married, I hoped for my father [to earn a degree]; after I was married, I hoped for my father-in-law and then you [to earn a degree]. But none of my wishes were fulfilled." Although this is a common enough feeling, these were sad words. I am by nature unsophisticated, and I like to speak about people's shortcomings directly. As a result, people often resent me. My wife admonished me frequently, but to my shame I did not change. When I was away from home, I was fortunate to befriend virtuous scholars, which would please my wife when she heard about it. In our spare time, I would discuss with her whether some individual was capable and virtuous and whether a current development was positive or not. She was always able to think deeply on the matter. Therefore, if I did not return home, that would be it; but, when I did return, I felt I was in the company of a close friend. Her maternal uncle served as a magistrate in Guangdong, but my wife did not have the slightest wish for his help. The way her brother treated her was quite distanced, but she did not have even a tiny bit of resentment about it. My capacity for forgiveness is nothing like hers.

I once said to my wife: "Please do not die. Wait until I have some money and am able to buy a coffin for you, and then you can die." I kept delaying for more than ten years after I pronounced these words. This year, *xinmao* [1831], I spurred myself to action and was determined to get it done. I borrowed money to purchase lumber and had a carpenter make [a coffin]. Doing this has made me feel a little better. I regretted that, when my father died, the lumber [for his coffin] was inferior. I also felt deeply about what happened to my aunt who married into the Yao family and to my seventh uncle. I swore in front of the spirits that I would not allow myself a sumptuous burial. That was to punish myself and make my heart a little settled. The reason why I diligently made an effort for the burial of my wife is that I do not have the virtue of [the Han dynasty scholar] Fu Weiming and do not dare use my wife and children to realize my aspirations. I also did this to repay my wife for her exertions on my behalf on the two major burials.

My wife came from an eminent family in Tongcheng. Her great-great-grandfather—the honorable Minjie—was named Lin; her great-grandfather, named Jianxun, was a military commander of Xinghan Township in Shaanxi; her grandfather, named Yan, held a Presented Scholar (*jinshi*) degree from the year *guiwei* [1763]. She is the daughter of Zhantai, a county student. In the past, my father was good friends with my wife's uncle Qiyuan, who held a Presented Scholar degree from the year *xinyou* [1801]. He liked my poems and prose, and praised me in front of his brother and sister-in-law. Therefore, they married their daughter to me.

The elegy reads:

> [Even] at times of leisure, one dare not look forward to a peaceful life.
> This is normal for human beings.
> Heaven punishes me severely, which has brought hardships on you.
> The good and the bad are not constant—this is confusing,
> Yet your disposition is so sincere and concentrated as if you forget these things.
> I inscribe these words for you to see, because I want you not to feel sad when you die.

My words are truthful and unembellished; through them your
virtuous deeds will shine.

Source: Fang Dongshu 方東樹, *Kaopanji wenlu* 攷槃集文錄, Xuxiu siku
quanshu edition (Shanghai: Shanghai guji chubanshe, 2002),
1497:11.439–41.

Notes

1. Martin W. Huang, *Intimate Memories: Mourning and Gender in Late Imperial China* (Albany: State University of New York Press, 2018), 15–22.
2. Created by writers from Tongcheng (Anhui), this major literary school of the Qing period emphasized moral meaning and a concise and unadorned style of prose writing.
3. The names Han Learning and Song Learning derived from the dynasties with which the two schools were closely associated in their intellectual approach and methodology. Han Learning dominated in the High Qing period (roughly the eighteenth century), and Song Learning revived in late Qing.

Further Reading

Barr, Allan H. "Marriage and Mourning in Early-Qing Tributes to Wives." *Nan Nü: Men, Women and Gender in China* 15.1 (2013): 137–78.

Huang, Martin W. *Intimate Memories: Mourning and Gender in Late Imperial China.* Albany: State University of New York Press, 2018.

——— "Negotiating Wifely Virtues: Guilt, Memory, and Grieving Husbands in Seventeenth-Century China." *Nan Nü: Men, Women and Gender in China* 15.1 (2013): 109–36.

Lu, Weijing. "Writing Love: The *Heming ji* by Wang Zhaoyuan and Hao Yixing." In *Gender and Chinese History: Transformative Encounters*, edited by Beverly Bossler, 83–109. Seattle: University of Washington Press, 2015.

Mann, Susan. "Dowry Wealth and Wifely Virtue in Mid-Qing Gentry Households." *Late Imperial China* 29.1 (2008): 64–76.

A Wife's Moving Tribute

Epitaph for Mr. Zeng (Zeng Yong 曾詠, 1813-1862),
by Zuo Xijia 左錫嘉 (1831-1896)

TRANSLATED BY GRACE S. FONG

An educated woman and highly accomplished poet chooses to author
her husband's epitaph at the time of his burial, eighteen years after his
death fighting the Taiping rebels. In addition to portraying her husband as a principled and caring local official, the funerary biography
contains rich details about the trauma inflicted by the Taiping Rebellion in Jiangxi.

AFTER THE STABLE AND PROSPEROUS REIGNS OF THE EMPERORS
Kangxi (r. 1662–1722), Yongzheng (r. 1723–1735), and Qianlong (r. 1736–
1795) in the eighteenth century, at the turn of the nineteenth century,
the Qing dynasty began to confront successive waves of social unrest
and violent upheaval as well as increasing aggression resulting from the
global expansion of Western imperialist powers. By mid-century, the Qing
dynasty had fought and lost the First Opium War (1839–1842), which
resulted in the ceding of Hong Kong to Britain, the British entitlement
to import opium freely into China, and, in addition, the opening of five
coastal treaty ports where foreigners held extraterritorial rights. While
beset by the pervasive problem of opium addiction among the populace,
the Qing government also had to deal with insurrections and uprisings

in various parts of the empire, the earliest being the millenarian White Lotus Rebellion (1796–1804) in central and western China. Some White Lotus rebels formed the Nian Society, which later led the Nian Rebellion (1853–1868) in eastern and northern China. In the same period, the Taiping Rebellion (1850–1864) spread from the south northward to the southeastern provinces and came near to attacking the capital, Beijing. Lastly, throughout the nineteenth century, periodic Muslim rebellions afflicted border areas from Yunnan in the southwest to Gansu in the northwest.

When Zuo Xijia's husband, Zeng Yong (1813–1862), died in 1862, the Taiping Rebellion had for twelve years ravaged the Jiangnan region (comprising the provinces of Jiangsu, Zhejiang, and Anhui), the economic and cultural heartland of the Qing Empire. What began in 1850 as a god-worshiping Christian sect among disaffected Hakka peasants in rural Guangxi in the southwest, led by failed examination candidate Hong Xiuquan (1814–1864), rapidly evolved into a huge militant force that swept northward while waging a full-scale civil war against the Qing government. Depending on their response, civilians were converted, conscripted, or massacred along the war path. Nanjing was captured in 1853 and made the capital of the Taiping Heavenly Kingdom. For over a decade, vast numbers of the population suffered the violence and disorder inflicted by the Taiping armies as well as the Qing government troops sent to fight them; an estimated twenty million people lost their lives during the Taiping upheaval.

As detailed by Zuo Xijia in her epitaph for her husband, Zeng Yong, he had been fighting the Taiping rebels in his official post as prefect of Ji'an in Jiangxi when he was recruited by Zeng Guofan (1811–1872), the Qing official and military leader who eventually succeeded in vanquishing the rebellion. Zeng Yong joined the Qing forces in the strategic county of Anqing (Anhui), which had been recovered from Taiping occupation, but he soon died of illness in a military camp. In the following year (1863), Zuo Xijia braved the perils of an arduous journey up the Yangzi River to transport her husband's coffin back to his hometown near Chengdu in Sichuan.

In 1880, eighteen years after Zeng Yong's death, Zuo Xijia wrote her long and moving epitaph for his final burial in his hometown, Huayang. As she recounts, Zuo Xijia was Zeng Yong's fourth "successor" wife, his first three wives having died in succession without issue, the first even before they were married. Zuo Xijia hailed from the highly reputed scholar-official Zuo lineage of Yanghu County (Jiangsu). Their mother having died when they were small, she and her equally talented sisters were educated by their father at home; she was especially noted for her skills in poetry and painting. Eighteen years her husband's junior, Zuo Xijia gave birth to three sons and six daughters, who were all quite young when Zeng Yong died and whom she raised as a young widow in her early thirties. Zuo Xijia begins the epitaph with an explanation of how she came to write it. More than any other kin, more than any of their grown children, Zuo Xijia would have had the most intimate and detailed knowledge of all stages of her husband's life. As she indicates in her introduction, she ultimately dispensed with the customary step of writing a record of conduct as a draft to invite someone else, an "eminent person," to write the epitaph. Instead, she took up the brush to write it herself. As a learned woman and an accomplished poet, Zuo had the literary means and cultural knowledge at her disposal to produce a formal but poignant epitaph commemorating her beloved husband's life and career, in which her role, as she perceived it, was central. To underline their intimate connection, she addressed Zeng Yong directly using the second-person pronoun "you" (*jun* 君).

Epitaph for Mr. Zeng, Chief Minister of the Court of the Imperial Stud and Prefect of Ji'an, Jiangxi, Conferred Posthumously by the August Qing Dynasty

Alas! This is the tomb of my husband. After you passed away, the family moved around for eighteen years. Only recently was I able to obtain one *mu* [one-sixth of an acre] of land to bury you in your native place. I had wanted to compose your record of conduct and beg an eminent gentleman to write an epitaph on the basis of it. But, when I held the brush and thought back on you, tears streamed down, which for a long time kept me from finishing it. This year my physical condition is deteriorating, and I worry that I may soon die. Then it would be my fault if your firm convictions and conscientious efforts were not passed down in the family records. Therefore, on the occasion of privately giving you the posthumous name Kanghui [Peaceful and Kind], I have taken on the task of writing down its significance and making known what I am able to say about you.

A native of Huayang County in Chengdu [Sichuan], your taboo name was Yong, courtesy name Yongyan, and style name Yincun. The descendants of your ancestor Wucheng migrated to Jiangxi. During the Yuan dynasty some migrated to Changle [Fujian], and only during the Kangxi reign of our dynasty [1662-1722] did some settle in Huayang, making them Huayang men. Your grandfather's taboo name was Huichao and that of your father, Xiuying. Because of your office, your father was given the posthumous title Grand Master for Palace Counsel. Your grandmother was Madam Wang, your successor grandmother Madam Zhang, and your mother Madam Liu; your mother was given the posthumous title Lady of Virtue.

Innately intelligent, as you grew older you developed into a filial son and caring brother. For generations your family had farmed for a living. When you were an adolescent, you worked in the fields alongside your parents. It was not until you were fourteen that you began to apply yourself to learning. During the day, you still worked on the farm with your father, but at night you studied tirelessly. Before long, you could compose essays. In spring of the *yiwei* year in the Daoguang reign period [1835], you were appointed a government student. As the provincial examinations were to be held that autumn, you studied the classics and histories with increased concentration, gaining full understanding. You wrote *Notes on Reading the Histories* in several chapters. With regard to the *The Book of Songs*, *The Analects*, and *The Classic of Filial Piety*, you thoroughly analyzed the strengths and weaknesses of the commentaries by Han and Song Confucian scholars. Every day you wrote several thousand words by way of annotations and corrections. Often you would say that the essentials of learning are to be clear in commenting on the Classics and to identify the moral principles, and that the essentials of personal character are to be strict in self-discipline and lenient toward others. You came close to attaining this Way.

In the *jiachen* year [1844], you passed the Presented Scholar (*jinshi*) examination and were appointed secretary in the Ministry of

Revenue. Subsequently you were promoted to director. At the time, a powerful official had charge of the ministry. He sent someone to ask for your allegiance. You calmly replied, "I am from a farming family and have no experience with seeking wealth and rank by devious means." Unsure what to do, the messenger left. For fourteen years, you remained in the Ministry of Revenue, all the while neither accepting gifts from outside nor letting private considerations influence you.

In the merit evaluation of the eighth year of the Xianfeng reign period [1858], you were placed in the top rank, and your name was listed for employment in the circuits and prefectures. The next year, at the emperor's directive, you were appointed to inspect water transport at Jinmen [Tianjin]. On completion of that assignment, you were appointed prefect of Ji'an in Jiangxi. When you took leave of the powerful senior official on your departure, he again hinted that he would like you to keep him informed of what was going on outside the capital as well as in it, but you acted as if you did not understand what he wanted. Someone near you stepped on your foot [to warn you of the danger of offending the superior], but you looked away, your expression unchanged. In the end, you did not utter a single word. At the time people were amazed at your composure.

When you arrived in Ji'an, the city wall was in bad shape on all sides, with piled up rubble blocking the roads. All that remained were a few wrecked battlements. On arrival, you fortified the city walls and completed construction of a government granary. You grieved at the sight of white bones everywhere in the fields, so you disbursed funds and ordered the four subprefectures to collect [the bones] and bury them. When your superior sent you an order to set up a commercial tax station,[1] you submitted a letter saying, "Given the distress of the people, no merchants come here. If we add to their burdens, how will they be able to bear it?" Townspeople who read your letter all wept, and in the end the tax station was not established. By looking after the common people and educating the scholars, you enabled them to manage their fields and make plans to mutually protect each other, thus helping them become more self-reliant.

In spring of the eleventh year [of the Xianfeng reign period, 1861], the bandits [Taiping rebels] from the Yue region [Guangdong and Guangxi] again attacked Ji'an. You climbed the ramparts and fiercely guarded the city. Even when the bandits attacked again, they were not able to break through. When the siege reached a critical stage, you sent urgent dispatches several times, which resulted in the assignment of two generals to come to your aid—Li Jinyi, who was called Cannon Charging at Heaven, and Lu Desheng, the assistant regional commander of Ji'an—both of whom were surrendered bandits who had accepted appointments in our army but secretly stayed in touch with the bandits. When they arrived, they demanded money [for expenses]. You could not bear to exploit the already traumatized population, so used your own salary to provide funds. Li then pretended to go out to fight, subsequently returning to report that the bandits were stretched thin and could not even mount a defense of their positions. He requested that the county and prefecture march their soldiers out of the city to ambush the bandits, who would surely flee. You went out to supervise the troops. Then Lu opened the city gate to let the bandits in, and Li followed suit. When you learned of their treachery, you pulled out a dagger, intending to cut your own throat. Those nearby, shouting and wailing, stopped you, so you were not able to kill yourself. When you then tried to drown yourself, they pulled you out of the water. Tearfully they said, "Sir, if you die, what will happen to us? Dying wouldn't help matters. It's better to fight. If we win, you will have no worries. If we do not win, we promise to die with you. You must not refuse!" You forced yourself to get up, selected five hundred well-trained braves, and sent the strongest ones to enter the city at night and set fire to the stores of gunpowder. The bandits were thrown into confusion. Taking advantage of the chaos, you vanquished them. The bandits fled, and you took back the city. However, Lu and Li swiftly sent a letter to report the victory and received a grand reward. [By contrast,] because they criticized you, you were demoted, which made you feel shame but not resentment. Later the treason of Lu and Li was exposed, and they were executed.

At that time Mr. Zeng Wenzheng [Zeng Guofan, 1811–1872], who was supervisor of the army of Jiangxi and Jiangsu, learned of your integrity and sent an express document to have you transferred [to his unit]. But the people of Ji'an submitted a letter begging to retain you. The prefect also gave you responsibility for restoring order [in Ji'an]. Only after Mr. Zeng wrote a letter in his own hand to urge you with all sincerity did you go and join the Thunderclap Army in its campaigns to suppress the bandits.[2] Your merit was described in a memorial to the emperor, and your old rank was restored. But before long you died at the army base fighting the Taiping rebels. You were compensated according to regulations regarding dying of disease while in military service and given the posthumous title of chief minister of the Court of the Imperial Stud. In addition, one son was to be appointed county magistrate through the protection privilege.

You stood tall and handsome with a thin beard. Your features were graceful and awe-inspiring. By nature, you were straightforward and loyal, honest and diligent, and unaffected by praise or criticism. You loved books your whole life; those you copied by hand filled several trunks. It is my regret that all your writings and books were destroyed by fire during the war.

You were born on the third day of the ninth month in the Jiaqing reign period [1813] and died at age fifty on the second day of the inter-calary eighth month in the first year of the Tongzhi reign period [1862]. You were first betrothed to Madam Zhong, who died before the wedding. You then married Madam Zhang and [after she died] Madam Dan, neither of whom gave birth to any children. You then adopted your younger brother's son, Guangxi, as your eldest son. I was the last to be married to you and gave birth to three sons. Guangxi was an expectant appointee as prefectural registrar and promoted to county magistrate. The second son, Guangxu, was appointed county magistrate through the protection privilege. The third, Guangmin, is a student in the county school; and the fourth is Guangwen. I also gave birth to six daughters. The eldest married Liu Bishuai of Xindu and was widowed at a young age; the second married Yuan Xuechang of Yanghu; the third married Lin Shangchen of Nanyun; the fourth married Wu Zhongying of Tongliang; the fifth married Zhang Xiang-ling of Hanzhou; the sixth married Wei Guangying of Xindu.

As soon as I received the news that you had fallen ill, I rushed to go to you but was delayed by a windstorm at Lake Poyang. The terrible news came while I was crossing the lake. In your final testament, you wrote, "My parents are still alive. It is my hope that you will return to serve them. I dare not expect that my coffin could be returned there; I can be temporarily buried in Ji'an. When our sons are established, they can then transport the coffin back for burial." Alas! What pain! If your bones did not return home, there would be no reason for me to bring the children home on my own. Looking at the little ones sojourning away from home, separated from our kin, I felt utterly alone. We would probably die of either destitution or distress. What then would happen to my in-laws?

The following year, I accompanied the coffin going upstream from Jiangxi through deserted passes on a dangerous and difficult route and barely made it home. Shedding tears, I painted *Solitary Boat Entering Shu* and sent letters to inform the various friends and relatives. Because your coffin had been returned home, I drew strength from your spirit and served my parents-in-law until they passed away, then buried them as prescribed by the *Rites*. Our four sons have grown up; they are all married and have become officials. Our six daughters have all married. We have six grandchildren. Alas! Finally, my responsibilities are somewhat lighter!

On the eighth day of the third month in the sixth year of the Guangxu reign period [1880], I buried you according to ritual on the southern side of Shipaique, north of Chengdu. What grief! In the deep spring forever hidden, when will we be buried together? I think of your virtuous conduct in life and worry that it will not be known in later ages. I dare to engrave this account on pure stone to record it for eternity. The eulogy reads:

Eminent in loyalty and purity
Was my lord in his time.
You esteemed the Way and your learning flourished.

Virtuous and filial, sincere and sympathetic,
A farmer devoted to your occupation.
Upright and straightforward,
You looked after the people,
Governing with kindness and harmony.
When the violent bandits encroached
The generals assigned were crafty and traitorous.
Aroused by your spirit of self-sacrifice
The forsaken city was reestablished.
Following the supreme general on the southern expedition
You again exerted yourself in meritorious service.
Anxious about His Majesty's business, you worked hard,
Care-worn, you finally lost your life.
In the end our emperor's favor
Brought posthumous honors.
The protection privilege reaches posterity
Its light shines endlessly.
For a thousand ages in the spirit valley
Ten circles of cold pines.
The engraved epitaph in the dark palace
Forever conveys your loyalty.

Source: Zuo Xijia, *Lengyinxianguan shigao shiyu wencun* 冷吟仙館詩稿
詩餘文存 (Dingxiang: Dingxiang guanshu, 1891), *Wencun*.4a–7b, in
Jiangnan nüxing bieji erbian 江南女性別集二编, edited by Hu Xiaoming
胡晓明 and Peng Guozhong 彭国忠 (Hefei: Huangshan shushe, 2010),
2:1417–20; also in Ming Qing Women's Writings, http://digital.library
.mcgill.ca/mingqing/search/results-work.php?workID
=112&language=eng.

Notes

1. These tax stations levied taxes on internal trade, with the proceeds used to pay the soldiers who were fighting the Taiping Rebellion.
2. The Thunderclap Army was led by the famous Hunanese general Bao Chao (1828–1886) under Zeng Guofan.

Further Reading

Biographical Dictionary of Chinese Women: The Qing Period, 1644–1911, edited by Lily Xiaohong Lee et al. Armonk, NY: M. E. Sharpe, 1998.

Fong, Grace S. "Engendering Lives: Women as Self-Appointed and Sought-After Biographers." In *Representing Lives in China: Forms of Biography in the Ming Qing Period, 1644–1911*, edited by Ihor Pidhainy, Roger Des Forges, and Grace S. Fong, 197–226. Ithaca, NY: Cornell East Asia Program, 2018.

———. "A Widow's Journey during the Taiping Rebellion: Zuo Xijia's Poetic Record." *Renditions* 70 (2008): 49–58.

Mann, Susan. "The Lady and the State: Women's Writings in Times of Trouble during the Nineteenth Century." In *The Inner Quarters and Beyond: Women Writers from Ming through Qing*, edited by Grace S. Fong and Ellen Widmer, 283–313. Leiden: Brill, 2010.

Meyer-Fong, Tobie. *What Remains: Coming to Terms with Civil War in 19th Century China*. Stanford: Stanford University Press, 2013.

TEACHING GUIDE

Listed below are several questions for each selection to help stimulate classroom discussion. Some would also work well as short writing assignments.

Selection 1. Three Short Eastern Han Funerary Biographies

1. Do the three subjects of these epitaphs come from similar sorts of families? What kinds of virtues are attributed to them? Are these virtues gendered?
2. In what ways do these funerary biographies differ from conventional biographies? What do these differences tell you about the functions of funerary biographies?
3. What are the major differences in the literary style of these three pieces?

Selection 2. A Chinese General Serving the Northern Wei State

1. According to the epitaph, what are Sima Yue's main accomplishments? What facts of Sima Yue's life (described in the introduction to the selection) were not mentioned in this epitaph? What do you think are the reasons behind such omission?
2. Why did a descendant of the rulers of the (Han Chinese) Jin dynasty thrive in the northern (non-Han) court? Is it odd that he served in a military capacity? What can you see of the interaction and interchange between Han elite and Xianbei elite from this funerary biography?
3. What role did Sima Yue play in fortifying the borderlands between the Northern Wei and the Chinese states to the south? How might his

military successes have encouraged the Northern Wei emperor to move his capital to Luoyang? Why was this move significant?

Selection 3. A Twice-Widowed Xianbei Princess

1. What are the reasons behind Madam Yuan's Buddhist conversion? Does her case help explain the important role of elite women in the spread of Buddhism in the early medieval period?
2. The epitaph depicts Madam Yuan as a woman exemplifying Confucian virtues. In your opinion, does it endorse her Buddhist pursuits as well? How so?

Selection 4. Authoring One's Own Epitaph

1. Should we read these epitaphs as autobiographies? What were the authors' motives for writing accounts of themselves?
2. Although both epitaphs nominally portray their subjects as pursuing a life influenced by Daoist ideas and practices, the circumstances of those lives were quite different. For example, Wang Ji lived in a rustic setting where he interacted regularly with various locals, whereas Wang Xuanzong dwelt in a cave on a sacred mountain where he interacted primarily with other recluses. What other ways can you identify in which the representations of their understanding of "the Way" and/or their lifestyles were similar or different?

Selection 5. Wives Commemorating Their Husbands

1. What do these two texts tell you about Tang women's perceptions of family relations, marital love, gender roles, and social status?
2. What are the similarities and differences between these two texts? What do these similarities and differences tell you about the Tang dynasty?

Selection 6. A Married Daughter and a Grandson

1. What do these texts tell you about perceptions of family, kinship, marriage, gender roles, and childhood in Tang China?
2. What are some elements of funeral practice mentioned in these two texts that you find interesting? What do they tell you about Tang society?

3. Identify types of emotion conveyed in these texts. In your opinion, were these emotions historically or culturally specific? How so?

Selection 7. A Nun Who Lived Through the Huichang Persecution of Buddhism

1. How would you define Nun Zhi's religious, ethnic, and gender identities? In what ways was her life experience both unique and common in human history?
2. How was sibling affection portrayed in this text? In what ways did such sibling relations reflect Chinese culture and tradition?

Selection 8. An Envoy Serving the Kitan Liao Son of Heaven

1. According to this epitaph, what were Han Chun's main achievements? In your reading, what motivated the author to highlight these accomplishments?
2. In what ways did this epitaph help you understand the Kitan (Liao) dynasty?
3. What passages in the epitaph point to Han Chun's cultural identity? How do you interpret them?

Selection 9. Epitaphs Made Widely Available

1. In what ways are these Song Luzhou epitaphs similar to or different from the other Tang or Song epitaphs that are collected in this anthology?
2. Identify the differences between the three Luzhou epitaphs in terms of content and literary style. What can account for the changes in epitaph writing over the course of the eleventh century?

Selection 10. A Friend and Political Ally

1. In writing the epitaph for Shi Jie, the author, Ouyang Xiu, strived to portray him as an ideal Confucian gentleman. What elements contribute the most to that portrayal?
2. How would you describe Shi Jie as a person? What do you learn about Shi Jie's family and social life from this epitaph?
3. How did Ouyang Xiu demonstrate that he was Shi's true friend?
4. What insight does this epitaph offer concerning the relationship between politics and literary or biographical writing?

Selection 11. Preserving a Father's Memory

1. What can you infer about Song intellectuals' understandings of filial piety from this epitaph?
2. What was Chao Juncheng like as a person? What were some of his main interests?
3. In recounting the "unremarkable" life experience of Chao Juncheng, the author Huang Tingjian seemed to have a concept of what an ideal official would be like. What do you think were some of Huang's ideas? Do you see any tension in Huang's portrayal of Chao?
4. Both Shi Jie (Selection 10) and Chao Juncheng died in their forties. What problems did their relatively early deaths create for their families?

Selection 12. A Gentleman without Office

1. What aspects of Wei Xiongfei's life interest you the most? Why?
2. In what ways does this epitaph help you understand Song local society, commercialization, wealth, and village life?

Selection 13. Wives and In-Laws

1. What do these two epitaphs tell you about the examination culture of the Song dynasty?
2. What are some characteristics of an ideal man and woman highlighted by the author, Yao Mian? Compare and contrast such portrayals with the men and women eulogized in earlier (or later) selections.
3. What does the funerary inscription for Yao Mian's wives tell you about the household role of women in the Song dynasty? What were their duties and responsibilities, and what power and privileges did they have?
4. Both the Yao and Zou families belonged to the elite, yet wealth and social standing could not protect them from various family crises. What do these epitaphs reveal about the dangers and uncertainties facing elite families in this period?

Selection 14. A Clerk Promoted to Official under the Mongols

1. What qualities were viewed as admirable in a clerk in this epitaph?
2. Why does the author give so much attention to Mr. Su's service in Karakorum?

3. What features of the Yuan (Mongol) government bureaucracy can be seen in this epitaph?

Selection 15. A Mongol Rising to the Defense of the Realm

1. Does this epitaph help you understand the fall of the Yuan dynasty? How?
2. Selections 14 and 15 are epitaphs for men in north China in the early and mid-fourteenth century. How different are the social circles in which these men participated? What does this reveal about society in Yuan period north China?
3. What features of the Mongol kinship system can be seen in this epitaph?
4. Why do you think non-Han people like the Mongols used Classical Chinese as a scribal language while also maintaining their own languages?

Selection 16. A Merchant Aspiring to Gentlemanly Virtue

1. What are some gentlemanly virtues assigned to Merchant Cheng in this epitaph? What do such depictions tell you about the social and historical milieu of the Ming dynasty?
2. The author seems to suggest that mercantile wealth should not be considered a burden on one's virtue. What are some of his main arguments?
3. What connections do you see between commercial wealth and kinship organization?

Selection 17. A Ming General Turned Warlord

1. In depicting a great military general, this epitaph reveals a wide range of perceptions of masculinity, heroism, and loyalty in late imperial China. Give some examples.
2. What have you learned about military strategies and battle operations in late imperial China from this epitaph?

Selection 18. A Brother Remembers His Sister

1. What aspects of the relationship between a married woman and her natal family are highlighted in this epitaph?

2. Compare Selection 18 to Selection 7, "A Nun Who Lived Through the Huichang Persecution of Buddhism." What differences do you see in the understandings of sibling affection, womanly virtue, or family relations?

Selection 19. A Chinese Bannerman Expert in Waterworks

1. What were Jin Fu's main achievements? Was his military background relevant to his work on rivers and canals?
2. What made keeping the rivers and canals flowing challenging? What could go wrong?
3. From this funerary biography, do you see ways the careers of Chinese bannermen differed from the careers of men recruited through the examinations?
4. Based on this epitaph, how would you characterize the Qing bureaucracy?

Selection 20. A Woman Determined to Die

1. What do you learn from this epitaph about the life of Madam Dai?
2. Does this epitaph help you understand the "cult of widow chastity"? In what ways?
3. Why did members of the local elite support honors for Madam Dai? Did they have anything to gain?

Selection 21. A Wife's Sacrifices

1. In what ways is this epitaph unconventional?
2. Can you think of anyone as self-sacrificing as Madam Sun? Does Fang show any ambivalence about his wife's always putting his needs first?
3. What do you make of Fang asking his wife to put off dying until he could afford a coffin? Did it make a difference?
4. Compare and contrast perceptions of marital love, womanly virtue, and gender roles as seen in this epitaph with those in previous epitaphs.

Selection 22. A Wife's Moving Tribute

1. What do you learn about the relationship between husband and wife in the Qing from reading this epitaph? Illustrate with examples.

2. How do epitaphs written by wives for their deceased husbands compare to those written by husbands for their deceased wives?

Questions for Groups of Selections

1. Reread the four funerary biographies for men who served non-Han rulers (Selections 2, 8, 14, 19). What do you learn about alien dynasties from them? Why do the authors put little emphasis on ethnicity?
2. Consider the eight funerary biographies for women (Selections 1, 3, 6, 7, 13, 18, 20, 21). Do they have much in common? Which of the differences among them would you attribute to change over time, either in ideals of womanly conduct or of literary style? Pick one to analyze more closely.
3. Several inscriptions are for men who did not hold office (Selections 1, 5, 9, 12, 16). How are they described? Which of their activities get the most praise? Are there significant changes over time?
4. Think about the funerary biographies you have read in terms of their value to historians. What are their strengths as historical sources? What are their limitations? Give examples from the funerary biographies that you have read to substantiate your arguments.

CONTRIBUTORS

BEVERLY BOSSLER is professor of history at the University of California, Davis. Her research focuses on social, intellectual, and gender history in Middle Period China (Tang, Song, Yuan). She is the author of *Powerful Relations* (1998) and *Courtesans, Concubines, and the Cult of Female Fidelity in China, 1000–1400* (2013), and is the editor of *Gender and Chinese History: Transformative Encounters* (2015).

TIMOTHY DAVIS is Asian Studies Librarian at Brigham Young University and a scholar of the social, cultural, and literary history of early medieval China. His book *Entombed Epigraphy and Commemorative Culture in Early Medieval China* (2015) was the first monograph in English on the religious and social functions of early *muzhiming*.

ALEXEI KAMRAN DITTER is associate professor of Chinese at Reed College. His research explores interactions between social and textual practices in medieval Chinese literature, focusing in particular on questions of place, genre, and memory. He is a coeditor of *Tales from Tang China: Selections from the "Taiping guangji"* (2017). Most recently, he is completing a monograph studying genre and memory in medieval Chinese literature and coediting an anthology of late medieval entombed epitaph inscriptions.

YONGTAO DU is associate professor of history at Oklahoma State University. His research focuses on locality-polity relationships in late imperial China. He is the author of *The Order of Places: Translocal Practices of the Huizhou Merchants in Late Imperial China* (2015).

PATRICIA BUCKLEY EBREY is Williams Family Endowed Professor of History at the University of Washington. Over the course of her career, she has worked on the social, cultural, and political history of China, especially of the Song dynasty. Her current research interests include migration in Chinese history. Her *Cambridge Illustrated History of China* (1996) and *Chinese Civilization: A Sourcebook* (1993) are both widely used in classes. She won prizes for *The Inner Quarters: Marriage and the Lives of Women in the Sung Period* (1993) and *Accumulating Culture: The Collections of Emperor Huizong* (2008).

GRACE S. FONG is professor of Chinese literature and Richard Charles and Esther Yewpick Lee Chair in Chinese Cultural Studies at McGill University. She has published widely on Classical Chinese poetry and women's writings in late imperial China. Her publications include *Herself an Author: Gender, Agency, and Writing in Late Imperial China* (2008) and the coedited volumes *The Inner Quarters and Beyond: Women Writers from Ming through Qing* (2010) and *Representing Lives in China: Forms of Biography in the Ming-Qing Period* (2018). She is director of the online digital archive and database Ming Qing Women's Writings (http://digital.library .mcgill.ca/mingqing).

R. KENT GUY is professor emeritus of history and East Asian studies at the University of Washington. He has worked on the social, political, and intellectual history of the Qing dynasty and is the author of *Qing Governors and Their Provinces: The Evolution of Territorial Administration in China, 1644–1796* (2010) and *The Emperor's Four Treasuries: Scholars and the State in the Late Ch'ien-lung Era* (1987). He is currently at work on a book on impeachments in the middle Kangxi reign.

MARK HALPERIN is associate professor of Chinese languages and cultures at the University of California, Davis. His research focuses on medieval Chinese literature, religion, and literati culture. He is the author of *Out of the Cloister: Literati Perspectives on Buddhism in Sung China, 960–1279* (2006) and has written several articles about how Confucian scholar-officials portray religion.

XING HANG is associate professor of history at Brandeis University. His research focuses on the East Asian world order, maritime East Asia, Eurasian comparative history, the Ming-Qing transition, overseas Chinese, and Chinese nationalism and identity. He has published articles on Chinese mercantile networks and port settlements in early modern maritime Asia.

MARTIN W. HUANG is professor of Chinese literature at the University of California, Irvine. His research focuses on literati self-representation, desire, and masculinities as they are explored and represented in late imperial Chinese culture. He is the author of *Literati and Self-Re/Presentation: Autobiographical Sensibility in the Eighteenth-Century Chinese Novel* (1995), *Desire and Fictional Narrative in Late Imperial China* (2001), *Negotiating Masculinities in Late Imperial China* (2006), and, most recently, *Intimate Memory: Gender and Mourning in Late Imperial China* (2018).

TOMOYASU IIYAMA is associate professor at Waseda University. His research interests lie in the history of north China during the tenth to seventeenth centuries. His major publications include *Mō hitotsu no shijinsō: Kingen jidai kahokushakai to kakyo seido* (Local literati and civil service examinations in north China during the Jin and Yuan eras, 2011) and articles on family and genealogical rituals during the Jin and Yuan dynasties and late imperial China.

JEN-DER LEE is research fellow at the Institute of History and Philology, Academia Sinica, Taiwan. She examines legal and medical history from a gender perspective. Most of her work focuses on early imperial China, but she has recently extended her interest to women's encounters with law and medicine in modern China and Taiwan. Her publications include two books (*The Death of a Princess*, 2001, and *Gender and Health Care between the Han and Tang Dynasties in China*, 2008, both in Chinese), four edited volumes, and many articles.

WEIJING LU is associate professor of history at the University of California, San Diego. Her research focuses on late imperial gender, social, and cultural history. She is the author of *True to Her Word: The Faithful Maiden Cult in Late Imperial China* (2008, winner of the Berkshire Conference of Women Historians first book prize) and guest editor of a special issue on China for the

Journal of the History of Sexuality (2013). Most recently, she is completing a book on marriage and intimacy in Qing China.

LANCE PURSEY is currently completing a PhD in medieval history at the University of Birmingham. His research uses epitaphs to investigate the cultural salience of cities in Kitan (Liao) society and the connection between power, place, and identity.

ANNA M. SHIELDS is professor of East Asian studies at Princeton University. Her interests include literary history and the emergence of new literary genres and styles in late medieval China, the sociology of literature, and the role of emotions in classical literature. She is the author of *Crafting a Collection: The Cultural Contexts and Poetic Practice of the Collection from among the Flowers (Huajian ji)* (2006) and *One Who Knows Me: Friendship and Literary Culture in Mid-Tang China* (2015). Most recently she is working on a new book that examines the shaping of the Tang dynasty literary legacy in the Five Dynasties and Northern Song.

MAN XU is associate professor of history at Tufts University. She specializes in Song history, with a particular focus on family and kinship, local society, material culture, and gender. She is the author of *Crossing the Gate: Everyday Lives of Women in Song Fujian (960–1279)* (2016). Most recently, she is working on a book manuscript that investigates the transformation of local elites in north China from the seventh to the twelfth centuries.

PING YAO is professor of history at California State University, Los Angeles. Her research interests include medieval Chinese women's experiences in everyday life and religious practice. Her English publications include two textbooks, *Sharing the World Stage: Biography and Gender in World History* (coauthor, 2007) and *East Asia: A Documentary History* (coauthor, 2016); an anthology, *Gendering Chinese Religion: Subject, Identity, and Body* (coeditor, 2014); and a monograph in Chinese, *Women's Lives in Tang China* (2004).

JOLAN YI is professor of history at National Taiwan University. Her research focuses on gender and family in late imperial China. She is the author of *Sangu liupo: Mingdai funü yu shehui de tansuo* (Three aunties and six grannies: Women and society in Ming China) (2002), *Shixue yu xingbie: Mingshi "Lienüzhuan" yu Mingdai nüxingshi zhi jian'gou* (Historiography and gender: Biographies of women in the *Ming History* and the construction of women's history) (2011), and numerous articles on historiography and the history of gender and the family in late imperial China.

CONG ELLEN ZHANG is associate professor of history at the University of Virginia, specializing in the social and cultural history of the Song dynasty. Her publications include *Transformative Journeys: Travel and Culture in Song China (960–1279)* (2011) and *Record of the Listener: Selected Stories from Hong Mai's "Yijian zhi"* (translator, 2018). Most recently, she is completing a monograph on filial piety in the Northern Song.

INDEX

Abaoji (r. 916–926), 84, 86, 90
academies, 113, 117, 252
adoption, 143, 152, 174, 178, 265
An Lushan Rebellion (755–763), 69
Analects, 57n5, 61, 64nn1,2, 65nn3,5, 73, 94, 142, 149, 153, 156nn3,8,12, 262
ancestor/ancestry, 56, 107, 122, 159, 168, 173, 186–87, 224, 262; diminished interest in, 15; elevating/glorifying, 9, 25; recorded in epitaphs, 6, 8, 15, 102,
ancestral rites/sacrifices/offerings/ worship, 4, 105, 107, 110, 113, 131, 142, 170, 184, 250; ancestral shrines, 97, 186, 224, 237
Ancient Style Prose Movement, 13, 14, 47, 48
Anhui, 223, 227–30
aristocratic families, 40–41, 67, 78, 101
authorship, 101, 103
autobiography, 48

banditry, 95–96, 176–77, 229. *See also* uprisings
bannermen, 223
Beijing (Yan region) 84, 87, 90, 91, 94, 97, 98, 191, 197
biographical writing, 3–6. *See also* autobiography
Book of Rites, 27, 61, 73, 106, 187
Book of Songs, 27, 61, 65n4, 93, 106, 243, 255, 262

brother-in-law, 217
brothers, 25–27, 76–77, 145, 167, 186, 244–45, 256; as author of epitaph, 53–57, 78–82, 212–21. *See also* siblings
Buddhism, 40, 41, 69, 72, 73, 75–76, 98, 133, 135, 251; Buddhist monasteries, 31, 76, 77, 79; Buddhist monks and nuns, 12, 40–44, 77–82, 131; Buddhist sects, 159, 166, 173; Buddhist services, 73, 168, 245; criticism of, 111, 113, 119; persecution, 77, 80; Pure Land Buddhism, 68–69, 73
burial. *See* funeral and burial practices/ ceremonies

Cai Hang (1193–1259), 151
calligraphy, 4, 8, 14, 28, 73, 99, 102, 108, 160, 175
Cao Yin (fl. 7th century), 59–60, 62–63
Chang'an, 12, 31, 47, 49, 61, 62, 67, 69, 70, 73
Chao Buzhi (1053–1100), 123, 124, 125, 126, 127
Chao Juncheng (1029–1075), 122–28
chaste widow, 219, 241–42
Chen Hou (1074–1123), 103, 108–10
Cheng Silian (1235–1296), 165
Cheng Weiqing (1531–1588), 182–89
children, 15–16, 68, 116, 214, 217, 265–66; deaths of, 67, 68, 69, 72–73

civil service examination system, 59–63, 103, 130, 132, 145, 158–59, 183, 219, 242–44; accusations of favoritism in, 88; *Daodejing* in, 51; local, 139, 145; prefectural, 216; provincial, 214, 216, 244, 251, 256, 262; study for, 183, 219, 244; success in, 13, 16, 63, 112, 114, 126, 139–41, 149, 184, 262. *See also* literati elite

Classic of Changes, 186, 243

Classic of Filial Piety, 73, 149, 262

classics, Confucian. *See* Confucianism

clerk, 158–70

commercialization, 130, 183–85, 191

concubines/concubinage, 43, 91, 139, 142, 143, 150, 167

Confucianism, 111–13; Confucian classics, 59, 61, 110n1, 119, 122, 192, 242, 251, 262; Confucian learning, 48, 111, 113, 130, 131, 159, 185; Confucian revival movement, 111–13; Confucian ritual, 62, 168; Confucian temple, 164; Confucian virtues, 41, 184. *See also* ancestral rites; Confucius; family rituals; filial piety; Han Yu (768–824); Mencius; mourning; Yang Xiong; Zhu Xi

Confucius, 50, 112, 119

Culai (Academy), 113

Culai (Mountain), 116, 118, 119, 120

Culai (Mr.). *See* Shi Jie

cult of *qing,* 241, 243, 250

Daodejing, 51, 58n15

Daoism, 12, 40, 47–57, 61, 75–81, 111, 113, 119; Daoist rites, 245; three major Daoist traditions (Shangqing, Tianshi, Lingbao), 51

daughter-in-law, 105, 107, 139, 217, 218, 248, 254

Deng Tingzhen (1776–1846), 252

diplomacy, 83, 84, 87, 92–93, 94, 95, 96–97

Du Chun, 123, 124, 127

Du Yan (978–1057), 119

Dugu Ji (725–777), 69–70

Duke of Zhou, 56, 119

Dunhuang, 78, 94

education, 103, 113, 183. *See also* academies; civil service examination system; Confucianism; Imperial University; literacy, female

elegy (*ming*), 6

elite. *See* literati elite

Elliot, Charles, 252

emperors, 112, 117, 118, 147, 156n10, 169, 194, 225–27, 230–40, 265; Abaoji (Liao, r. 916–926), 84–86, 90; Chongzhen (Ming, r. 1628–1644), 194, 205; favor of, 25, 96, 97, 149, 178–79, 204; Gaozu (Tang, r. 618–635), 51, 60, 62; Huizong (Song, r. 1100–1126), 174; Jingmu (Northern Wei, r. 428–451), 42; Kangxi (Qing, r. 1622–1722), 230–32; Lizong (Song, r. 1224–1265), 132; marriage to, 38n3; Qianlong (Qing, r. 1735–1796), x, 253, 259; Renzong (Song, r. 1022–1063), 114, 127; Renzong/Ayurbarwada, (Yuan, r. 1311–1320), 161; Shengzong (Liao, r. 982–1031), 95; Taizong (Tang, r. 626–649), 60; Wu (Liang, r. 502–549), 33; Wu (Liu Song, r. 420–422), 31–32; Wuzong (Tang, r. 840–846), 77; Xiaowen (Northern Wei, r. 471–499), 32, 39–42; Xingzong (Liao, r. 1031–1055), 97; Yongzheng (Qing, r. 1723–1735), 259

empresses, 24, 91; Chengtian, 98; Ling (491–528), 40; Lingtian (Liao), 90, 91; Wenming (441–490), 40; Wu (Tang, r. 690–705), 51–52, 75–76

envoy, 83, 84, 85, 87, 93, 95, 96–97, 99

epitaphs (*muzhiming*), 4–18; for friends, 111–24; for husband, 59–64, 259–67; for merchants, 182–89; for military men, 30–38, 172–80, 190–210; for non-Han, 39–46, 172–80; and politics, 111–16; and record of conduct, 123; requested by sons or disciples, 14, 120, 123, 125; self-authored, 47–57; for sister, 75–82, 212–21; for wives and parents, 62, 123–24; for women, 23–25, 39–46, 66–72, 75–82, 142–55, 212–21, 241–49, 250–58

ethnicity, 16–17, 39–41, 78, 83–99, 172–75

examination system. *See* civil service examination system

exemplary women, 213, 219, 241–58. *See also* women: virtues of

factionalism, 84, 111–12, 114, 115, 117, 118, 140, 216, 219; "Discourse on Factions," 114

faithful maidens, 241–42

family rituals, 113, 224

Fan Zhongyan (989–1052), 112

Fang Dongshu (1772–1851), 251

filial piety, 4, 61, 68, 108, 122–26, 131, 184, 245, 247–48; filial son, 16, 113, 122, 125, 262. See also *Classic of Filial Piety*; funeral and burial practices/ceremonies

First Opium War, 259

Fu Bi (1004–1083), 120

Fujian, 192, 229, 239n2, 279

funeral and burial practices/ceremonies, 9–15, 17, 23, 51, 54, 107, 208, 236, 254–55; condolences, 25, 36, 205; delayed, 34, 36–37, 114, 116, 125; expenses, 97, 116, 124, 135, 255; experts, 9, 13, 102–3; graveyards, 10, 113, 168; joint-burial, 62, 97, 105, 241–49; moving bodies, 31; reburial, 67, 143, 147; temporary burial, 11, 64, 67, 73, 135; tombs, 88. *See also* mourning

funerary biographies/inscriptions. *See* epitaphs

Gansu, 88, 97

Gao Fang (1264–1328), 165

gender. *See* women

genealogy, 116, 237, 237

geomancy, 132

Goryeo. *See* Korea

Grand Canal, 222, 225, 230, 232, 233, 234, 239n5

graveyards. *See* funeral and burial practices/ceremonies

Guangdong, 195

Guangxi, 195, 260

Han Derang, 91, 92

Han Kuangmei, 90–91

Han Kuangsi, 91

Han Learning, 251

Han Qi (1008–1075), 112, 120

Han Yu (Liao general), 91, 92

Han Yu (768–824), 13, 112, 113, 119

Han Zhigu, 90

He Jian (686–742), 59–62, 63–64

Hebei, 91, 92, 94–96

Heilongjiang, 85, 96

Henan, 30, 63, 81, 168, 177, 178, 180

Historical Records (Shiji), 3, 211n3, 243

Hong Xiuquan (1814–1864), 260

horse riding, 92, 93, 98, 164, 176

Huang Tingjian (1045–1105), 122–25

Hubei, 32

Huichang Persecution of Buddhism, 77, 80

husband-wife relations, 62, 68, 69, 70–71, 243, 250–58; husband, epitaph for, 260–67; primary wife, 45; successor wife, 40, 42, 260–61. *See also* marriage; widows

imperial surname, 86, 91, 92

Imperial University, 113, 115, 119, 120, 145, 151, 188

Inner Mongolia, 86, 87, 90, 91, 93

irrigation canals, 228–29

Jia Rang (fl. 7 BCE), 236–37

Jiangsu, 222, 223, 225, 226, 265

Jiangxi, 61, 114, 238n2, 259, 260, 261, 262, 263, 265, 266
Jilin, 85, 96
Jin Fu (1633–1692), 222–40: illness and death, 235–36; plans for river work, 230–32
Jin Zhiyu, 224–26, 235–36, 238
jinshi. See civil service examination system
joint epitaph, 62, 242, 248
Jurchen, 16, 85, 191–94, 197

Kaifeng, 85, 93, 127, 159, 160, 174, 177
Kangxi Emperor (r. 1622–1722), 230–32; southern tour, 233–34
Karakorum, 161, 162
Khosila, 161
Kitan language, 88
Kitan Liao, 83–99, 117
Kong Dan (fl. 182), 23, 24, 26–28
Korea, 84, 85, 87, 93, 95, 96, 191, 192, 197–99, 209

Learning of the Principle, 112. *See also* Confucianism
Learning of the Way, 112. *See also* Confucianism
li (proper conduct), 131, 134. *See also* Confucianism
Li Jinyi, 264
Li Jiqian (963–1004), 93
Li Shuji, 140, 146, 148
Li Xiuji, 140, 148
Li Yishan, 140, 147, 148, 153
Li Yuanhao (1003–1048), 118
Liang Jian (d. 1042), 104–6
Liaoning, 90, 94, 95, 96, 224
literacy, female, 60, 142, 149, 150, 153
literati elite, 4–5, 13, 75, 101, 111–28, 159, 167, 174, 182–85
Liu Aita (d. 1630), 204–5, 209
Liu Bang (256–195 BCE), 88
Liu Yu, Song Emperor Wu (r. 420–422), 31–32

Liu Zongyuan (773–819), 13, 136
local histories, 4
Luoyang, 23, 31–33, 40, 49, 71, 73, 76, 172, 178; as Northern Wei capital, 11, 33, 35, 39
Luzhou, 101–4

Ma Jiang (34–106), 10, 23, 24–25
Madam Dai (1666–1687), 241–49
Madam Dugu (785–815), 66–72
Madam Fang (Qian Huan, 1600–1668), 212–21
Madam Plum Mansion (Zou Miaozhuang, 1230–1257), 142–55
Madam Sun (1769–1833), 250–58
Madam Xin (fl. 742), 59–60
Madam Zhou (fl. 7th century), 59–61
maids, 108, 214–15, 218, 220
Manchus, 16, 191, 193, 194, 209, 222–24
Mangshan, burial ground, 11, 12, 44
Mao Qiling (1623–1716), 17, 194, 242, 243
Mao Wenlong (1579–1629), 190–211
marriage, 41, 70–71, 141, 212, 255, 260–61, 265–66; age at, 78; arrangements, 26, 70, 98, 140, 142, 150–51, 154–55, 218, 237, 257; connections/networks/alliances, 5, 12, 13, 40, 67–69, 138–46, 149, 173, 175; in-laws, 138–56, 266; remarriage, 40, 96. *See also* concubines/concubinage; husband-wife relations; widows
Mencius, 64n1, 112, 117, 119, 120; mother of, 43, 45, 80
merchants, 163, 182–89
military households, 172, 190–91, 224
military men, 30–38, 40–42, 91–98, 172–80, 190–210, 232, 257, 260; epitaphs for, 30–38, 172–80, 190–210; lowly position of, 190, 203
Ming army, 223–24, 227
Mongol conquest, 159
Mongolia, 85, 87, 92, 94, 161
Mongols, 159, 161, 172–80

mothers, 16, 59, 78, 109, 152, 214–20, 245
Mount Tai Academy, 113, 118
mourning, 122, 123, 126, 260–61, 265–66;
    rules, 140, 141
muzhiming. See epitaphs

natal family, 212–15, 254. *See also*
    marriage
Neo-Confucianism. *See* Confucianism
Nian Rebellion (1853–1868), 160
non-Han. *See* ethnicity
Nun Zhi/Zhi Zhijian (812–861), 75–82
Nurhaci (Emperor Taizu of Qing), 204–5

omens, 143, 154
ordo, 85, 87, 94, 95
Ouyang Xiu (1007–1072), 111–16, 120; as
    epitaph writer, 115; "Discourse on
    Factions," 114

Pan Shizheng (585–682), 52
parallel prose, 13, 113
Pass of the Mountains and Seas
    (Shanhaiguan), 191, 196, 199–201, 205,
    209, 211n2
physiognomy, 139, 140, 144, 145
Pingcheng (N. Wei Capital), 32
poetry, 133, 142, 251, 261
Pure Land Buddhism, 68, 69, 73

Qian Chengzhi (1612–1698), 212–15
Qianlong Emperor, x, 253, 259
Qingli Reform, 112, 113, 114, 116. *See also*
    factionalism
Quan Deyu (759–818), 14, 66–70

Rebellion of Three Feudatories, 229
rebellions. *See* uprisings
record of conduct (*xingzhuang*), 7, 123, 188,
    196, 261; compared to epitaph, 213
Red Turban Rebellion, 173–75
reincarnation, 68, 69, 73, 216
Ruan Yuan (1764–1849), 251

Sayin Čidaqu (1317–1365), 172–81
scholar residing at home (*chushi*), 131
scholar-official elite. *See* literati elite
servants, 108, 150, 173, 215, 216, 218, 220, 224
Shaanxi, 162, 175, 180, 235, 257
Shandong, 116, 120
Shanhaiguan. *See* Pass of the Mountains
    and Seas
Shanxi, 84, 92, 93, 98, 235
Shazhou, 87, 89, 94, 97, 98
Shen Fu (1763–1832), 251
Shi Bing, 112, 117
Shi Jie (1005–1045), 111–21; "On the Central
    Kingdom," 119; "The Mirror of the
    Tang,"119; "Poem on the Sagacious
    Virtue of the Qingli Reign," 114, 118;
    "On Strange Writing,"119
Shulu Ping (Liao Empress Yingtian),
    90, 91
Shun (sage king), 119
siblings, 75–77, 149, 160, 212–15, 216, 219,
    221, 254. *See also* brothers; sisters
Sichuan, 118, 127, 131–32, 176, 260
silver mines, 88
Sima Chuzhi (390–464), 31–32, 34
Sima Guang (1019–1086), 224, 237
Sima Jinlong (d. 484), 32–33, 34
Sima Qian (d. 86 BCE), 3
Sima Yan (236–290), 31
Sima Yi (179–251), 31
Sima Yue (462–508), 30–38
sisters, 75–82, 141, 143, 154, 212–21. *See also*
    siblings
Six Records of A Floating Life, 251
Song learning, 251
Song Qi (998–1061), 126
Song-Liao relations, 83–84
sons. *See* children
Southern Capital, 118, 119
Su Shi (1037–1101), 124, 125, 127
Su Tianjue (1294–1352), 159, 162
Su Xun (1009–1066), 152
Su Zhidao (1261–1320), 158–70

Sun Fu (992–1057), 113, 117
Susong Academy, 252. *See also* academies

Taiping Rebellion (1850–1864), 259, 260,
    264–65
Taishan (Mount Tai) Academy, 113, 117
Taizu, Emperor of Qing. *See* Nurhaci
Tang-Song transition, 17, 101–2
Three-Year Rites, 122. *See also* mourning
tomb. *See* funeral and burial ceremonies
travel, 16, 87, 94, 186, 230, 251–52, 256
Treaty of Chanyuan, 83–84, 87, 93
tribute, 84
Tuoba, 31–32, 39–40

uprisings, 93, 96, 161, 173–75, 259–60.
    See also Nian Rebellion; Rebellion of
    Three Feudatories; Red Turban
    Rebellion; Taiping Rebellion; White
    Lotus Rebellion
Uyghur Khanate, 84

Wang Cheng (d. 1042), 106–8
Wang Daokun (fl. 16th century), 183
Wang Shizhen (1634–1711), 182, 223, 228
warfare, 92, 93, 96, 174, 191, 195–210, 227
Wei Liaoweng (1178–1237), 131–34
Wei Xiongfei (1130–1207), 132–36
well-field system, 228
Western Xia, 84, 87, 92, 93
White Cloud Society, 159, 165–66
White Lotus Rebellion (1796–1804), 260
widows, 16, 39–46, 80, 108, 219, 241, 243,
    261, 265; widow chastity, 241, 246
wives, 10, 60–61, 98, 116, 120, 138–43,
    148–55. *See also* husband-wife
    relations
women: epitaphs by, 18, 59–65, 260–67;
    epitaphs for, 23–25, 59–61, 66–72,
    142–55, 212–21, 241–49, 250–58; as
    household managers, 250, 252; literacy
    of, 142, 149, 150, 153; poetry of, 142,
    153–54; virtues of, 103–5, 107, 213, 219,

246–47. *See also* marriage; husband-
    wife relations; widows
Wu Zhongshan (ca. 92–172), 23, 23, 25–26

Xianbei, 11, 30–32, 39–46
Xiao (Kitan clan), 88, 91, 92
Xiao He (d. 193 BCE), 88
Xing Luan (464–514), 41, 42
xingzhuang. See record of conduct
Xiongnu, 31

Yang Xiong (53 BCE–18 CE), 113, 119
Yangzi River/delta, 31, 36, 56, 183, 225, 228,
    230, 232, 234, 260
Yanjing (Beijing), 87, 90, 94, 97
Yanzhou, 112, 116
Yao (sage king), 119, 146
Yao Mian (1216–1262), 138–40; and civil
    service examinations, 139, 141, 145, 149;
    economic status of, 139, 140, 144, 149,
    154
Yao Nai (1731–1815), 251
Yao Tianfu (1229–1302), 165
Yellow River, 128, 222–35, 238
Yelü (Kitan clan), 85, 86, 88, 91, 92
Yelü Lihu, 91
Yelü Zhixin, 92
Yu (sage king), 119
Yu Ji (1271–1348), as author, 17, 158–70
Yuan Cheng, Prince Wenxuan (467–519),
    40–42
Yuan Chonghuan (1584–1630), 201
Yuan Chuntuo (475–529), 39–46
Yuan Weiqing, Prince Xihe, 44

Zeng Guofan (1811–1872), 260, 265
Zeng Yong (1813–1862), 259; official career
    of, 262–64
Zhang Zhu (1287–1368), 172, 174–75
Zhao Mengfu (1254–1322), 160
Zhejiang, 165, 195, 239n2, 242
Zhi Mo (fl. 860), 75, 76, 78
Zhu Xi (1130–1200), 152, 224, 237, 242

Zhuangzi, 49–50, 61

Zou Miaoshan (1228–1249), 139, 142, 147, 148–49, 153

Zou Miaozhuang (1230–1257), 139, 142, 143, 147, 148–55

Zou Yilong (1204–1255), 139–41, 144–48, 149; economic status of, 142, 146; support of scholars, 141, 142, 144, 146

Zuo Xijia (1831–1896), 259; talents (poetry and painting), 261, 266

www.ingramcontent.com/pod-product-compliance
Lightning Source LLC
Chambersburg PA
CBHW020834060726
R18530900001B/R185309PG47498CBX00001B/1